School Crime and Policing

School Crime and Policing

❖

WILLIAM L. TURK

Editor
University of Texas—Pan American

M.L. DANTZKER

Series Editor

Upper Saddle River, NJ 07458

Library of Congress Cataloging-in-Publication Data

School crime and policing / [edited by] William L. Turk.
  p. cm.
Includes bibliographical references and index.
ISBN 0-13-092491-1
  1. School violence -- United States -- Prevention. 2. Schools -- United States -- Safety
measures. I. Turk, William L.

LB3013.32.P65 2004
371.7'82 -- dc21

2003048242

Editor-in-Chief: Stephen Helba
Director of Production and
  Manufacturing: Bruce Johnson
Executive Editor: Frank Mortimer, Jr.
Assistant Editor: Korrine Dorsey
Editorial Assistant: Barbara Rosenberg
Marketing Manager: Tim Peyton
Managing Editor—Production: Mary Carnis
Manufacturing Buyer: Cathleen Petersen
Production Liaison: Denise Brown

Full Service Production: Naomi Sysak
Composition Management and Page
  Makeup: Integra Software Services
Design Director: Cheryl Asherman
Design Coordinator: Miguel Ortiz
Cover Designer: Carey Davies
Cover Photo: Spencer Grant,
  PhotoEditInc.Com
Cover Printer: Phoenix Color
Printer/Binder: Phoenix Book Tech

Pearson Education LTD.
Pearson Education Singapore, Pte. Ltd
Pearson Education Canada, Ltd
Pearson Education–Japan
Pearson Education Australia PTY, Limited
Pearson Education North Asia Ltd
Pearson Educaçion de Mexico, S.A. de C.V.
Pearson Education Malaysia, Pte. Ltd

10 9 8 7 6 5 4 3 2 1
ISBN 0-13-092491-1

To my children:

I am proud of who you are, what you have accomplished, and *all* you will achieve in the future.

> Billy, the facilitator
> Kristy, the organizer
> Michael, the worker
> Cullen, the dreamer

Contents

❖

About the Authors

❖

Ahmed, S. Faruq, at the time this article appeared in *The School Administrator,* was a principal associate at the architectural and design firm of Burt Hill Kosar Rittlemann Associates, Butler, PA.

Ardis, Chris, is in her nineteenth year of teaching. Originally from Peoria, Illinois, Chris graduated from MacMurray College in Jacksonville, Illinois, with a degree in deaf education. She began her career as a teacher of the deaf in McAllen, Texas. Several years later, she started the American Sign Language as a Foreign Language program for McAllen Independent School District. She currently teaches ASL at McAllen High School. She is also a certified journalism teacher. Chris writes a weekly column for the McAllen newspaper, The Monitor, which focuses on education, family, and life in general.

Aultman-Bettridge, Tonya, is a researcher with the Colorado Department of Human Services, Division of Youth Corrections. She received a Bachelor of Arts degree in sociology and a Bachelor of Science degree in journalism from the University of Colorado, Boulder, and a Master of Criminal Justice degree from the University of Colorado, Denver. Currently, she is a Ph.D. student in the Graduate School of Public Affairs at the University of Colorado, Denver. Previous research efforts include a state-level analysis of trends in juvenile homicide, youth gun violence prevention strategies, lethal and nonlethal intimate partner violence, and safe school planning efforts. She has also served as co-principal investigator for evaluation research projects for the Anti-Defamation League and the Asian Pacific Development Center in Denver, Colorado.

Berner, Cindy N., is currently a Master's degree candidate and teacher's assistant in the Department of Criminal Justice at the University of Texas–Pan American. She holds a Bachelor's degree in criminal justice from Michigan State University and plans to pursue her doctorate degree.

Essex, Nathan L. (Ph.D.), at the time this article appeared in *The School Administrator,* was professor and Dean of the College of Education, University of Memphis.

Fey, Gil-Patricia, at the time this article appeared in *The School Administrator,* was a research assistant in the College of Education, Division of Policy Studies and Educational Leadership, Arizona State University, Tempe, AZ.

Green, Mary W., is associated with the Sandia National Laboratories in Albuquerque, New Mexico.

Kosar, John E., at the time this article appeared in *The School Administrator,* was the president of the architectural and design firm of Burt Hill Kosar Rittlemann Associates, Butler, PA.

Linton, Eugene P., at the time this article appeared in *The School Administrator,* was Superintendent, Mercer County Educational Service Center, Celina, OH.

Longoria, Thomas, Jr. (Ph.D., Texas A&M University, 1994), is an associate professor of public administration at the University of Kansas . He has previously published in journals such as the *Social Science Quarterly*, *Urban Affairs Review*, and *State and Local Government Review*. He is currently working on a project examining nonprofit organizations along the U.S.-Mexico border.

Mack, W. R. III (Ph.D., Texas A&M University, 1999), is an assistant professor of political science at the University of Texas at El Paso. He has previously published in *American Politics Quarterly* and the *Texas Journal of Political Studies*. He is currently working on manuscripts relating to telemedicine use in rural Texas and the legislative influence of the president in Congress when the president orders the use of military force in international affairs.

Manganaro, Lynne L. (D.P.A., Arizona State University, 1997), is an assistant professor of political science at the University of Texas at El Paso. She has previously published in *Political Research Quarterly* and *Urban Affairs Quarterly*.

Mihalic, Sharon (M.A.), has for the last five years directed the Blueprints for Violence Prevention Initiative at the Center for the Study and Prevention of Violence at the University of Colorado. She has examined the evaluations of numerous violence-prevention programs and has had major input into the selection of the Blueprints programs. She is a coauthor or contributing author on the 11 Blueprints books. She provides the oversight for four major projects funded by the Office of Juvenile Justice and Delinquency Prevention to replicate the Blueprints programs in multiple sites nationwide. Other research includes several articles in the areas of marital violence, drug use, and the effects of adolescent employment on delinquency.

Nelson, J. Ron (Ph.D.), at the time this article appeared in *The School Administrator,* was an associate professor of education in the Division of Psychology in Education, at Arizona State University, Tempe, AZ.

Roberts, Maura L. (Ph.D.), at the time this article appeared in *The School Administrator,* was an assistant professor of education in the Division of Psychology in Education, at Arizona State University, Tempe, Arizona.

Sickmund, Melissa (Ph.D.) is a senior research associate at the National Center for Juvenile Justice. She joined the National Center for Juvenile Justice in 1986. She holds a Ph.D. in social psychology from the University of Maryland. She is coauthor of the *Juvenile Offenders and Victims* reports and is principal investigator for custody data for OJJDP's National Juvenile Justice Data Analysis Project. She has also been involved with the National Juvenile Court Data Archive, authoring its annual *Juvenile Court Statistics* and *Offenders in Juvenile Court* reports and numerous other reports based on Archive data. Before joining NCJJ, Dr. Sickmund was a statistician with the Bureau of Justice Statistics and an analyst with the Federal Bureau of Prisons.

Snyder, Howard N. (Ph.D.) is the Director of Systems Research at the National Center for Juvenile Justice. He has been the Director of Systems Research at the National Center for Juvenile Justice since 1981. Dr. Snyder has directed several projects funded by the U.S. Department of Justice. The National Juvenile Justice Data Analysis Project is designed to improve the quality, utility, and availability of information on juvenile crime, victimization, and the justice system. As a part of this effort, he and his colleagues have authored the *Juvenile Offenders and Victims* series of reports.

Stephens, Ronald D. (Ph.D., University of Southern California), currently serves as executive director of the National School Safety Center. His undergraduate and graduate degrees are in the field of business management. Dr. Stephens holds the California teaching credential, administrative credential, and Certificate in School Business Management. Dr. Stephens has conducted more than 1,000 school security and safety site assessments throughout the United States. Dr. Stephens serves as consultant and frequent speaker for school districts, law enforcement agencies, and professional organizations worldwide. He is author of numerous articles on school safety as well as the author of *School Safety: A Handbook for Violence Prevention.* Additionally, he serves as the executive editor of *School Safety,* America's leading school crime prevention news journal. His career is distinguished by military service in Vietnam.

SyWassink, Rick (Major), is the chief deputy at the Muscatine County, Iowa, Sheriff's Office. His law enforcement career started in the Cedar Rapids, Iowa, Police Department in 1974. Major SyWassink holds a B.A. in criminal justice from Mt. Mercy College with advanced studies from the University of Iowa, Iowa State University, and St. Ambrose University. Major SyWassink is an adjunct professor of criminal justice at Iowa Wesleyan

College and has trained emergency medical personnel, law enforcement officers, and educators in crime scene response, school violence, and responding to school violence situations.

Stetzner, Kate, at the time this article appeared in *The School Administrator,* was Superintendent of the Butte, Montana, public schools.

Turk, William L. (Ph.D., University of Texas Arlington), is an assistant professor of political science at the University of Texas–Pan American in Edinburg, Texas. He has recently published *When Juvenile Crime Comes to School* (The Edwin Mellen Press, 1999), an in-depth look at and analysis of school crime in 50 Texas school districts. He has published in academic journals and extensively in private industry press. He is currently working on a book about special districts in Texas.

Yeagley, Raymond, at the time this article appeared in *The School Administrator,* was Superintendent, Rochester School Department, Rochester, NH.

Preface

School crime has been on the public agenda for almost 30 years. Violent and dangerous acts occur with some regularity at schools across the country and have for some time. The acts were dismissed by citizens and hidden by education officials. School principals were well aware of the fights on school property, the acts of vandalism, and the weapons confiscated every school year. It was an issue that never reached the "identification of a problem" stage.

Individual acts of crime and whole school disruptions during the rock and roll era, the civil rights movement, the Vietnam War protests, and the dramatically changing lifestyle in post-WWII America did not seem to grab our attention. *Blackboard Jungle* and *Rebel Without a Cause* came closer to alerting Americans that something at school had changed. The advent of congressional hearings in 1975 signaled the beginnings of a fairly recent national concern with school crime.

My hope is that this book will contribute in some small measure toward a better understanding of the problem of school crime, yet I sincerely hope it also offers some possible solutions. It is no accident that this book's content is weighted toward suggested solutions of the problem. Four of the 13 chapters are geared toward an analysis of the problem, while the remaining nine are oriented toward resolution.

The first chapter asks the question: Why is there school crime? The answer is because there is juvenile crime. The larger question of why juveniles or adults commit crimes remains to be answered. Scholars, philosophers, theologians, and others have struggled with this conundrum across the ages. The inability of human beings to consistently obey even the simplest of rules seems to be part and parcel of our basic nature. Chapter 1 is designed to give that overview of juvenile crime in present-day America.

The authors of Chapters 2 through 4 use published data to describe the status of crime occurring in and around schools in the United States, California, and Texas. By examining an overview of school crime in the United States and then specifically looking at the two largest states, it is hoped the reader will gain a clear perspective of the state of crime in schools at this date. What crimes are being committed? Who are the criminals? Who are the victims? What, exactly, are the dimensions of the problem?

The remainder of the book is devoted to working on solutions for the problem identified so conclusively in these first chapters. Chapter 5 addresses the concept of planning for safe schools. Planning is the keystone in the arch of successful safe school management. The very essence of planning is to see opportunities, threats, strengths, and weaknesses. Planning shapes the whole area encompassed by the idea of safe schools. Richard Stephens writes from experience in the field in detail and with conviction. Crime is going to happen in your school; be prepared through proper planning.

Dr. Stephens, who has devoted his life's work to safe schools, then follows with best practices for developing safe schools in Chapter 6. He offers concrete suggestions on how to proceed and especially how to cooperate with local police officials to combat school crime. In my view, cooperation with local police authorities is essential for all schools. Their expertise and experience are invaluable to the school system. No school district can, or should, attempt to "go it alone." "Building community partnerships" is not just common sense; it is imperative. Chapter 6's discussion of "campus access and control," "administrative leadership," "school climate," "student behavior, supervision, and management," "staff training," and "student involvement" is rife with guidance for building safety into the school. The School Crime Assessment Survey in Appendix A is invaluable for an accurate inventory of a school's crime-prevention readiness.

Following along on the recommendation from the previous chapter, Chapter 7 features the work of a practicing police officer. He writes from a practical perspective about the on-site operations during or immediately after a criminal incident. The questions this chapter answers is: Who is in charge, and how do we proceed? Being able to respond to a criminal incident quickly and expeditiously will make all the difference between a catastrophe and a manageable situation. This chapter reinforces the imperative for cooperation—cooperation between schools, parents, and the community holds the greatest promise for solutions to school crime. Rick SyWassink presents the police department's role in the community as a model for this cooperation.

Chapter 8 is devoted to hearing from a classroom teacher. Frontline personnel who are on the spot every single school day offer a unique perspective. Chris Ardis writes in first person, unusual in academic tomes such as this. When she requested my permission to write this way, I did not hesitate to respond positively. Teachers' relationships with their students are personal. Motivations for teaching are many, but what is most often heard runs along the lines of "I feel as though I'm making a difference in the lives of my students." It does not get much more personal than that. Ms. Ardis's observations demand our attention; school crime is so much more than data—it is human life. Read what she writes.

The school administrators responsible for the overall supervision of their charges on a daily basis have a story to tell. Taken from the pages of *The School Administrator* are the six short articles in Chapter 9 that highlight some of the many considerations of administrators as they deal with the school crime problem. Protecting the due process of law for all students, profiling students, designing safer physical surroundings, and hiring a weapon-carrying police officer are all topics that deserve the reader's attention.

Technology plays a part in the solution of the school crime problem. Most school districts cannot afford to conduct their own studies of the types of security products available on the market today. Nor are they in a position to evaluate the strengths and weaknesses of these products and their expected effectiveness in a school environment. Video cameras, video recording equipment, metal detectors, handheld scanners, x-ray baggage scanners, and entry-control technologies are discussed. Author Mary Green, writing for Sandia National Laboratories, is a neutral, nonbiased third-party evaluator with no product to sell, rent, service, or guarantee. Chapter 10 is required reading for all schools investigating additional equipment to address school crime on their premises.

Chapters 11 and 12 are simply an exhaustive presentation of prevention programs of all sizes, colors, and stripes. The two authors review an enormous number of programs designed to prevent school crime. If they had just reviewed the literature of this multitude of programs, they would have done yeomen's work. However, Sharon Mihalic and Tonya Aultman-Bettridge went far beyond a review of existing programs. They set themselves to the task of systematically assessing and evaluating the various programs. Simply stated, assessment is an evaluation of the degree to which a program accomplishes its stated objectives. These authors have done an exemplary job of identifying, reviewing, and evaluating an astronomical number of prevention programs. If you are in the school crime prevention business, this chapter is a MUST read.

The final chapter, lucky 13—meant as a summarizing and concluding chapter—pulls everything together. Additionally, it presents findings from a local student survey, which offers some insights into questions relating to the "perception" and "reality" of school crime.

It has been my intention to present a book that is short on theory, but long on pragmatic information. My hope is that all those concerned with school safety will include this book on the reference shelf behind their desks, to be consulted as conditions require. I see this book as a reference source, a silent consultant if you will, to be read the first time for initial information and immediate action, but to be retained for continual direction. Good reading!

William L. Turk
University of Texas–Pan American
Edinburg, Texas

1

Juvenile Offenders and Victims: 1999 National Report

Howard N. Snyder and Melissa Sickmund

John Dewey, in his now classic Democracy and Education (1916), observed that schools are but a reflection of the communities that accommodate, nourish, and populate them. His chapter "Education as a Social Function" stresses the point that schools are necessarily a part of their surrounding environment. If, as the great educator says, schools are a reflection of their environment, it is then necessary to view the original image itself, making possible a comparison of the reflection with its progenitor. It is appropriate to take the reality of school crime and include the realities of the communities that surround the schools.

The reality of school crime is that it is "location-specific" juvenile crime. That is, school crime is simply juvenile crime that occurs on the property of a public school. The subject of school crime is of great interest because of this location. Historically schools in the United States were places of reverence, of learning, of sanctity. Incidences of minor disruption at school were met with swift punishment. Therefore, the commission of serious crime at school has been and is considered abhorrent.

To understand the overall context of school crime properly, it is necessary to observe what is happening in the extended community, that is, the nation as a whole. What is the status of juvenile crime in the United States? Answering that question will shorten the journey toward answering the question, Why is there school crime in the United States?

Juveniles by definition are persons who have not attained many years of age. Commonly, a person who has not reached the chronological age of 18 is considered a juvenile. For over a century, the U.S. criminal justice system has treated juveniles differently from adults. The public must constantly be reminded that juveniles are different. The fact is obvious, yet so obvious that it is frequently forgotten.

Gathering accurate data on the criminal activities of juveniles is difficult under the best of circumstances. Their parents, their teachers, and society, many times protect juveniles because of their youth in general. Many juvenile offenders are never brought to the attention of the criminal justice system in the commission of minor/major criminal acts.

> Many crimes are never even reported to police and never become part of official crime statistics. The National Crime Victimization Survey found that in 1997, 42% of the serious violent crimes committed by juveniles were ever reported to police. In 1997, police agencies learned about 51% of sexual assaults by juveniles, 40% of robberies by juveniles, and 42% of aggravated assaults by juveniles. These percentages have not changed appreciably in the last 20 years (1999 National Report [full citation follows] p. 63)

Juveniles may not be reported and may not be arrested, or if arrested are not referred to juvenile courts and, thus, are not included in official police or court data. The juvenile justice system uses a number of techniques in an attempt to capture the full extent of juvenile crime in the United States.

One of the very best and most comprehensive studies of juvenile crime in the United States is Howard N. Snyder and Melissa Sickmund's Juvenile Offenders and Victims: 1999 National Report (Washington, DC: Office of Juvenile Justice and Delinquency Prevention, 1999). This publication presents information culled from a number of sources, in a valiant effort to present an accurate picture of juvenile crime nationally. The publication draws data from many sources, including the following: the Bureau of Justice Statistics' Nation Crime Victimization Survey; the Federal Bureau of Investigation's National Incident-Based Reporting System and its Uniform Crime Reports; the National Institute on Drug Abuse's Monitoring the Future Study; the Office of Juvenile Justice and Delinquency Prevention's National Juvenile Court Data Archive; the Bureau of Labor Statistics' National Longitudinal Survey of Youth; the Centers for Disease Control and Prevention's Youth Risk Behavior Surveillance Survey; the National Youth Gang Survey; the Bureau of Alcohol, Tobacco and Firearms' Youth Crime Gun Interdiction Initiative; and, of course, the Bureau of the Census.

A good deal of what follows in this chapter is taken from the 1999 National Report. Immediately below, a complete rendition of the Table of Contents is given for the benefit of the reader. This publication should be on the shelf of every person who works with America's youth. It is an indispensable and constantly utilized reference source.

Table of Contents

Chapter 1: Juvenile population characteristics
  Juvenile population
  Juveniles in poverty
  Living arrangements of juveniles

JUVENILE POPULATION CHARACTERISTICS

Juveniles in the United States today live in a world much different from that of their parents or grandparents. Problems experienced by children at the turn of the century are the products of multiple and sometimes complex causes. Data presented in this chapter indicate that in many ways conditions have improved in recent years, but only marginally. For example, the proportion of juveniles living in poverty has declined recently, but juveniles are still far more likely to live in poverty today than 20 years ago. Similarly, teenage birth rates have declined in recent years but still remain high. Fewer children are being raised by two-parent families as well. Although high school dropout rates have fallen for most juveniles, the rates are still too high, especially in an employment market in which unskilled labor is needed less and less. (p. 1)

In 1998, more than 70 million persons in the United States were below age 18, the age group commonly referred to as *juveniles*. This represents 26% of the total U.S. resident population. The juvenile population fell to its lowest level in nearly three decades in 1984, to below 63 million individuals. Since that year, the juvenile population has increased gradually and is projected to do so well into the next century.

Race and Ethnicity

Between 1995 and 2015, the number of black juveniles is expected to increase 19%, American Indian juveniles 17%, and Asian/Pacific Islander juveniles 74%, while white juveniles will increase 3%. Along with race, the Bureau of the Census also classifies persons by their ethnic origin. Hispanic juveniles (who can be of any race, but are primarily classified racially as white) will increase 59% between 1995 and 2015. Over this period, the number of white non-Hispanic juveniles will decrease 3%. (p. 2)

Poverty

In 1997, the poverty threshold for a family of four was $16,400. Juveniles under age 18 were 26% of the U.S. population, but were 40% of all persons living below the poverty level in 1997.

The proportion of children living in poverty varied by race and ethnicity [Table 1.1]. In 1997, poverty rates for black juveniles and juveniles of Hispanic origin (37%) were far greater than the rates for white (16%) and Asian (20%) juveniles. Due to the proportion of white children in the U.S. population, however, the majority of children living in poverty were white. In 1997, 9 million white juveniles, 4 million black juveniles, and 0.6 million Asian/Pacific Islander juveniles were living in poverty—this included 4 million juveniles of Hispanic origin.

Nontraditional Families

The proportion of children living in two-parent homes declined from 85% to 68% between 1970 and 1997. This roughly paralleled an increase in the percentage of children living with only their mother. While most children (85%) in single-parent families lived with their mothers in 1997, an increasing proportion were living with their fathers. In 1997, similar patterns were seen in the proportion of children living with nonworking parents and the proportion living in poverty. The proportion of children living with a nonworking single parent was more than twice the proportion living with two nonworking parents (34% vs 14%). Children were most likely to live in poverty when living with only their mother. (p. 8)

Education

In the 1950s, a high school education was an asset when entering the work force. In today's society, a high school diploma or its equivalent is often a minimal requirement for obtaining entry-level jobs or for continuing education or training.

Despite the increased importance of completing high school, the completion rate among persons ages 18–24 and not still in school has increased only slightly since 1972 when it was 83%. In 1996, completion rates were about the same for males and females

TABLE 1.1   Percent of Families with Children in Poverty

	1978	1997
All races	13%	16%
White	9	13
Black	34	30
Hispanic	24	30

Note: Race proportions include persons of Hispanic ethnicity. Persons of Hispanic ethnicity can be of any race; however, most are white. (p. 5)

ages 18–24. The rate was lower among Hispanics (62%) than among non-Hispanic whites (92%) or blacks (83%). (p. 12)

A 1992 study reported that 4 in 10 dropouts said they left high school because they did not like school or because they were failing. As many males as females said they left school because they could not get along with their teachers. More males than females dropped out because of school suspension or expulsion.

While overall most dropouts reported school-related reasons for leaving school, most female dropouts reported family-related reasons. (p. 13)

JUVENILE OFFENDERS

Homicide

Based on the Federal Bureau of Investigation's (FBI's) Supplemental Homicide Report (SHR) data, 18,200 persons were murdered in the U.S. in 1997—the lowest number in more than a generation. Of these murders, about 1,400 were determined by law enforcement to involve a juvenile offender; however, the actual number is greater than this. *[7.7% of all murders involve a juvenile offender]*

The 1,400 murders known to involve a juvenile offender in 1997 involved about 1,700 juveniles and 900 adults. Of all murders involving a juvenile, 31% also involved an adult, and 13% involved another juvenile. In all, 44% of all murders involving a juvenile involved more than one person. (p. 53)

Homicide and Urban Counties

Based on SHR data, 88% of the more than 3,000 counties in the U.S. reported no juvenile murderers in 1997. Another 6% of the counties had just one identified juvenile homicide offender in 1997. In fact, more than 1 in 4 juvenile homicide offenders (26%) in 1997 were in 8 counties. The major cities in these 8 counties (beginning with the city in the county with the greatest number of identified juvenile homicide offenders) are Chicago, Los Angeles, Houston, New York, Baltimore, Detroit, Philadelphia, and Dallas. As these 8 counties contain just 12% of the U.S. population, it is clear that homicide by juveniles is concentrated in a small portion of the U.S. geographic area. (p. 57)

Serious Violent Crime

According to the NCVS [National Crime Victimization Survey], in 1997 juveniles under age 18 were involved in 27% of all serious violent victimizations, including 14% of sexual assaults, 30% of robberies, and 27% of aggravated assaults.

Serious and violent victimizations in the U.S. peaked in 1993 at 4.2 million, the highest level since the NCVS began. Between 1993 and 1997, the number of serious violent victimizations with at least one juvenile offender dropped 33%, from 1,230,000 to 830,000. (p. 62)

Time-of-Day for Juvenile Crimes
School Days and Nonschool Days

The FBI's National Incident-Based Reporting System (NIBRS) collects information on each crime reported to law enforcement agencies, including the date and time that the crime was committed. Analyses of these data document that the most likely time for committing a violent crime is different for juveniles and adults.

In general, the number of violent crimes committed by adults increases hourly from 6 a.m. through the afternoon and evening hours, peaks at 11 p.m., and then drops hourly to a low point at 6 a.m. In stark contrast, violent crimes by juveniles peak in the afternoon between 3 p.m. and 4 p.m., the hour at the end of the school day.

The importance of this afterschool period in understanding the patterns of juvenile violence is confirmed when the days of the year are divided into two groups: school days (i.e., Monday through Friday, excluding holidays, in September through May) and nonschool days (all days in June through August, all weekends, and holidays). A comparison of the crime patterns for school and nonschool days finds that the 3 p.m. peak occurs only on school days. The time pattern of juvenile violent crimes on nonschool days is similar to that of adults, with a gradual increase during the afternoon and evening hours, a peak between 8 p.m. and 10 p.m., and a decline thereafter. Therefore, on both school and nonschool days, the level of juvenile violence is relatively low during the time period when juvenile curfew laws are in effect. (p. 64)

High School Students and Weapons

The 1997 Youth Risk Behavior Surveillance System found that 9% of high school students said that in the past 30 days they had carried a weapon (e.g., gun, knife, or club) on school property [Table 1.2]. This was half the proportion of students (18%) who said they had

TABLE 1.2   Percent of High School Students Who Had Carried a Weapon on School Property in the Past 30 Days

	Total	Male	Female
Total	9%	13%	4%
9th grade	10	15	5
10th grade	8	11	4
11th grade	9	15	3
12th grade	7	10	3
White	8	12	2
Black	9	11	8
Hispanic	10	16	4

(p. 68)

carried a weapon anywhere in the past month. Males were more likely than females to say they carried a weapon at school. (p. 68)

Illicit Drug Use Among High School Seniors

In 1998, 54% of all seniors said they had [sic] least tried illicit drugs. Marijuana was by far the most commonly used illicit drug: in 1998, 49% of high school seniors said they had tried marijuana.

Sixteen percent (16%) of high school seniors reported using stimulants, making stimulants the second most prevalent illicit drug after marijuana. In 1998, almost 1 in 10 seniors (9%) said they had used cocaine.

In 1998, 4 in 5 high school seniors said they had tried alcohol at least once; half said they had used it in the previous month. Even among 8th graders, the use of alcohol was high: one-half had tried alcohol and almost one-quarter had used it in the month prior to the survey. (p. 70)

Perhaps of greater concern are the juveniles who indicated heavy drinking (defined as five or more drinks in a row) in the preceding 2 weeks: 31% of seniors, 24% of 10th graders, and 14% of 8th graders reported this behavior.

Tobacco use was less prevalent than alcohol use. In 1998, 65% of 12th graders and 46% of 8th graders had tried cigarettes, and 35% of seniors and 19% of 8th graders had smoked in the preceding month. Of more concern is the fact that 22% of seniors, 16% of 10th graders, and 9% of 8th graders are currently smoking cigarettes on a regular basis. (p. 71)

Between 1975 and 1998, the proportion of high school seniors reporting use of marijuana in the 30 days prior to the survey fluctuated, peaking in 1978 and then declining consistently through 1992. Since then, reported use has increased, but the 1998 rate was still far below the peak level of 1978.

Students' reported use of alcohol also shifted from 1975 to 1998. After 1978, alcohol use fluctuated with a limited range thereafter, but the 1998 rate was far lower than the 1978 rate. (p. 75)

Youth Gangs

The 1996 National Youth Gang survey indicates that an estimated 31,000 gangs were operating in close to 4,800 U.S. cities in 1995. These gangs had more than 846,000 members, half of whom were under age 18 [Table 1.3]. These estimates are higher than those emerging from most previous gang studies. Regardless of whether this reflects actual growth in gang membership, more comprehensive surveying, or other factors, the 1996 survey makes clear that gang problems now affect more jurisdictions than ever before, including many smaller cities and rural and suburban areas with no previous gang experience. (pp. 77–78)

While the overall amount of school crime reported by students showed no significant increase between 1989 and 1995, the proportion of those students who reported the presence of gangs in their schools increased from 15% to 28%. Moreover, the violent victimization rate for students in schools where gangs were reported was 7.5%, considerably higher than the 2.7% rate for students in schools with no reported gang presence. (p. 79)

TABLE 1.3   Demographic Profile of Gang Members, 1995

Total Number	846,000 (100%)

Sex	
Male	90%
Female	10

Race/Ethnicity	
Hispanic	44%
Black	35
White	14
Asian	5
Other	2

Age	
14 or younger	16%
15–17	34
18–24	37
25 or older	13
	(p. 78)

LAW ENFORCEMENT AND JUVENILE CRIME

From the early 1970's through 1988, the number of juvenile arrests for Violent Crime Index offenses (murder and nonnegligent manslaughter, forcible rape, robbery, and aggravated assault) varied with the size of the juvenile population; that is to say, the arrest rate remained constant. In 1989 however, the juvenile violent crime arrest rate jumped to its highest level since the 1960s, the earliest period for which comparable data were available. The rate continued to climb each year thereafter until it reached a peak in 1994. In the 7-year period between 1988 and 1994, the rate surged 62%, straining the resources of the juvenile justice system and causing policymakers to ask what had changed.

The rapid increase was followed by a rapid decline. By 1997, the juvenile violent crime arrest rate was at its lowest level in the 1990's: just 7% above the 1989 rate, but still 25% above the 1988 rate. (p. 120)

JUVENILE COURTS AND JUVENILE CRIME

Age

Juveniles in all age groups contributed to increases in delinquency caseloads between 1987 and 1996.

Delinquency case rates rose substantially between 1987 and 1996 for most age groups.

In 1996, juvenile courts handled 61.8 delinquency cases for every 1,000 juveniles (youth subject to original juvenile court jurisdiction) in the U.S. population. The 1996 delinquency case rate was 34% greater than the 1987 rate. For all but the youngest age groups, delinquency case rates showed similar increases. The greatest increase was found for 15-year-olds. (p. 146)

Gender

Both male and female delinquency caseloads have increased in recent years, females more sharply.

Males are involved in 8 in 10 delinquency cases each year.

Although they constitute only half of the juvenile population, males were involved in about three-quarters of person, property, and public order offense cases handled by the courts in 1996 and in 86% of drug law violations cases. With the exception of drug cases, male proportions were slightly higher in 1987.

Compared with males, female delinquency caseloads grew at a faster pace.

The number of delinquency cases involving females rose 76% between 1987 and 1996, compared with 42% for males. The growth in cases involving females outpaced the growth for males for all but drug offense cases. (p. 148)

Race

In 1996, black juveniles were referred to juvenile court at a rate more than double that for whites.

Caseloads of black juveniles contained a greater proportion of person offenses than did those of other races. Property offense cases accounted for the largest proportion of cases for all racial groups, although among black juveniles, property cases accounted for fewer than half of the cases processed in 1996. For all races, drug offense cases accounted for the smallest proportion of the 1996 caseload. (p. 150)

White juveniles were less likely to be detained than black juveniles and juveniles of other races.

Secure detention was nearly twice as likely in 1996 for cases involving whites, even after controlling for offense. Detention was least likely for cases involving white youth charged with property crimes. Detention was most likely for cases involving black youth charged with drug offenses.

For black youth, the relative increase in the number of delinquency cases involving detention was greater than the relative increase in delinquency cases overall. For white juveniles and juveniles of other races, growth in the overall delinquency caseload was greater than the growth in detention caseload. (p. 154)

A View from Recent Juvenile Arrest Records.   Howard N. Snyder. "Juvenile Arrests 1999," *Juvenile Justice Bulletin*, NCJ 185236, December 2000. Washington, DC: Office of Juvenile Justice and Delinquency Prevention. www.ncjrs.org/html/ojjdp/jjbul2000_12_3/contents.html.

The 1999 murder rate was the lowest since 1966.

The juvenile share of the crime problem decreased in 1999.

In 1999, 27% of juvenile arrests were arrests of females.

Juvenile arrests disproportionately involved minorities.

The chance of being murdered varies with age, gender, and race.

Juvenile arrests for violence in 1999 were the lowest in a decade.

Few juveniles were arrested for violent crime.

Juvenile arrests for property crimes declined substantially in recent years.

Most arrested juveniles were referred to court.

From the Administrator

After peaking in 1994, juvenile violent crime arrests, which had increased substantially since the late 1980's declined dramatically. The juvenile arrest rate for violent crime in 1999 was 36% below its peak in 1994 and from 1993 to 1999, the juvenile arrest rate for murder decreased a remarkable 68%— to its lowest level since the 1960's. The number of juvenile arrests have declined in every violent crime category despite an 8% growth in the juvenile population from 1993 to 1999.

Such encouraging news, however, should not result in complacency or lead us to reduce our efforts to combat violent juvenile crime. Rather, to further reduce the levels of juvenile violence and other juvenile offending, we should continue and expand our work in States and communities across this country to prevent and control delinquency and strengthen the juvenile justice system.

Juvenile Arrests 1999 provides a summary and analysis of national and State juvenile arrest data presented in the FBI report *Crime in the United States 1999*. It offers a road map of where we have been, while identifying trends that can help us to tailor responses and target resources more effectively in order to support the development of healthy, law-abiding youth.

John J. Wilson
Acting Administrator

A View from Juvenile Court Cases.   The Summary table (Table 1.4) gives an overview of juvenile crime nationally over a period of seven years. The general picture shown here, over that time period, is that about 8% of all juvenile crimes are "violent offenses," about 39% of all juvenile crimes are "property offenses," and over half, or 53%, are "delinquency offenses." The general pattern of juvenile crime is weighted toward property crimes and relatively minor offenses, which would be normally attributable to youthful offenders.

Juvenile violent crimes show an "average" 41% increase from 1990 to 1996, which is a very striking and alarming finding. Homicides, rapes, aggravated assaults, in fact all crimes

TABLE 1.4   Summary of Delinquency Cases Disposed by Juvenile Courts by Reason
for Referral, 1990–1996 (in thousands)

Reason for Referral	1990	1991	1992	1993	1994	1995	1996	Avg.
Total offenses	1,320	1,413	1,484	1,515	1,605	1,703	1,758	1,543
Case rate[1]	51.7	54.4	55.8	55.8	58.2	60.7	61.8	
Violent Offenses	97	109	121	124	135	141	137	123
Homicide	2	2	2	3	3	3	2	
Rape	5	6	6	7	6	7	7	
Robbery	28	31	33	35	37	39	37	
Aggravated assault	62	70	79	80	88	93	90	
Property Offenses	564	613	617	593	594	619	623	603
Burglary	146	154	158	149	142	139	141	
Larceny	342	381	381	374	382	416	422	
Motor veh. theft	71	72	71	63	61	53	52	
Arson	7	7	8	8	9	11	9	
Delinquency Offenses	658	691	746	798	877	943	998	816
Simple assault	128	139	155	171	184	204	217	
Vandalism	100	112	118	119	124	120	120	
Drug law violations	71	65	73	91	125	159	176	
Obstruction of justice	80	76	80	90	102	109	126	
Other[2]	278	298	320	328	343	351	359	

[1]Number of cases disposed per 1,000 youth (ages 10–17) at risk.

[2]Includes such offenses as stolen property, trespassing, weapons offenses, other sex offenses, liquor law violations, disorderly conduct, and miscellaneous offenses.

Source: www.census.gov/prod/2001pubs/statab/sec05.pdf. February 16, 2001.

in this category, have increased, with a slight dip down in the very last year included. Comparably, property offenses have "on average" increased by only 10%, and delinquency offenses have increased by 52% during the seven-year period. The reader should note that delinquency offenses, that is, those offenses that are least serious, account for the greatest number of juvenile crimes, and the greatest percentage of increase. Simple assault, vandalism, trespassing, disorderly conduct, and other miscellaneous offenses are included in this general category of crimes.

Note should also be taken of how police professionals categorize various types of crime. Four specific crimes are considered "violent" because these crimes are specifically aimed at or committed against other individuals. These are serious crimes. The other two categories are crimes against property and crimes associated with being a juvenile.

Figure 1.1 is intended to give a visual representation of the three groupings of juvenile crimes nationally over the seven-year period, as shown in the Summary table. As can be seen from the figure, the delinquency offense and property offense categories are by far the most numerous and have been so over the entire period. Juveniles are mostly involved in minor and property offenses. Violent offenses are the most serious and the most alarming. The fact that this category has grown over time is of great concern. However, it is crucial to recognize that these crimes, while showing an increase, constitute a relatively small percentage of the total crime committed by juveniles. Must society be concerned with even this "small 8%"? Of course! Violent crime, serious crime is the topic of much of the concern of school officials, they are concerned with all school crime, but serious crime presents the greatest threat. However, let us not lose sight of the "big picture," which in this case shows an overall pattern whereby 92% of juvenile crime is classified as nonserious property and minor juvenile offenses.

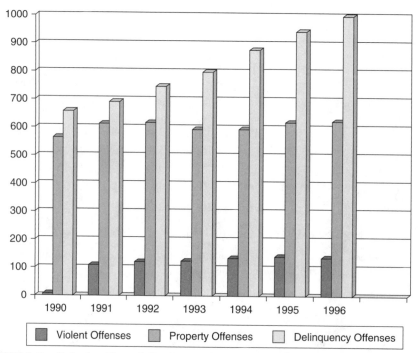

FIGURE 1.1   Relative Size of the General Categories of National Juvenile Crime

2

School Crime in the United States: A Brief Analysis of Patterns and Trends

Lynne L. Manganaro and Thomas Longoria, Jr.

Public policy, simply put, is everything that government does and does not do. The series of events that leads government either to do something or not to do something can be thought of as the public policy process; that is, the process by which government deliberately decides to engage in an action or not engage in an action. It is generally accepted that the public policy process contains a number of identifiable stages. The first and perhaps most important stage in the process is problem recognition.

Before the legislative branch of government considers an issue, before an executive agency administers a program aimed at an issue, and before the judicial branch interprets a conflict arising out of some issue, that issue must first be recognized as a problem requiring government attention. Not every problem or issue requires public attention, particularly at the local level. Many public issues are resolved informally, without the need for any specific governmental action. Many issues, problems, or conflicts have been around for years, without arousing any great degree of public perception. Only after a problem has been recognized can that issue be placed on the public policy agenda; then it will compete with other issues for consideration.

School administrators, faculty, staff, parents, students, and the public at large have known since the first public school was opened in the United States that at school there has been some degree of petty theft, simple assault, disorderly conduct, destruction, or defacing of public property. It can be assumed that in the first school attended by the first students in colonial America, some students carved their initials or names into benches or desks, that the outside privy was tipped over occasionally, that some of the boys engaged in fisticuffs from time to time and that some small personal item found its way into another person's possession. Leaders in the colonial public school movement discussed discipline at great length. Later, Horace Mann, John Dewey, and many others wrote and spoke of these sorts of things, which occurred at or near public schools. Hollywood was not engaging in pure fiction with the early 1950s movies Blackboard Jungle and Rebel Without a Cause. Switchblade knives, violence, assaults, rape, theft, and so forth are staples of these films.

The difference today is that those fictional renditions are far tamer than the reality found in some twenty-first-century public schools. Episodes in schools across the United States dwarf the fictional accounts by their violence, senseless-ness, and magnitude. School violence and crime are no longer simple, isolated incidents. Enough has happened to cause concern throughout the length and breadth of the country.

This chapter is designed to identify the problem of school crime from a national perspective. What is the REAL situation with crime and violence in the nation's schools? How extensive is it? Where is it happening, and who is engaged in it? How pervasive is it? What crimes are being committed at school, how often, and by whom? These authors look at three years of national data compiled jointly by the U.S. Departments of Education and Justice to find the answers to these questions.

How safe are U.S. schools? With the recent spate of school shootings, this question looms large among students, parents, school administrators, policy makers, and the general public. Although rare occurrences, the shootings generate a perception that schools in the United States are no longer safe venues for learning. A climate of fear affects both students and teachers. As a result, many resources and strategies have been employed over the last few years to address school violence and safety. A key component in trying to address school violence involves collecting data for decision makers. Until 1997 there were no centralized repositories of data on school safety available to interested parties. Most states, or for that matter local school districts, did not have comprehensive data collection strategies. If data collection strategies did exist, they were not uniform across districts or states. For example, one reporting agency included frying pans in a list of dangerous weapons. To address the growing public concern over school crime, in 1997 President Clinton directed the U.S. Departments of Education and Justice to prepare an annual report on school safety. The directive resulted in the *Annual Report on School Safety* (1998, 1999, 2000) (hereinafter *Annual Report*) and its compendium volume *Indicators of School Crime and Safety* (1998, 1999, 2000) (hereinafter *Indicators*).

The information presented in this chapter comes from two sources: the *Annual Report* and the *Indicators*. The *Annual Report* presents an overview of school crime and safety from data collected in the *Indicators*. Data collected in the *Indicators* come from five primary sources: the Bureau of Justice Statistics, the National Center for Education Statistics, the National Center for Health Statistics, the Centers for Disease Control and Prevention, and the Survey Research Center of the University of Michigan. When inter-preting the data, it is important to keep this in mind that data collection methodologies and coding of incidents vary. To supplement the aggregate statistics, this chapter also presents and discusses newspaper articles that provide more of the context for the collection, use, and interpretation of school crime data in practice. The various studies do, however, utilize a representative sampling of schools.

The reporting of school crime has likely increased over the years as a reflection of growing concern stimulated by triggering events and the media. Schools with recently adopted zero tolerance policies probably now report previously unreported incidents. Thus, reported levels of school crime, if shown to increase, may be biased at the individual school and, when aggregated, may be an artifact of the act of being reported. Even with concerns over data collection and methodology, the reports shed light on the issue of violence in U.S. schools. The remainder of this chapter presents a summary of the major findings of these reports, examines areas in which there have been substantial changes over time, and draws conclusions.

OVERALL TRENDS

For the period 1992 through 1998, there has been a significant decline in the number of nonfatal crimes against students ages 12 through 18. In 1992, there were 148 total crimes per 1,000 students, and by 1998 the number had decreased 32% to 100 total crimes per 1,000 students. Thefts also declined by 45%, from 100 per 1,000 in 1992 to 55 per 1,000 in 1998. Violent crime (about 50 per 1,000 students) and serious violent crime (about 8 per 1,000 students) rates have remained essentially the same for the last seven years. The trends related to school-based crime are roughly tracked by crimes against young people both at school, which also includes time en route to and from school, and away from school. Not surprisingly, the data reveal that there is typically more total crime and more theft against students away from school than at school. In particular, violent crimes and serious violent crimes against youth are higher away from school than in school (*Indicators,* 2000:5). For example, between July 1997 and June 1998, there were 35 murders and suicides at school, compared with 2,752 murders and suicides away from school (*Indicators,* 2000:2).

Generally there are few differences in the number of student victims of crime when considering gender, age, and urbanicity. The only exception is violent crimes, of which males as well as younger students (ages 12–14) are both more likely to be victims. Although the stereotype is that urban schools will report higher levels of crime generally and violent crime specifically, the data do not bear this out. For example, urban schools reported 49 violent crimes per 1,000, suburban schools reported 40 per 1,000, and rural schools reported 43 per 1,000 (*Indicators,* 2000:6). The typical school reported no serious violent crimes. Ninety percent of public schools did not report any serious violent crimes to the police in 1997 (*Indicators*, 2000:18).

However, crime does affect students in urban areas more, but in off-campus settings. Whereas there are no differences in violent crime rates on campus, students in urban areas are victims of violent crime at a rate of 65 per 1,000 compared with 50 per 1,000 in suburban areas and 25 per 1,000 in rural areas (*Indicators,* 2000:6). Based on these differences, we can conclude that urban schools are doing a satisfactory job in keeping students relatively safe compared with the hazards they face when not in school (*Indicators,* 2000:7). The on-campus/off-campus differences are dramatic in several cases. For example, in 1993, 42% of youth reported having been in a physical fight anywhere in the last 12 months compared with 16% of youth who reported having been in a physical fight on campus. By 1997,

37% of students reported being in a physical fight anywhere and 15% on school property (*Indicators,* 2000:12).

At the aggregate level, there has been a modest decline in criminal victimization from 1995 to 1999. In 1995, 10% of students reported being victims of a crime, compared with 8% in 1999. Most of this decline can be attributed to more dramatic decline in reported criminal victimization for students in grades six through nine. For example, the percentage of ninth-graders reporting crimes decreased from 12% in 1995 to 9% in 1999 (*Indicators,* 2000:8). While levels of property theft remained essentially the same from 1993 to 1997 within grade levels, there was a decline in reported theft when different student classifications were examined. For example, in 1997, 37% of freshmen reported property theft, compared to 28% of seniors (*Indicators,* 2000:15).

The next sections present more detailed information about different types of crimes against students and teachers.

CRIMES AGAINST STUDENTS

Theft

Theft continues to be a major source of school crime for both students and teachers. Table 2.1 reports the theft rate against students (per 1,000) ages 12 through 18 occurring at school or en route to or from school for a variety of demographic characteristics from 1992 to 1998. According to Table 2.1, thefts against males and females appear to be in decline since 1992. Even though the theft rates for both groups declined significantly between 1992 and 1998, thefts against students were more prevalent during the middle school years (12–14) compared to the high school years (15–18). For example, in 1992, 12- to 14-year-olds reported a theft rate of 105 per 1,000, compared with 87 thefts per 1,000 for the 15- to 18-year-old group. In 1998, these rates declined to 65 thefts per 1,000 and 53 per 1,000, respectively. By 1998 the differences between middle and high school theft victimization rates were not significantly different. Perhaps this is partly a reflection of the difficulty experienced during adolescence in general. Again, the data reveal that the rate has decreased over the time period examined.

With respect to ethnicity, Table 2.1 reveals that white and "other" students appear to be the victims of theft slightly more than do black or Hispanic students. These results could also be a function of differences in self-reporting rates between the groups. Again, even though theft remains the most common crime against students, the rates for all four groups appear to be declining over time. Finally, the urbanicity of the school impacts theft rates. Theft occurs more often in suburban schools compared with urban or rural schools. However, this could also be a function of reporting; suburban students may be more likely to report a theft than their urban and rural counterparts. The trend for theft rates regarding urbanicity also decreases between the reporting periods. Urban schools experienced a 26% decline, suburban districts a 46% decline, and rural districts a 38% decline.

Violent Crime

Violent crimes against students include serious violent crimes and simple assault. Serious violent crime includes rape, sexual assault, robbery, and aggravated assault. Table 2.2 reports the violent crime rate against students (per 1,000) ages 12 through 18

TABLE 2.1   **Number of Nonfatal Crimes Against Students Ages 12 through 18 Occurring at School or on the Way to or from School per 1,000 Students, Theft, 1992 to 1998**

Gender	1992	1993	1994	1995	1996	1997	1998
Male	105	101	97	92	78	64	59
Female	85	91	90	77	77	61	58
Age							
12–14	105	111	109	103	91	69	65
15–18	87	83	81	70	67	58	53
Race/Ethnicity							
White, non-Hispanic	105	106	101	93	83	67	60
Black, non-Hispanic	67	76	81	64	73	59	64
Hispanic	72	68	74	67	58	44	48
Other, non-Hispanic	110	70	71	80	72	72	57
Urbanicity							
Urban	92	84	78	78	76	63	68
Suburban	105	113	107	96	82	66	56
Rural	80	77	84	70	71	55	50

occurring at school or en route to or from school between 1992 and 1998 for a variety of demographic characteristics. The violent crime rate against males has declined by 19%, and even though the rate for females has remained constant, they are still less likely than males to be victims of violent crime. There appears to be a higher rate of violent crime perpetrated against students between the ages of 12 and 14, almost 2 to 1 for the inclusive years. However, the rate for both groups shows a decline overall.

In terms of race/ethnicity, a pattern between the four groups is harder to discern. Violent crime against students of each race/ethnic group occurs at similar rates, with the exception of the "other" category. For example, in 1998 the violent crime rate for white and black students was fairly even, with white students reporting a victimization rate of 45 per 1,000 and black students a rate of 48 per 1,000. Hispanic students reported a rate of 34 per 1,000. Across time, the data suggest that white students reported being victimized more consistently than the other three groups for the years 1992, 1993, 1995, and 1997. Hispanic students reported being victimized more during 1994 and 1996, and black students more during 1998. While violence against white, black, and Hispanic students appeared to have declined somewhat, violence against students identifying as "other" increased 68% over the reporting period.

TABLE 2.2   **Number of Nonfatal Crimes Against Students Ages 12 through 18 Occurring at School or on the Way to or from School per 1,000 Students, Violent, 1992 to 1998**

Gender	1992	1993	1994	1995	1996	1997	1998
Male	64	70	65	59	56	50	52
Female	32	46	47	41	30	29	33
Age							
12–14	67	16	78	73	60	54	60
15–18	33	9	38	31	30	29	30
Race/Ethnicity							
White, non-Hispanic	52	63	55	54	45	43	45
Black, non-Hispanic	46	52	59	47	32	36	48
Hispanic	41	50	63	46	51	32	34
Other, non-Hispanic	19	29	39	23	36	19	32
Urbanicity							
Urban	92	15	65	49	50	42	49
Suburban	105	12	62	57	48	46	40
Rural	80	11	37	39	24	24	43

Moving to the urbanicity (degree of urbanization within an area) of the school, we see that in 1992 a high of 105 violent incidents against students was reported in suburban schools. Table 2.2 reveals that 1992 was a peak year for violence against students regardless of the urbanicity of the school. Since then the rates have decreased, although, in general, suburban and urban schools report more violent crime than their rural counterparts. There has been a decline in violent crime in urban and suburban schools and an increase in the rural schools, so that by 1998, there were no significant differences. This change introduces a new area for concern and suggests that rural schools should develop an equally aggressive and proactive strategy to deal with violent crime.

Serious Violent Crime

Serious violent crime, although less prevalent in U.S. schools, remains a critical concern of school administrators in providing safe venues for children to learn. These are the incidents that make the evening news and fuel community concern over school safety. The *Indicators* in 2000 defines serious violent crime as rape, sexual assault, robbery, and aggravated assault. Table 2.3 reports the serious violent crime rate against students (per 1,000) ages 12

TABLE 2.3 Number of Nonfatal Crimes Against Students Ages 12 through 18 Occurring at School or on the Way to or from School per 1,000 Students, Serious Violent, 1992 to 1998

Gender	1992	1993	1994	1995	1996	1997	1998
Male	15	14	15	11	11	10	10
Female	5	11	10	6	6	5	8
Age							
12–14	16	16	18	13	9	10	14
15–18	6	9	9	5	8	6	6
Race/Ethnicity							
White, non-Hispanic	9	11	11	7	7	7	9
Black, non-Hispanic	18	22	15	13	12	8	12
Hispanic	10	9	22	11	15	10	11
Other, non-Hispanic		6	13	9	11	5	4
Urbanicity							
Urban	15	15	21	14	14	12	13
Suburban	10	12	13	7	8	8	7
Rural	6	11	4	5	4	2	11

through 18 occurring at school or en route to or from school between 1992 and 1998 for a variety of demographic characteristics. Looking at the serious violent crime rates displayed in Table 2.3 reveals that serious violent crime rates are *very low* compared to either theft or violent crime. Serious violent crime against students regardless of gender has remained fairly constant between 1992 and 1998. Again, in self-reports, male students are more likely to be victimized than female students.

Serious violent crime against students based on their race/ethnic background appears higher for black and Hispanic students compared with white students or students identified as other. In general, the rates for serious violent crime against black and Hispanic students are consistently higher across all years. Serious violent crime against white students appears relatively constant across all years. Finally, with respect to urbanicity, Table 2.3 suggests that serious violent crime against students occurs more frequently in urban schools. It also seems that serious violent crime is on the decline in suburban schools, but might be on the rise in rural schools. In 1998, rural schools reported a rate of 11 incidents per 1,000, an 83% increase. Only data from subsequent years will bear this out as a real change or change that is an artifact of data collection issues. In any event, the growth in serious violent crime in rural areas is an emerging issue and challenge for school administrators.

Bullying and Fighting

Bullying is typically viewed as a common and enduring schoolyard occurrence as much as is theft. However, there has been much speculation over the role that bullying plays in some of the school shootings. Some believe bullying has been a major catalyst in the more horrific instances of school violence. Unfortunately, it is difficult to get a handle on the level of bullying occurring in U.S. schools because of underreporting. For a myriad of reasons that include intimidation and lack of efficacy, most students never report bullying to school authorities. With President Clinton's directive to track school crime, the *Indicators* have begun to collect data on bullying. In 1999, 5.1% of students reported being bullied at school. In terms of gender, 5.4% of males reported being victims of bullying, compared with 4.8% of females.

Being a victim of bullying is more prevalent in middle school. For example, in 1999, nearly 1 in 10 of sixth and seventh graders reported being bullied at school. When this is broken down by gender, however, the differences are significant. Totals of 12.6% of sixth-grade boys and 10.9% of seventh-grade boys reported being victims of bullying, compared with 8.0% of sixth-grade girls and 7.0% of seventh-grade girls. For high school students, the bullying rates equalized for males and females. When looking at the overall totals for bullying, the data suggest that bullying is not a gender-specific behavior. However, the data also clearly show that the middle school years are more problematic for males than females.

Fighting is another relatively common schoolyard occurrence. The *Indicators* of 2000 reported data on students fighting in grades 9 through 12 for the years 1993, 1995, and 1997. The percentage of students who reported having been in a physical fight during the last 12 months (on school property) declined slightly from 16.2% in 1993, 15.5% in 1995, to 14.8% in 1997. For all three years, males (23.5%, 21.0%, 20.0%) were almost three times more likely than females (8.6%, 9.5%, 8.6%) to engage in fighting. Fighting occurred more frequently in the ninth grade and remained relatively constant across the three time periods (23.1%, 21.6%, and 21.3%). The breakdowns for the other grades are as follows: tenth grade (17.2%, 16.5%, and 17.0%), eleventh grade (13.8%, 13.6%, and 12.5%), and twelfth grade (11.4%, 10.6%, and 9.5%) (*Indicators,* 2000:61).

CRIMES AGAINST TEACHERS

Overview

Teachers are not immune to victimization. For example, the May 2000 slaying of Florida middle school teacher Barry Grunow by a 13-year-old student demonstrates that teachers are just as likely to be the primary target of violence. On average, between the years 1994 and 1998, there were 133,700 violent crimes against teachers at school and 217,400 thefts from teachers (*Annual Report,* 2000:8). Data for teacher victimization come primarily from teacher reports collected by various agencies previously identified. Unfortunately, the *Indicators* do not detail nonfatal teacher victimization to the same degree as student victimization.

Theft

Our nation's teachers experience theft at about the same rate as their students. The *Indicators* of 2000 reported aggregated data for theft against teachers for the years 1994 to 1998. In the data, the average annual number of thefts per 1,000 teachers is broken down by instructional level, gender, race/ethnicity, and urbanicity. The theft rate against teachers was lowest in elementary schools, at 39 thefts per 1,000, and highest for middle/junior high schools, at 67 thefts per 1,000, with senior high schools falling slightly below middle/junior high, at 63 thefts per 1,000. It should be remembered the theft rate against students was also the highest in middle/junior high. Female teachers experienced theft at a slightly higher rate than their male counterparts (53 versus 45 per 1,000).

Turning to race/ethnicity, Hispanic teachers reported the highest theft victimization rate (58 per 1,000), followed by white teachers (52 per 1,000), black teachers (41 per 1,000), and other teachers (37 per 1,000). While students in suburban schools are more likely to report being victims of theft, teachers in urban schools are more likely to report theft victimization. The theft rate against teachers in urban schools is 63 per 1,000, with suburban schools reporting a rate of 46 per 1,000 and rural schools a rate of 31 per 1,000.

Other Crime

Teachers are also subject to personal attacks and are more likely to be victims of violent rather than serious violent crime. Data from the *Indicators* of 2000, aggregated from 1994 to 1998, report the number of violent and serious violent crimes per 1,000 teachers for selected characteristics. In terms of instructional level, teachers are more likely to experience violent crime in middle school at a rate of 60 per 1,000, compared with high school (38 per 1,000) and elementary school (18 per 1,000). Serious violent crime against teachers occurs at a much lower rate, and the data show 5 incidents per 1,000 in elementary school, followed by 4 incidents per 1,000 in middle school, and 2 incidents per 1,000 in high school. Male teachers are twice as likely to be the recipients of both violent (53 incidents per 1,000) and serious violent (6 per 1,000) crime compared with female teachers (25 per 1,000 and 3 per 1,000) (*Indicators,* 2000:25).

According to the data, teachers in urban schools are more likely to be victimized than their suburban or rural counterparts. The violent crime rate against teachers in urban schools is 40 incidents per 1,000, compared with 24 incidents per 1,000 for teachers in suburban and rural schools. The serious violent crime rate is 5 incidents per 1,000 against teachers in urban schools, compared with 3 incidents per 1,000 for teachers in suburban and rural schools. The level of violent crime against teachers is approximately two times higher in urban schools than in nonurban schools. There is an urban effect for teachers but not for students, for whom rates of violent crime victimization are essentially the same (*Indicators,* 2000:25). Finally, white and Hispanic teachers reported being victims of violent crimes at a rate of 33 incidents per 1,000, compared with black teachers (24 incidents per 1,000) and teachers identifying as "other" (13 incidents per 1,000). For serious violent crime, teachers identifying as "other" reported 7 incidents per 1,000, compared with 5 for black and 4 for white teachers.

SCHOOL ENVIRONMENT

The perception that schools are unsafe prompts many students to carry weapons to school as a self-protection measure. However, the presence of weapons generates a vicious cycle in that it creates an intimidating and threatening atmosphere, making teaching and learning difficult (*Indicators,* 2000:29). The *Indicators* of 2000 summarized the percentage of students in grades 9 through 12 who reported carrying a weapon (gun, knife, or club) on school property at least 1 day in the past 30 for 1993, 1995, and 1997. Overall, the data indicate that the percentage of students who reported carrying a weapon to school during the specified periods has remained constant over time. In 1993, 11.8% of students reported carrying a weapon, compared with 9.8% in 1995 and 8.5% in 1997. Even with the slight decrease, nearly 1 in 12 students carried a weapon at least 1 day, a considerable level of risk for other students and teachers alike.

Male students are more likely than female students to carry weapons to school by a ratio of 3 to 1, even though the proportion of males carrying weapons has declined by 30%. While the incidence of carrying weapons to school decreased over the time periods, carrying weapons to school appears to be slightly more prevalent during the junior high years. Students in the 9th grade reported the highest percentage of weapon carrying for all three time periods with 12.6%, 10.7%, and 10.2%, respectively. The year 1993 found the highest percentage of students in grades 9 through 12 carrying weapons to school. These self-reports declined in 1995 and again in 1997 for all grades. The percentage of 10th graders carrying weapons declined by 33%, 11th graders by 21%, and 12th graders by 35% (*Indicators,* 2000:78).

If we compare the percentage of students who reported carrying weapons off campus to those who carried them only on school property, the numbers are significantly different by a factor of almost 2 to 1. For example, in 1993 the total number of students who reported carrying a weapon off campus was 22%, compared with 12% of students carrying a weapon on school property. Similar patterns hold for differences by gender. Males are more likely than females to carry weapons off campus. For example, in 1997, 28% of males reported carrying a weapon off campus versus 7% of females. It appears that nearly 1 in 3 male students reported carrying weapons off campus. The data also show that students are not carrying weapons on school property to the same extent that they are off campus. Over time, schools experienced a 25% decrease in students carrying weapons on school property, compared with an 18% decrease in students carrying weapons off campus. The data reveal that schools are relatively safer for students than their general environment, either as a function of perception or of security measures (*Indicators,* 2000:28).

SCHOOL CRIME AND VIOLENCE: OVERALL PATTERNS

Due to the nature of the data reported, it is difficult to make any definitive statements regarding the state of school crime and violence in U.S. schools. However, the data summarized do reveal some general patterns that are interesting to note. School crime (whether violence, theft, or bullying) appears more prevalent in the middle schools for both students and teachers. Males are more likely to be victims of violent crime, whereas females are more likely to be victims of theft. Rural schools, although not immune from violence or crime, appear relatively safe compared with their urban and suburban counterparts.

THE INTERSECTION OF AGGREGATE STATISTICS AND PUBLIC POLICY: WHAT CAN WE MAKE OF THESE "FINDINGS"?

The summary of national-level aggregate statistics is meant to round out general trends. As such, it is difficult to make substantial policy suggestions. For example, the impact of reporting requirements on increasing the number of reported school-based crimes is unknown and may be skewing the data. Zero tolerance has also had an impact on reporting of school-based crime, but to an unknown extent. In order to make more sense of aggregate statistics, a sampling of recent newspaper articles surrounding school crime and violence follows.

The Good News: Investments in Prevention Pay Off

The case of Aiken County schools in Georgia reminds the public that the ultimate public policy goal is to have no crimes in the schools. According to school superintendent Linda Eldride, "we're happy the numbers are down, but we would like to see them at zero." For example, during the 1998–1999 school year, 0.43 school crime incidents were reported per 100 students, compared with 0.66 the previous year. This decline is considered by local officials to be evidence that the school district's zero tolerance approach to school violence works (Throne, 2001). At the state level, the Georgia State Education Superintendent is confronting a growing rate—1.49 incidents per 100, up 8% from the previous year—and is attributing the increase to the fact that more schools are taking a strict approach and reporting more crimes (Throne, 2001). The decline in school crime incidents in Aiken County is being attributed to a conservative school board that supports zero tolerance and a character education component of the school curriculum. Despite the decline, the state education superintendent requested $14 million to add to the 250 police officers who currently patrol the schools.

School leadership that makes school safety a priority was also attributed to low school-based crime rates in Alachua County, Florida. According to a school board member, "fifty years ago, we didn't think about that . . . parents want to know, number one, if their children will be safe" (Carr, 2000). While intervention and making arrests consume much of the time of safety officers in middle and high schools, a school violence prevention program is in place for elementary school students who can, according to the first ever district security chief, still be turned around (Carr, 2000). Resource officers who spearhead the prevention efforts are paid through a combination of district money and state grants for a total of $719,411. The Alachua County Sheriff's deputies made a total of 142 arrests in areas such as drug or weapon possession and fighting.

The Bad News: Other Zero Tolerance "Costs"

The trade-off between more enforcement and more prevention is significant. The other side of zero tolerance has already been felt in a number of ways. Recently proposed legislation in California alleges that the civil rights of Latinos and African-American students are being violated due to zero tolerance policies, and that there should also be a national database of suspensions and expulsions so that statistical analysis can determine whether zero tolerance enforcement is having a disproportionate impact on minority students. The issue of disproportionate impact is significant because suspensions and expulsions are predictors of dropping out of school and subsequently dooming young persons to unemployment, underemployment, and/or low-wage jobs, and possibly a future defined by crime and drugs.

An FBI report urged school officials to be aware of students who are preoccupied with violence, skilled with weapons, and left out of peer groups (McQueen, 2000). A copy of the report *The School Shooter: A Threat Assessment Perspective* can be found at the Bureau's website, www.fbi.gov. James Kent, superintendent of the school district in which 17-year-old Kip Kinkle killed two teens at a high school, said that "the guide could have helped school officials pay closer attention to the boy, who had killed his parents at home before he left for school," and endorsed the use of such data and information (McQueen, 2000).

Concerns about the impact of the FBI report specifically, and the strategy in general, have been criticized. For example, after the release of the report, Vincent Schiraldi of the Justice Policy Institute, a youth advocacy think tank, stated that "I'm fearful once we start putting these things out, every principal in America is going to come up with the names of 10 kids" that fit the profile (McQueen, 2000). The report provides school teachers and administrators with a list of personality and behavioral traits such as "poor coping skills, access to weapons, signs of depression, drug and alcohol abuse, alienation, narcissism, inappropriate humor, no limits on or monitoring of television and internet use" (McQueen, 2000). The report was "intentionally vague" about what to do, according to an FBI official, because school shootings are a relatively rare occurrence. There is simply not enough data to create a profile.

Still, there is a considerable stigma associated with children who "act strangely." According to Bruce Hunder, a lobbyist who represents the American Association of School Administrators, "school leaders do keep an eye on children who act strangely. Often, troubled children are referred to the alternative classrooms and schools that have doubled in the last few years" (McQueen, 2000). Stigmatizing students through assignment to alternative classrooms and profiling remains a problem according to Schiraldi, noting that "I think when we're trying to figure out what makes kids tick, we ought to talk to parents, teachers, child psychologists, students themselves, not people called 'special agent.'"

Interestingly, being a boy was not listed as a risk factor or a characteristic as part of the FBI "profile." The discussion of school crime often notes the fact that boys indeed commit more crimes, both school and non-school based, than do girls. Boys do not fare well in U.S. schools. They are less likely to go to college, are more often placed in special education courses or labeled as slow learners, and are more apt to be diagnosed with attention deficit disorder and placed on more powerful prescription drugs than their female counterparts (Knickerbocker, 2001). Boys, for example, are more likely to withdraw to television and the Internet. This "escape and comfort—condoned if not encouraged by the adults in their lives—accelerates the separation from parents and other important adults" (Knickerbocker, 2001). Boys receive mixed messages from society about men and masculinity. They are pressured to be "cool, confident, and strong" and at the same time "sensitive and open with their feelings." Most boys withdraw or "clam-up," according to William Pollack, a psychologist (Knickerbocker, 2001). Another psychologist, Dan Kindlon, found that "boys are not taught how to handle their emotions . . . we just tell them to sit on it and tough it out" (Knickerbocker, 2001).

In addition to concerns about differential impacts on minority students and the consequences of "profiling," zero tolerance also impacts the ability to collect reliable and consistent data across school districts and states that can then be used in the decision-making process. Take the case of an 18-year-old Florida National Merit Scholar with a 3.75 grade-point average who was suspended from school, charged with a felony, jailed, and banned from her graduation—all for, unbeknownst to her, innocently leaving a steak knife on the floor of her car. Stories such as these demonstrate the need for consensus and uniformity on the definitions of such things as bullying, fighting, and particularly what constitutes a weapon. For example, if a student shoves another student, should it be reported to begin with, and if the decision to report is made, under what classification will shove be placed? What happens if a California school district defines shoving differently from a Texas school district, or when school districts within a state utilize different definitions? Generating an accurate picture of school crime and violence would be seriously undermined without consensus and uniformity in the reporting and data collection process.

THREATS OF VIOLENCE AND THE FEAR FACTOR

Threats of violence should be taken very seriously according to a study conducted by the U.S. Secret Service (*New York Times*, March 9 in *Naples Daily News*). The study, based on an analysis of 37 cases, found that "students who came to school with a plan to kill did not 'just snap.' They had plotted their attacks in advance and, in many cases, had aired their grievances to schoolmates, issued threats and otherwise left clues that might have been used to prevent the attacks" (*New York Times*, March 9 in *Naples Daily News*). This suggests that if serious violent crime is the issue, effective campaigns to encourage students to report threats without being made to feel the stigma of being a "tattletale" are highly significant. Creating a culture that fosters communication between students, teachers, and administrators—no matter the plausibility of the threat—becomes highly significant. Adults are often the last to know, according to former Education Secretary Richard Riley, which means that reliance on peers is crucial.

RISK PERCEPTION: WHICH ARE SAFER, SCHOOLS OR NEIGHBORHOODS?

The national statistics suggest at the aggregate level that schools are much more safe than neighborhoods. However, at least in the case of Nashville, and perhaps many other urban school districts, the risk perception is reversed. According to a survey conducted by *The Tennessean,* "A majority of Nashvillians feel very safe in their homes and walking in their neighborhoods at night, but fewer feel that way about the safety of the city's public schools" (Cheek, 1999). In the case of this particular survey, part of the difference is the potential impact of the Columbine shooting, in which 12 students, one teacher, and then two suicides created a media hype and more, possibly disproportionate, sensitivity to the issue of school violence. In any event, 14% of respondents felt that schools were not safe, compared with 6% who did not feel safe in their homes.

Echoes of Columbine

Any rumors of violence are taken more seriously after Columbine. For example, in Manatee County, Florida, "Rumors of violence and a suicide pact were enough to keep about 800 students home from one of the country's largest high schools . . . despite the fact that authorities weren't sure a threat had even been made" (*Naples Daily News,* 2001). In a nearby district, "heightened fears about school violence had the sheriff's deputies patrolling a middle school where an anonymous written threat was found, about 1,400 students stayed home" (*Naples Daily News,* 2001).

Post-Columbine Lessons: Working With, Not Against Youth

Few school districts have used the federal funds allocated to them to develop such programs and purchase computer software that generates a profile of a likely offender. This strategy of profiling can potentially harm innocent people, and again, accordingly, the solution lies in creating a culture and climate of open communication in which students feel a sense of shared responsibility (*New York Times,* March 9 in *Naples Daily News*).

DISCUSSION

This examination of recent data on school crime and violence results in several conclusions that may be useful to school administrators, teachers, and parents. First, the data clearly show that middle schools are a problem for both teachers and students. Middle school teachers experience higher rates of theft and violent crime compared with their high school counterparts. Middle school students are perpetrators and victims of substantial amounts of crime and violence on school property and off campus. In particular, adolescent boys are more prone to violence, physical fighting, and bullying, while adolescent girls experience theft and bullying to a greater degree than female high school students. Although the adolescent years are difficult in and of themselves, it appears that the schools are not immune to becoming another venue where these age-appropriate difficulties are being expressed. As such, tracking severity with meaningful classifications should be considered. For example, an assault by a sixth grader probably leads to less physical harm to the victim than if two seniors were fighting. In any event, interpretation should be sensitive to context, and prevention and program enforcement should be proportionate to the situation.

There has been an overall decline in rates across different types of school crime. These trends could be dismissed as part of the overall decline in crime in the United States in general. However, at least one explanation for the decline in crime rates overall is that there are, as a proportion, fewer young people who are predisposed to committing crimes in the population. The findings in this study therefore may also be relevant for our consideration of crime in the United States generally. If zero tolerance and other crime-reduction strategies are making schools safer by reducing school-based crime, these young people may be less likely to commit crimes as a cohort later in life. In other words, there may be broader societal benefits of school-based crime-reduction strategies and policies.

Another issue that needs to be considered by policy and decision makers is the reliability of the data. The reporting requirement mandated by President Clinton generates the need for consensus and uniformity in data collection effort by states and school districts. Data collection can be time-consuming and expensive; however, the benefits likely outweigh the costs—especially if school boards, administrators, parents, and the general public use the data to keep school crime on the agenda and make school crime prevention/enforcement and program evaluation a basic aspect of school administration. Because media coverage of sensational incidents can generate negative perceptions of school safety, timely and accurate information can also provide the needed counterbalance to calm public fears.

The convergence of victimization rates in urban, suburban, and rural schools suggests both the effectiveness of strategies in urban and suburban schools and the need for a response among school and community leaders in rural areas. Many school districts in urban and suburban areas have increased physical security on campuses through the use of metal detectors, hiring campus police, and conducting random locker searches. These strategies seem to be effective methods for reducing school crime, but may be prohibitively expensive options in rural districts. Rural districts are not immune to school crime even though their victimization rates are converging with urban and suburban districts. Consequently, effective data collection and sound program analysis of school crime should be used to pinpoint particular problem areas in all schools, thereby lowering programmatic costs.

Are U.S. schools safe? After a review of available national statistics, it appears that violent and serious violent crime has in fact declined over time. This is good news for students, parents, teachers, and school administrators whose immediate concern focuses on the physical safety of the school environment. Zero tolerance, conflict resolution programs, and tighter security measures generated in the wake of the initial school shootings appear to be working to reduce the incidence of violent crime. However, more common are fights and bullying which remain prevalent in middle schools, as well as thefts against both students and teachers. Although there is a myriad of reasons why students are engaged in school shootings, being the victims of bullying has been cited as a major factor. Consequently, more effort should be focused on reducing bullying during the middle school years. On a positive note, these behaviors (bullying and fighting) somewhat decline during the high schools years.

The public's perception of school safety also remains a defining factor in the debate over whether U.S. schools are safe. While national statistics indicate a decline in school violence, there remains considerable public concern over the issue of school safety. The media's coverage of these events may inadvertently fuel community fears that schools are full of gun-toting students. Focusing on the heinousness of the events to the exclusion of reporting that these events are statistically quite rare gives the general public the perception that they are commonplace. In addition to the many preventative programs and increased security measures that have been implemented, school districts should focus more attention on educating the community regarding the findings of aggregated national data which present a more complete picture of school safety.

REFERENCES

Annual report on school safety (2000). Washington, D.C.: Departments of Education and Justice.
Annual report on school safety (1999). Washington, D.C.: Departments of Education and Justice.
Annual report on school safety (1998). Washington, D.C.: Departments of Education and Justice.

Carr, Cathi (2000). Area schools relatively safe. www.gainesvillesun.com/news/articles/ 01-26-00d.shtml. January 26.

Cheek, Duren (1999). Poll shows effects of school violence. www.tennessean.com/sii/ 99/06/22/poll22.shtml. June 22.

Indicators of school crime and safety (2000). Washington, D.C.: National Center for Education Statistics. Bureau of Justice Statistics. www.ed.gov/offices/OESE/SDFS/publications.html. October.

Indicators of school crime and safety (1999). Washington, D.C.: National Center for Education Statistics. Bureau of Justice Statistics. October.

Indicators of school crime and safety (1998). Washington, D.C.: National Center for Education Statistics. Bureau of Justice Statistics. October.

Knickerbocker, Brad (2001). Young and male in America: It's hard being a boy. www.csmonitor.com/durable/1999/04/29/text/p1s3.html. August 1.

McQueen, Anjetta (2000). What makes a violent student? www.staugustine.com/stories/ 090700/nat_20000907.001.shtml. September 7.

Throne, Katie (2001). School crime down in Aiken County. augustachronicle.com/stories/ 010100/met_203-8713.000.shtml. February.

3

School Crime Reporting in California

Tonya Aultman-Bettridge

Continuing with a discussion of "problem identification," this chapter is included to give the reader a feeling for school crime as it is being reported in the nation's most populous state. Many of the same terms, concepts, and reporting techniques are available in this chapter as in Chapter 2.

Of interest here is that California itself is reporting actual occurrences of crime on the state's public school campuses, as opposed to data from surveys, which is where much of the information contained in Chapter 2 is from.

Recent national attention has been focused largely on dramatic, highly violent school incidents, such as mass shootings by students. However, specific details of these tragedies have drawn attention to other types of school violence and crime.[1] Information regarding histories of bullying, previous threats, and past acts of delinquency preceding some school shootings may have made schools more aware of crime and violence occurring on campus. In addition, the early discovery of some threats and/or plans for violence (whether genuine or not) illustrates the importance of a reliable mechanism for reporting school crime. The issue of bullying in particular has come to the attention of the public and many policy makers (see, for example, Elliott & Salazar, 2001). This newly focused attention on school crime and violence issues has prompted a demand for comprehensive and reliable information on the prevalence of crime in U.S. schools.

School incident reporting can serve a variety of purposes. In many cases, school record keeping regarding crime incidents can serve to assist officials in sharing all available information about youth who may be demonstrating a need for prevention or intervention efforts. In other cases, these reporting systems can track trends and patterns in crime in order to assess the exact nature and extent of crime in American schools.

Perhaps more importantly, school incident reporting systems can also serve an additional vital function—that of safe school planning. Stephens (1998) has identified a thorough incident reporting system as a vital component of any plan designed to ensure the safety of school personnel and students. Accurate record keeping regarding school crime can provide schools with target priority areas (property crimes vs. person crimes, for example) or, depending on the detail of the system, can pinpoint particular problem areas within the school campus (the parking lot, bathrooms, etc.) for some types of crime.

The utility of accurate reports regarding the extent and nature of school crime and violence is evident. However, for a variety of reasons, these demands can be difficult to meet. Generally, information on school crime and violence can come from three different sources: victims of crime, self-reports of offenders, and official record keeping by schools and police agencies.

METHODS FOR MEASURING SCHOOL CRIME

Several sources of information are available to measure national levels of school crime. These sources primarily rely on victims' and offenders' reports of incidents occurring on campus. In addition, official reports (via arrest statistics) may also be used to estimate general amounts of crime. Each of these sources of information has its own strengths and weaknesses, and all have the ability to provide general information about prevalence rates of certain types of crimes on school campuses. Victim and offender reporting generally have the advantage of capturing crime not reported to authorities. On the other hand, these types of reporting are prone to various errors. Official arrest statistics are limited by the fact that much crime against juveniles is not reported to authorities. The benefit of many of these mechanisms is that they may be used to estimate school crime more specifically and allow for comparisons between areas (states, cities, school districts, etc.).

One possible source of school crime information is the school crime subsection of the National Crime Victimization Survey (NCVS). This national survey collects information from crime victims regarding the types of victimization experienced, along with details about the crimes and the perpetrators (if known) as well as the locations of the events (Finkelhor & Ormrod, 1999). A primary advantage of using national crime victimization data to estimate amounts of crime occurring in the United States (regardless of where the crime occurs) is the ability to account for unreported victimizations. A recent report of 1995 and 1996 NCVS data (Finkelhor & Ormrod, 1999) estimated that only 28% of violent crimes and 10% of thefts against juveniles become known to police.

However, juveniles do often report their crimes to other authorities, most likely school officials. This does not, however, translate directly into those victimizations being reported to police, underscoring another important reason for strong reporting systems. Violent crimes against juveniles occurring outside of school are more likely to become known to authorities than are victimizations occurring at school, with 37% of victimizations outside of school being reported (by either the victim or someone else), compared with only 15% of in-school victimizations. However, in-school crimes are more likely to be reported to some authority (49%), compared with nonschool crimes (41%). Holding with the pattern of juvenile crimes being reported less frequently than crimes against adults, younger youth are less likely to report victimizations than are other juveniles (Finkelhor & Ormrod, 1999).

While using NCVS data to estimate school crime on a national, state, or city level can be very useful, there are many limitations in the information available. First, the NCVS asks questions only regarding certain, typically more serious, crimes. This means that many issues, such as bullying, harassment, or weapons possession, that are particularly important to school officials are not measured. Additionally, the NCVS collects victimization information only on persons ages 12 and over. This means that although information is available at the high school and middle school ages, little can be determined about victimizations at elementary schools. Finally, the survey does not request details about a particular school, so information is limited to a "big picture" view.

Information on levels of school crime and violence can also come from self-reports on the part of students (both offending and victimization) via school-based surveys. Typically, theses surveys are conducted with either all students in the school or, more likely, a sample of students selected to represent the entire student body accurately. These surveys can ask students about delinquent acts that they have committed, been the targets of, or witnessed occurring at school. Two of the more well known of these surveys are the Youth Risk Behavior Surveillance system (YRBS) and the Monitoring the Future survey (MTF). Both of these are in-school surveys completed by students on a regular basis.

The YRBS occurs in participating schools every two years. Questions are grouped around six "priority" health risk behaviors identified as such by the U.S. Department of Health and Human Services. Measures include factors leading to both intentional (violence) and unintentional (accidents) injury, tobacco use, drug and alcohol use, sexual behavior (related to sexually transmitted diseases and unintended pregnancies), unhealthy dietary behavior, and physical inactivity (Kann et al., 2000). The YRBS includes a national school-based survey (based on a representative sample of schools and students) as well as state, regional, and local surveys conducted by various local educational and health agencies. The MTF survey is a similar data collection effort, administered yearly to eighth-, tenth-, and twelfth-grade students in participating schools (Medical Economics Company, 2000). Like the YRBS, this survey focuses on youth health issues, emphasizing alcohol, tobacco, and other drug use primarily, but it also includes a variety of school indicators, including delinquent behavior and attitudes toward the school environment (Kann et al., 2000).

Student self-report measures of school crime have the advantage of providing information at the individual school level, which can then be totaled to estimate school crime in a school district, state, and so on. Also, in addition to surveys of students, surveys of teachers, other school officials, and parents can be used to augment and validate information gleaned from students. However, these data do have limitations. Primarily, student self-reports are open to error made by students in estimating when incidents occur and how often, as well as the potential for students to over- or underreport delinquent behavior (whether their own or others'). National surveys done with self-report measures of delinquency, however, do indicate that these data are quite reliable and valid, and despite possible flaws, still represent better measures than official arrest statistics (Elliott & Salazar, 2001).

Another important note regarding both self-report measures and victimization surveys is that limitations of resources make it impossible to ask all students about their experiences. For example, it would be impossible to survey every student in every school even just once in his or her school career, due to time and resource constraints. Therefore, amounts of school crime must be made from a sample of students. In this respect, data collected will only be as good as the degree to which the sample is representative—that the students actually surveyed really represent all of the students in that school, state, city, and so forth.

Finally, information on school crimes is available often through official police contacts and/or the record-keeping systems of individual schools or school districts. In some ways, this information may be the least complete. Although not subject to the potential errors of victim reports or offender self-reports on criminal behavior, these systems are likely to considerably underestimate actual amounts of school crime. First, many crimes occurring on school property may not be brought to the attention of school staff, because victims who are unwilling to report incidents are not otherwise brought to the attention of adults. Even in those cases in which delinquent acts (those behaviors that would be crimes if committed by adults) are brought to the attention of school officials, they are dealt with through traditional school discipline policies and, in many cases (such as minor vandalism or petty theft), may not seem appropriate for referral to a police agency. As previously outlined, a low percentage of violent crimes occurring at school ever come to the attention of police (15%), and less than half are even reported to officials at the school (Finkelhor & Ormrod, 1999).

STATE MANDATES FOR SCHOOL CRIME REPORTING

Calls for closer attention to issues around violence and crime in schools have made decisions regarding which acts require police intervention and which do not more ambiguous than in the past. In some ways, the issue is complicated further by the presence of police on many school campuses in the form of school resource officers. States around the country have, in the last 10 years, begun attempts to improve reporting of school crime as well as informing schools about crimes committed off campus by their students. Some information regarding specific school shootings, Columbine in particular, have prompted questions about whether some incidents of school violence might be prevented if early warning signs could be better detected in students (U.S. Department of Education, 2000).

Across the country, legislatures have made collecting and reporting information regarding youth delinquency, regardless of place of occurrence, a priority. Many of these laws have been prompted by beliefs that the more people who have information about a youth's delinquent history, the more early warning signs will be identified and perhaps violent youth will be the target of intervention at earlier stages (U.S. Department of Education, 2000). Regardless of intent, however, between 1994 and 2000 almost every legislature in the country either passed new legislation or amended old statutes requiring the reporting of delinquent acts or making allowances for information sharing at the discretion of various authorities.

Between 1994 and 2000, at least 31 states passed some form of legislation either requiring or allowing more open communication between police/courts and school administration. Twenty-one of these states made it mandatory that schools either report to police certain (usually serious or violent) offenses or, in some cases, report any act that, if committed by an adult, would constitute a crime. In 18 states, legislatures passed laws authorizing a freer exchange of information between schools and juvenile justice or police agencies, at the discretion of the parties involved. Some of this legislation also provides protection for school officials disclosing information about a juvenile (National Conference of State Legislatures, 2001).

States have also begun placing greater burdens on schools to report incidents occurring on campus or during school-sponsored events. Two states have recently passed laws requiring school officials to notify officials in other school districts regarding serious delinquency or sexual offenses when a student transfers to a new school. Three states have required parents to notify schools if their children commit certain serious, delinquent acts at the time of occurrence or when the child moves to a new school. At least 21 states mandate some kind of reporting to police or the courts regarding either specific or, in some cases, all delinquent offenses occurring at school or during a school-sponsored event. Of these states, 9 require that an official reporting system or study of offenses at school be put into place, with most mandating annual reports to the legislature.

REPORTING SCHOOL CRIME IN CALIFORNIA

California is one of those states that has mandated a standardized reporting system and requires that its department of education compile and report yearly statistics on crime incidents occurring at school, during school-sponsored events, or while students are traveling to or from school. California's reporting system dates back to 1984, when the legislature mandated that the California Department of Education maintain a data system to be used for assessing prevention program needs (CA Penal Code Section 628 et seq.). In 1995 requirements for reporting were augmented, with the state passing legislation mandating a standardized form to be used by all schools (excepting charter schools) to report school crime, as defined by the California School Safety Assessment (CSSA) program (California Department of Education, 2001).

The mandatory CSSA form requires schools to record the date, time, and location of each of the following incidents:

Crimes Against Persons

Assault with a deadly weapon
Battery
Homicide
Robbery/extortion
Sex offense(s)

Property Crimes

Arson ($100 or more)
Burglary (any amount)
Graffiti ($100 or more)
Theft ($50 or more)
Vandalism ($100 or more)

Drug and Alcohol Offenses

Use of alcohol/drugs
Possession of alcohol
Possession of drugs
Possession of drug paraphernalia
Possession of alcohol/drugs for sale
Sale and/or furnishing of alcohol/drugs

Other

Bomb threat
Destructive/explosive devices
Loitering/trespassing
Possession of weapon(s)

In addition, the reporting form requests information on the suspect (if known) and the victim, in the cases of a crime against a person. These descriptions include only the gender of the suspect/victim and that person's status (student at the school or nonstudent for suspects; student, nonstudent, certified employee, classified employee, or other for victims). The identity of neither the victim nor the suspect is included in the reporting form. Forms are accompanied by information on definitions of crime and guidelines for which crime should be reported.[2]

The CSSA program has been implemented in each California school district beginning with the 1995–1996 school year. To date, five years of data are available to compare trends and patterns of school crime in California. The remainder of this report focuses on the results of CSSA data collection efforts, discussing current patterns[3] in California school crime, trends in school crime from 1995–1996 to the 1999–2000 school year (the most recent year for which data are currently available), and implications for how this information can inform school violence tracking, prevention, and intervention efforts (California Department of Education, 2001).

PATTERNS OF SCHOOL CRIME IN CALIFORNIA

Violence

For the 1999–2000 school year, the highest rates of reported crimes were crimes against persons, or violent crimes,[4] as compared to property, drug, or other offenses. Offenses relating to possession of weapons or destructive/explosive devices or making bomb threats, however, remain the lowest rates of violence-related offenses reported in California schools. Figure 3.1 illustrates these differences by type of offense.

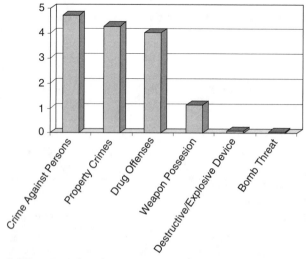

FIGURE 3.1   California School Crime Rates, 1999–2000 School Year, by Type of Offense (Rate per 1,000 Students)

While person crimes have the highest incident rates, this rate is driven almost entirely by reports of battery, the least serious of these crimes (Figure 3.2). In the 1999–2000 school year, more than 23,000 incidents of battery were reported, compared with approximately 2,100 assaults with a deadly weapon, 1,500 sex offenses, 1,200 robbery/extortion incidents, and 4 homicides.[5]

Consistent with national statistics (Federal Bureau of Investigation, 2000), homicide remains the lowest form of violent crime reported in schools, with California reporting four homicides for the school year 1999–2000. Descriptions of four homicide events in California schools provided by the National School Safety Center (NSSC) (2001) suggest that none of these homicide events was gun related, contrary to typical juvenile homicide patterns (Arrendondo et al., 1999). Two of the deaths recorded by NSSC were the result of kicking/ beating, one involved a knife, and in the fourth, a student was intentionally hit with a car.[6]

The highest rates of crimes against persons were reported for County Office of Education (COE) programs and California junior high/middle schools, followed by high schools (Figure 3.3). Elementary schools reported the lowest incidence of crimes against persons.

The majority of crimes against persons were committed against students by other students. In the 1999–2000 school year, 88% of violent crime victims were students, with the remaining victims being certified staff (6%), classified staff (3%), or other (3%). Most victims were male (68%). These proportions were similar for suspects.

Overall, the most recent year of California data regarding school violence matches national patterns. The violent crimes that generally receive the most attention and are the source of greatest concern are the most rare. Weapon possession, for example, made up only 8% of all school crime reported in 1999–2000. Bomb threats, possession of explosives, and

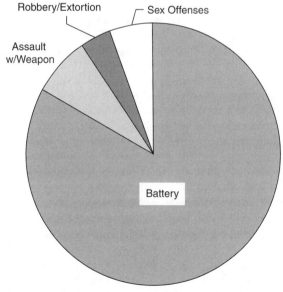

FIGURE 3.2   Crimes Against Persons, 1999–2000 School Year, Proportion by Type of Offense

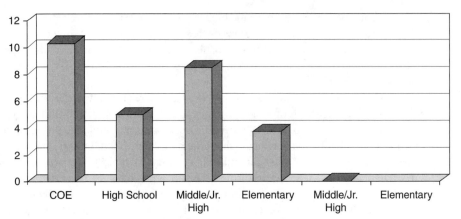

FIGURE 3.3   Crimes Against Persons, 1999–2000 School Year, by School Type
(Rate per 1,000 Students)

homicides combined made up only a little over 1% of all crimes reported by California schools. Based on homicide trends of the late 1990s,[7] of the approximately 300 yearly juvenile homicide victims in the state of California, only 4 (approximately 1%) were killed while at or traveling to or from school.

Knives are the predominant form of weapon used in offenses in California schools. Over 70% of weapons possession offenses were for the possession of a knife. In comparison, only 5% involved a firearm, while 24% involved the possession of another kind of weapon. In crimes against persons, no weapon was used in 91% of offenses. In only 2% of incidents were knives involved. Firearms were used in 1% of crimes against persons, while 6% involved the use of some other weapon.

Higher incidences of less severe violence, such as battery, indicate that the larger problem facing schools are incidents that may be better construed as "bullying" problems. These incidents, while less serious in their violence, can contribute to an overall negative school environment and lead to more serious problems in the future (Elliott & Salazar, 2001; Stephens, 1998).

Property Crimes

Property crimes were surpassed by crimes against persons as the most common offense type reported in California schools in 1999–2000. However, property crime still represented a substantial portion of crimes reported by schools—29% of all school crime incidents (compared with 32% for crimes against persons). Estimates of losses to the school district resulting from property crimes alone reached nearly $24 million for the 1999–2000 school year.

Of these offenses, vandalism occurred most frequently, with California schools reporting a rate of 1.7 incidents per 1,000 students (Figure 3.4). This was followed by thefts of greater than $50 (rate of 1.15), burglary (0.70), and graffiti (more than $100, rate

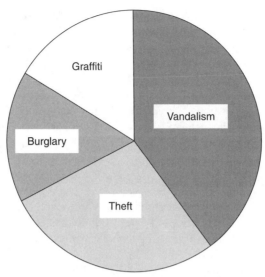

FIGURE 3.4   Property Crimes, 1999–2000 School Year, Proportion by Type
of Offense

of 0.67). The least common property crime was arson, with 0.05 incidents reported for every 1,000 students, representing only about 1% of all property crime.

High schools experienced the highest rates of property crimes, followed by middle/junior high and elementary schools (Figure 3.5). County Office of Education (COE) programs experienced the lowest rates of property crimes. These offenses not only were more frequent in high schools but also resulted in far greater economic losses to California

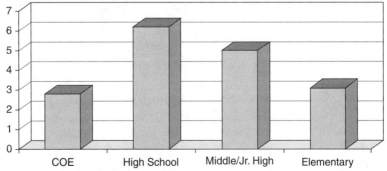

FIGURE 3.5   Property Crimes, 1999–2000 School Year, by School Type (Rate
per 1,000 Students)

school districts. The estimated losses due to property crimes for high schools were $10.59 per student, compared with $8.74 in losses per student for all other school types combined.

Arson disproportionately accounted for property damage in schools, when compared to its incidence rate. While making up only about 1% of all property crime, arson accounted for 41% of the dollar losses reported by school districts, for a total of over $10 million. The most prevalent property crime, vandalism, accounted for 31% of dollar losses, similar to its proportion (37%) of all property offenses. Theft, while making up 28% of all property crime, accounted for only 7% of dollar losses. Graffiti, making up 16% of property crime, constituted the least of all property damage (5%).

Drug and Alcohol Offenses

Drug- and alcohol-related offenses were reported at a slightly lower rate (4.1 per 1,000 students) than property crimes (4.3 per 1,000 students). The vast majority of drug and alcohol offenses reported by California schools involve possession/use of drugs and alcohol on campus (Figure 3.6). In contrast, far fewer incidents of sale or possession with intent to sell drugs and alcohol were reported for the 1999–2000 school year.

Differences among school types were more marked for drug- and alcohol-related offenses than for other types of school crime. High school rates of drug and alcohol offenses (11.3) were more than twice as high as rates in COE programs (5.1) and middle/junior high schools (3.8) (Figure 3.7). Elementary schools, not surprisingly, had the lowest rates of drug and alcohol offenses, with the total rate for all offenses less than 1 incident per every 1,000 students.

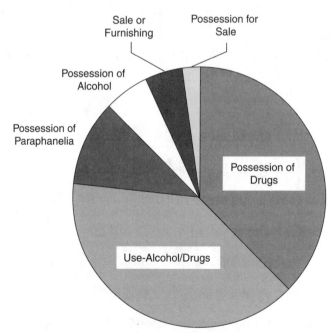

FIGURE 3.6   Drug- and Alcohol-Related Offenses, 1999–2000 School Year, Proportion by Type of Offense

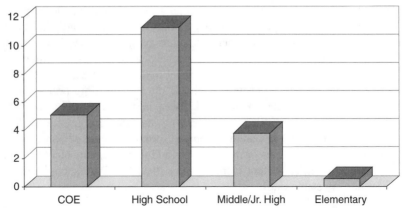

FIGURE 3.7   Drug and Alcohol Offenses, 1999–2000 School Year, by School
Type (Rate per 1,000 Students)

Summary of Patterns of School Crime in California

Overall, patterns of reported school crime in California indicate that more minor crimes
are those most in need of attention by schools. Very serious, violent types of crime
remain relatively rare, even in a state with traditionally high proportions of state
juvenile violent crime (Snyder & Sickmund, 1999). However, those crimes considered
most serious, while rare, do result in a considerable amount of loss, both monetarily
and in human costs. Four youth died violently in California schools during the
1999–2000 school year.[8] Further, while arson remained one of the least often reported
crimes, it accounted for nearly half of all dollar losses for California school districts
during the year.

TRENDS IN SCHOOL CRIME IN CALIFORNIA

After five years of a standardized reporting system in California schools, enough data are
available to examine some emerging trends in school crime.

However, as is the case when any new kind of system is put into place, there
are unavoidable problems and issues. Therefore, in interpreting these trends, it is important
to keep in mind that any system is only as good as it is implemented. Therefore, as a system
is implemented over a longer period of time, it is possible that improvements in reporting
may lead to an apparent increase in crime, which is not reflective of the actual incidence of
crime. Similarly, differing areas may do better or worse in implementing a reporting system.
Therefore, one school may seem to have higher rates of crime than another because reporting is better, not because there is actually more crime.

These issues have long been a weakness in official crime reporting in general, and it
is very difficult to statistically account for differences in reporting. As a result, it is always
important that the reader keep in mind other differences (besides actual differences in
crime) that may be the reason for increasing/decreasing trends or differences in crime
reported by different areas. However, examining patterns, despite limitations, can often

reveal vital information about changes taking place that school and police officials must keep in mind as they plan and adapt school safety policies and procedures.

Crimes classified as "other," including weapons possession and bomb threats, have been relatively stable since the standardized school crime reporting was implemented in California during the 1995–1996 school year (Figure 3.8). Further, school property crimes have exhibited a slight decrease during this time period. In contrast, crimes against persons, which exhibited declines in the 1995–1996 and 1997–1998 school years, have been increasing over the past three years. In fact, for the first time since the record-keeping system was implemented, crimes against persons have surpassed property crimes in their rates of incidence. In addition, drug and alcohol offenses have experienced a slight, consistent increase since the 1997–1998 school year, after three years of relatively stable rates.

Crimes Against Persons

Person crime rates declined by nearly 9% between the 1995–1996 and 1997–1998 school years. However, since then rates have increased, rising 7% between 1997–1998 and 1998–1999 to its initial levels. Between 1998–1999 and 1999–2000 school years, rates of crimes against persons jumped 17%. This increase was driven by an upswing in battery and sex crimes occurring on school campuses. Rates of robbery and assault with a deadly weapon have remained roughly the same over the five years for which data are available (Figure 3.9). However, incidents of battery have increased 29% since 1997–1998. Rates of sex crimes increased 62% over that time, although remaining at a fairly low rate of person crimes. During 1999–2000 sex crimes were reported at a rate of 0.26 incidents per 1,000 students, higher for the first time since reporting began than the rate of robbery (0.21).

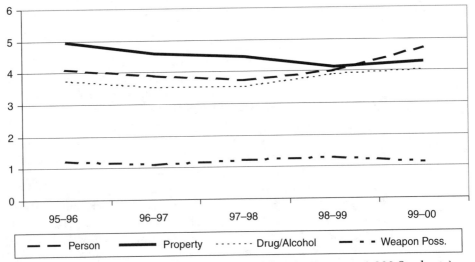

FIGURE 3.8 Trends in School Crime in California (Rate per 1,000 Students)

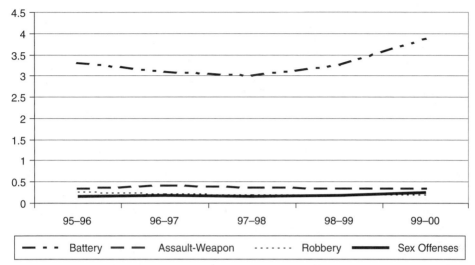

FIGURE 3.9 Trends in Crimes Against Persons, by Offense (Rate per 1,000 Students)

The increasing trend in crimes against persons was evident across school types, with the exception of California high schools (Figure 3.10). Elementary schools experienced the most steady and sustained increase in violent crime rates. For these younger grades, violent crimes rose from about 1.8 incidents per 1,000 students to a rate of more than 3.0 incidents per 1,000 students, an increase of about 66%. County Office of Education programs trends show a "spike" in violent crime rates between the 1997–1998 and 1998–1999 school years, with the trend showing a small decrease since that time. However, rates for the 1999–2000 school year remain more than 65% higher than when the reporting system began in 1995–1996. Rates also increased slightly for middle and junior high schools. Despite these recent increases in crimes against persons in other schools, in the five-year period violent crime rates declined fairly steadily for high school students, from a high rate of 6.5 in the 1995–1996 school year to a rate of about 4.8 in the 1999–2000 school year. This represents a decrease of nearly 30% over five years.

The numbers of school homicides have changed very little over the five-year reporting period, fluctuating from year to year by only one to two incidents. The four homicides reported for 1999–2000 were two incidents lower than the previous reporting year and identical to the number of incidents reported for 1997–1998, as well as the year prior, consistently representing less than one-hundredth of a percent of all school crime reported.

Property crimes decreased overall over the five-year period, increasing slightly (4%) during the most recent year of reporting (Figure 3.11). Typically, property crimes represented the most frequent type of crime occurring on California school campuses. However, steady declines in property rates, combined with increases in person crimes, led to rates of person crimes that were higher than those of property crimes for the first time in the five-year period.

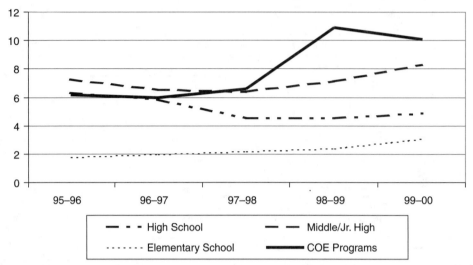

FIGURE 3.10   Trends in Crimes Against Persons, by School Type (Rate per 1,000 Students)

As property crimes have declined, so too have the costs to school districts associated with losses due to these offenses. Over the five-year period, district losses are down by about 3%. However, fluctuations in amount of district losses have been extreme over that time. Estimated losses from property crimes have hovered at just over $4.00 per student each year, except for the 1997–1998 school year, when losses dropped to less than $3.00 per student.

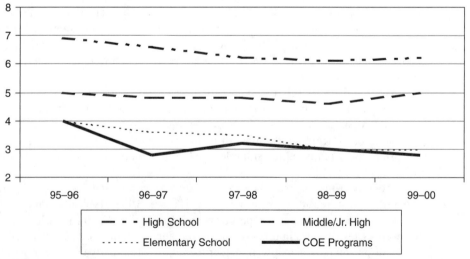

FIGURE 3.11   Trends in Property Crime, by School Type (Rate per 1,000 Students)

This rate jumped to its highest number, $4.33 per student (over $25 million total), in the 1998–1999 school year. A decrease in the most recent year of reporting has brought loss figures to the stable rate that was exhibited in the early years of reporting, with California schools still reporting over $23 million in losses due to property crimes in the 1999–2000 school year.

Losses continue to be high, despite the fact that property crime rates are declining or remaining stable in all types of schools. This may be due, in part, to the fact that while most types of property crimes are down, California schools have seen fairly sharp increases in arson offenses, which, as stated previously, account disproportionately for monetary losses due to property crimes. As discussed earlier, arson accounted for less than 1% of property crimes reporting during the 1999–2000 school year, yet contributed to nearly half of the overall losses.

Property crime declines were sharpest for elementary schools, with rates falling 25% over the reporting period. Rates fell similarly for COE programs. For middle and high schools, property crimes stayed fairly stable over the five-year reporting period, fluctuating slightly from year to year.

Drug and Alcohol Offenses

Overall, reported rates of drug and alcohol offenses rose substantially only in COE programs, while rising slightly in high schools (Figure 3.12). Middle and junior high schools saw rates decrease until 1997–1998, then rise most recently back up to levels slightly lower than those reported in the first year of the standardized system. For elementary schools, rates remained stable and very low.

Drug and alcohol offenses were reported more frequently throughout the period at the high school levels. However, the sharp increase in drug and alcohol offenses reported in

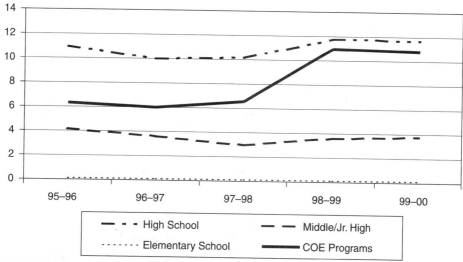

FIGURE 3.12   Trends in Drug and Alcohol Offenses, by School Type (Rate per 1,000 Students)

COE programs brought their rates very close to the higher rates of high school students. Rates remained low and generally decreasing for younger students, those in elementary and middle/junior high schools, indicating that at least in reported offenses, drug and alcohol use trends in California do not reflect a lowering of the age at which drugs and alcohol are present at school.

Weapon Offenses

Across all schools, both weapon possession offenses and assaults using weapons remained nearly unchanged during the five-year reporting period. In California schools across the board, the number of reported weapon possession offenses is down about 7% from the 1995–1996 rate of 1.22 offenses per 1,000 students. Similarly, rates of reported assaults with a deadly weapon remain identical to the 1995–1996 rate of 0.35 offenses per 1,000 students. Overall, it seems that the last five years of the 1990s in California did not see the higher rates of student weapons carrying that may have been indicated by media coverage of school shootings. Also, these findings from California schools are corroborated by findings from the national Youth Risk Behavior Surveillance system, which indicates that weapon possession among high school students has declined steadily since 1995.

USING SCHOOL CRIME INFORMATION

The information collected through CSSA can potentially serve many purposes. On a statewide level, policy makers might make more informed decisions regarding appropriate responses to school crime by having a better understanding of the problem. School districts and individual schools can use their individual data to determine individual needs of the school (or district) and to prioritize resource allocation for combating school crime. As trends and patterns become apparent over time, more target prevention and intervention efforts can be made. Finally, long-term data can help schools to evaluate their progress in fighting school crime and identify and document successful approaches.

At the state level, policy makers can use CSSA reports to make more informed decisions regarding policy by having a greater understanding of the problem. Perhaps more importantly, school crime data collected in the program can help to temper concerns regarding increases in school crime that are fueled by rare, but highly publicized events. The data presented here do not support the notion that overall school crime is increasing at an alarming rate. The more serious and violent crimes, in fact, have been stable over the life of the project.

Individual schools and districts can benefit a great deal from this information. Looking, for example, at fairly strong increases in battery at the elementary school level may result in some school officials shifting priorities for prevention efforts to those grades. High school administrators, also, may be interested in targeting knives and other weapons as stringently as they target guns in their prevention and intervention efforts, given that the possession and use of these weapons is more prevalent than firearms. As schools create plans for creating a safe and crime-free environment, it is vital that this information inform the planning process. Schools can individualize safe school plans to tailor prevention and intervention strategies to meet the unique needs of their students. Also, schools have the opportunity to monitor progress and outcomes of prevention and intervention efforts by studying long-term trends.

The scope of information made available through a reporting system such as the CSSA programs demonstrates the potential for schools throughout the country to mount a reasoned, strategic attack on the problem of crime in our country's schools. Further, the careful collection and presentation of data can help to dispel myths of school crime and better inform the public and policy makers about the reality of school crime and its costs.

ENDNOTES

1. Acts committed by youth (depending on state law and specific type of offense) that would be considered crimes if committed by adults are usually categorized as acts of "delinquency." Therefore, juveniles do not commit "crimes," but instead are "delinquent." For purposes of simplicity and clarity, the more generally recognizable term *crime* will be used in place of the more legally accurate term *delinquency* in this chapter.
2. Please note that these reporting forms and this system are designed for submission to the California Department of Education for the purpose of compiling and reporting statistics for planning and evaluation purposes. Crime incidents that fall under legal requirements for reporting to local authorities would still be reported to those agencies, based on local policies and procedures.
3. In most cases, crime patterns and trends will be reported in rates per 1,000 students, rather than in absolute numbers. By reporting rates rather than absolute numbers, changes in population do not falsely inflate or deflate the amount of crime reported.
4. In this case, battery, assault with a deadly weapon, robbery/extortion, or sex offenses.
5. Homicides are not reflected in Figure 3.2 because its percentage of all crimes against persons is too small to display on the graph (0.01%).
6. These descriptions are taken from the National School Safety Center's report "School Associated Violent Deaths." Four homicides were identified on this list. However, NSSC uses media accounts and informal reporting procedures to compile this list. Therefore, it is not possible to verify that the four homicides listed by NSSC match the four incidents reported through California's official reporting system.
7. The last four years of homicide data currently available from the Federal Bureau of Investigation in the *Supplementary Homicide Reports* (1995–1998) show that an average of 305 youths were victims of homicide yearly.
8. This does not include youth committing suicide on school property.

REFERENCES

Arrendondo, S., Aultman-Bettridge, T., Johnson, K., & Williams, K. (1999). *Youth handgun violence: A national study with trends and patterns for the state of Colorado.* Boulder, CO: Center for the Study and Prevention of Violence.

California Department of Education (2001). *California Safe Schools Assessment: 2000 results.* Sacramento, CA: California Department of Education.

California Department of Education (2000). *California Safe Schools Assessment: 1999 results.* Sacramento, CA: California Department of Education.

Elliott, D. S. and Salazar, K. (2001). *Creating Safe Communities and Safe Schools: Results from Colorado Statewide County Forums on Youth Violence.* Boulder, CO: Center for the Study and Prevention of Violence.

Federal Bureau of Investigation (2000). *Supplemental Homicide Reports*. Washington, DC: U.S. Department of Justice.

Finkelhor, D., & Ormrod, R. (1999). Reporting crimes against juveniles. *Juvenile Justice Bulletin,* November. Washington, DC: Office of Juvenile Justice and Delinquency Prevention.

Kann, L., Kinchen, S. A., Williams, B. I., Ross, J. G., Lowry, R., Grunbaum, J. A., & Kolbe, L. J. (2000). Youth Risk Behavior Surveillance – United States, 1999. *Journal of School Health, 70,* no. 7, 271.

Medical Economics Company (2000). The 25th annual Monitoring the Future Survey. *Contemporary Pediatrics, 17,* no. 2, 15.

National Conference of State Legislatures (2001). "Juvenile Justice State Legislation in 2001." *www.ncsl.org/public/catalog.*

National School Safety Center (2001). *School-associated violent deaths*. Thousand Oaks, CA: National School Safety Center.

Snyder, H. and Sickmund, M. (1999). Juvenile Offenders and Victims: 1999 National Report. Washington, DC: Office of Juvenile Justice and Delinquency Prevention.

Stephens, Ronald D. (1998). Safe school planning. In D. S. Elliott, B.A. Hamburg, & K. R. Williams (Eds.), *Violence in American schools*. New York: Cambridge University Press.

U.S. Department of Education (2000). *Early warning, timely response: A guide to safe schools.* Washington, DC: Government Printing Office.

4

School-Based Violent Crime in Texas

W. R. Mack, III and Thomas Longoria, Jr.

Continuing the discussion of problem identification, we now move to the second most populous state in the nation, Texas. Looking at actual crime data gathered by that state will give the reader an appreciation of the nature, size, and scope of the school crime problem.

In the elections of 2000, both Democrats and Republicans proclaimed that education was near the top, if not at the top, of their legislative agendas. Much of the discussion centered on school vouchers, national proficiency exams, and the competency of American students in reading, mathematics, and science. Yet, in the mid-to-late 1990s, discussions about education at the state level often concerned the issues of violence and crime on school campuses around the country as well as the safety of students, faculty, and administrators. Texas was among those states that wrestled with this issue. For example, "zero tolerance" policies that remove students from classrooms who deal drugs, carry a gun, commit aggravated assaults, and so on, and separate them from the local school population in alternative education programs, became more widespread. Furthermore, school shootings like those in Littleton, Colorado, and Pearl, Mississippi, have spurred students, parents, teachers, and administrators in school districts all over Texas to seek methods and programs through which to make schools safer and to identify those students who may be at risk to pursue criminal activity.

Perspective on Texas school crime can be gained by examining several available sources of analyses, including the Texas Youth Risk Behavior Survey (1998), the Texas School Safety Center Needs Assessment (1999), the Violence and Weapons in Texas Schools report (1999), and the state auditor's Report on Safe Schools Program (1999).

The general conclusion of such studies is that Texas school crime is in decline, or holding constant, in numerous categories. These trends run parallel to the decline or leveling off of school crime nationally, particularly in the area of violent crime arrests (Violence and Weapons in Texas Schools, 1999:1).

Understanding school-based crime in Texas demands consideration of the social and demographic characteristics of the state that impact children and youth. For example, Texas ranks at the bottom of many indicators of children's economic security (Center for Policy Priorities, 2001).

According to the new census data released in 2000, and an analysis presented in the 2001 *Kids Count Data Book*, the size and diversity of the youth population is growing more dramatically in Texas than elsewhere and will "amplify the demand for education and social services to support these children as they emerge into maturity" (Center for Policy Priorities, 2001).The percentage of children in poverty in Texas (ranked 41st among the 50 states) exceeds the national rate and the state is at the bottom of rankings of child well-being (Center for Policy Priorities, 2001).

In a number of other areas with relevance to the school-based crime, the news is equally distressing. For example, Texas is ranked 28th in teen violent death rate, 48th in teen birth rate, 41st in dropout rate, and 44th in teen idleness (Center for Policy Priorities, 2001). With growing percentages of at-risk youth, and with little in the way of constructive activities to take part in, it is not surprising that gang membership and associated crime are significant. El Paso, for instance—with three school districts (El Paso, Ysleta, and Socorro) that are over 75% Latino—had the highest level of both incidents of gang violence and numbers of firearms and other weapons confiscated. Statewide, from 1994 to 1997, the number of incidents of gang violence increased by 56% from 5,736 to 8,959, before declining in the 1997–1998 school year to 6,879 incidents. These statistics cannot be ignored.

This chapter is divided into three sections. The first section reviews basic descriptive data about the frequency and pattern of school violent crime in Texas. This review illustrates that the urban/rural distinction is a key aspect of understanding Texas school-based crime. In the second section, regression analysis is used to better understand the potential influence of county-level characteristics, including urbanicity, ethnicity, and socioeconomic attributes on levels of school-based violence. The third section is a summary of how specific schools districts in Texas have addressed school-based crime.

SCHOOL CRIME IN TEXAS

Although there are many dimensions of school crime in Texas, perhaps the most important ones to reflect upon are the levels of violence and the possession of weapons. When individually reported incidents in all Texas counties are considered, the typical county has few or no incidents. As will be outlined, some very large urban counties skew the averages. The ranges for the number of incidents is considerable for gang violence (0 to 1,054, mean 27.1, standard deviation 108.8), assaults on students (0 to 8, mean 230, standard deviation 791), assaults against teachers (0 to 817, mean 17, standard deviation 71), firearms confiscated (0 to 134, mean 2.3, standard deviation 10), and other weapons confiscated (0 to 1,379, mean 29, standard deviation 122).

While the typical school is safe, the "average" school does experience a significant number of incidents of violence and weapon seizures. This level of violence fosters feelings of fear that undermine the education process, affect the perceptions that adults have of the public schools and students themselves, and have ramifications for "white flight," weakening support of the public school system, failed bond elections, and associated "image" problems. The image that Texas schools are rife with violence, however, is not the reality in most cases. This section outlines school-based violent crime, weapons possession, and gang activity, as well as the efficacy of school violence prevention and enforcement efforts. The chapter also addresses the many differing views of the school environment from the various stakeholders in school districts—students, parents, teachers, administrators, and police.

Violent Crime

According to one study, "Texas is one of 19 states in which the juvenile violent crime arrest rate declined faster than the national rate. In 1997, the violent crime index for the United States was 412 for every 100,000 juveniles between the ages of 10 and 17, while the index for Texas was only 296. Individual state indexes ranged from 64 to 1,015 (Illinois) in 1997" (Lam-Yip, 2000:2). Still, in 1998, 11.7% of students in Texas reported carrying weapons to school, compared to 8.5% nationwide (Lam-Yip, 2000:6). Teachers, of course, are not immune to school-based violence. Assaults against teachers and staff average out to 1.23 per 1,000 students with an average of 4,665 incidents from 1994–1995 to 1997–1998 school years (Violence and Weapons in Texas Schools, 1999:2). This potential for violence, enhanced through the carrying and use of weapons, certainly exists in Texas schools and constitutes a threat to students, teachers, and administrators alike.

When asked if the community is more or less violent than local schools, the majority of respondents believed that communities were more violent (Texas School Safety Center, 2000:4). Using a five-level scale, 26% reported "no known violence or rebellious activity," 52% reported "limited risk with sporadic violent acts," 15% reported an "emerging, slowly escalating problem." Far fewer people viewed their school in crisis-like terms, with only 5% reporting "major intimidation—regular fights—verbal insults" were the norm and 2% insisting that the "school is controlled by fear and regular acts of violence"(Texas School Safety Center, 1999:4).

In 1997, 7.4% of students had been threatened or injured in school with a weapon one or more times during the previous year compared to 5% of the students sampled in the 1998 Texas YRBS (Lam-Yip, 2000:4). In 1998, there were "more than 63,000 assaults and more than 8,000 weapons confiscated in Texas public schools" (Violence and Weapons in Texas Schools, 1999:1). Although these levels of violence are high, "some types of school violence have declined in recent years—most likely because of programs designed to improve safety in schools and in the community" (Violence and Weapons in Texas Schools, 1999:1).

Texas followed similar trends in areas of juvenile crime generally. From 1985 to 1994, the rate of juvenile violent crime arrests (both in and out of school) nearly tripled. However, since 1994 there has been a decline in the juvenile crime rate (Violence and Weapons in Texas Schools, 1999:1). In looking at the data, it appears that large increases in school crime have been concentrated in the rate of assaults of students against students (a 27% increase from 1996–1997 to 1997–1998). However, the rates for other types of violence in Texas schools are not increasing as swiftly as many suggest and in some cases are declining (Violence and Weapons in Texas Schools, 1999:1).

Gang Membership

In Texas, with a significant Latino population, gang membership and associated crime is a concern for parents, teachers, administrators, and policy makers. For example, of the major urban counties, El Paso County, with the largest percentage of Latinos, has the highest rate of school-related gang violence of 2.2 per 1,000 students (Violence and Weapons in Texas Schools, 1999:2). It is important, however, to note that the lowest rate of gang-related violence in major urban areas is in Bexar County (0.3 per 1,000), with the second highest percentage of Latino students (Violence and Weapons in Texas Schools, 1999:2).

Of course, the presence of gangs has an impact on the school violent crime rate, and any level of gang activity is an important risk factor. For instance, "the violent victimization rate for students in schools where gangs were reported to be present was 7.5 percent compared to 2.7 percent for students in schools where gangs were not present" (Lam-Yip, 2000:4). The number of gangs in schools appears to be on the rise around the state. Lam-Yip finds that "between 1989 and 1995, the percentage of schools with at least one gang increased from 18 to 28 percent" (2000:4). The number and rate of school-related gang violence incidents have grown slightly from the 1994–1995 school year to the 1997–1998 school year (from 5,736 [1.6 per 1,000] to 6.879 [1.8 per 1,000]). However, there was a spike in the number in 1996–1997 to 8,959 (2.3 per 1,000) (Violence and Weapons in Texas Schools, 1999:2). In 1996, it was estimated that 420,000 gang members were juveniles, with most of them between the ages of 15 and 17. "In Texas, 3.5 percent of the students who responded to the TXYRBS indicated they were currently in a gang. Almost 10 percent were previously gang members" (Lam-Yip, 2000:4).

Gang-related violence and weapons possession often go hand in hand. In Texas, the number of firearms confiscated average at a rate of 0.125 per 1,000, with an average of 623 confiscations from 1994–1995 to 1997–1998 (Violence and Weapons in Texas Schools, 1999:2). Furthermore, the number of other weapons confiscated was taken at an average rate of 1.93 per 1,000 students with an average of 7,261 confiscations from 1994–1995 to 1997–1998 school years (Violence and Weapons in Texas Schools, 1999:2). In the same study, it was determined that 22.2% of Texas students carried a weapon of some kind during a 30-day period, compared to 18.3% nationally (Violence and Weapons in Texas Schools, 1999:7). One reason that this number is comparatively higher than the national average is that many more students in Texas report carrying hunting rifles in their vehicles (Violence and Weapons in Texas Schools, 1999:7).

URBAN DISTRICTS

Any discussion of crime in Texas schools that does not distinguish between large urban counties from the rest of the state would be misleading. According to one report, the five largest urban counties in Texas (Bexar, Dallas, El Paso, Harris, Tarrant) experience a large portion of the violence and weapons found in the state (Violence and Weapons in Texas Schools, 1999:2). When looking at the total number of violent incidents and weapon confiscations, these five counties report 44% of all occurrences of gang violence, 42% of assaults against students, 44% percent of assaults against teachers and staff, and 53% of all weapon confiscations (Violence and Weapons in Texas Schools, 1999:2).

Though these five urban counties contribute the bulk of the total number of incidents of school violence that occurred in the state, urban population is not seemingly a reliable predictor of school-based violent crime. For example, Bexar County has a rate of 13 assaults per 1,000 students, whereas Harris County has a rate of 6.1 per 1,000 students (Violence and Weapons in Texas Schools, 1999:2). In addition, there is no consistency within counties. For example, El Paso County has the highest rate of weapons confiscated (9 incidents per 1,000 students), the second highest rate of assaults against students (30.6 per 1,000), but the lowest rate of assaults against teachers (0.3 per 1,000 students) (Violence and Weapons in Texas Schools, 1999:2). Table 4.1 presents these rates for all of the main categories of school crime in major urban counties in Texas.

This variation in incident rates in ostensibly similar urban counties is surprising. Whether these variations are a function of true differences in the nature and scope of school-based violence, variations in reporting procedures (Markley, 1995), or the presence or absence of different crime prevention and enforcement programs (or some combination of these factors) cannot be determined without additional information. A study documenting these potential sources of variation would be a useful, yet costly, next step.

Does Urbanicity Matter? A Quantitative Analysis

Another way to make sense of variation in school-based violence is to examine differences in school violence in all Texas counties and assume that variations in reporting, crime prevention and enforcement programs, and other factors are randomly distributed. In terms of the total amount of violent school-based crime, urban counties certainly account for a higher proportion than rural counties. However, this section considers whether the rate of school-based violent crime is higher in urban areas. In other words, is there a linear relationship between the level of school-based violence and urbanicity? One perspective suggests that urban counties—which have poverty, school overcrowding, more violent communities, and higher percentages of at-risk students—should have higher rates of school-based crime. While this expectation is logical, there have been some findings that suburban districts have higher rates of school-based crime in areas such as theft. For example, a survey done by the Texas Department of Public Safety in conjunction with the Texas Education Agency survey found that "midsize suburban school districts are more prone to crime than big urban districts" (Markley, 1995).

The bivariate relationship between the percentage of urban residents in a county and the violent crime rate is statistically significant. Table 4.2 presents the bivariate regression analysis with the percent urban as the independent variable and the number of incidents as the dependent variable. Not surprisingly, as the percentage of urban residents in the county increases, so does the number of gang-related incidents. All of the models presented in Table 4.2 are statistically significant; however, in some cases urbanicity has a much larger impact.

According to the regression analyses, for every 1% increase in urban residents in the county, there are 1.2 more incidents of gang violence in schools, 9 more assaults against students, nearly 1 more teacher assault (0.75), 1 more firearm confiscated, and 1.2 more seizures of other types of weapons.

Using the data to make predictions and estimates is informative and useful. However, the finding that there are more incidents in heavily urban areas with more students is not

TABLE 4.1   Reported Incidence of Violence and Weapons in Large Urban Counties (rate per 1,000 students)

County enrollment		Incidents of school-related gang violence		Assaults against students		Assaults against teacher/staff		Number of firearms confiscated		Number of other weapons confiscated	
		Number	Rate	Number	Rate	Number	Rate	Number	Rate	Number	Rate
Bexar	254,806	661	0.3	3,308	13.0	412	1.6	62	0.2	492	1.9
Dallas	383,410	526	1.4	3,962	10.3	412	1.1	52	0.1	390	1.0
El Paso	153,115	334	2.2	4,689	30.6	39	0.3	18	0.1	1,379	9.0
Harris	624,154	1,054	1.7	3,787	6.1	817	1.3	134	0.2	738	1.2
Tarrant	250,153	429	1.7	8,993	35.9	228	0.9	24	0.1	940	3.8

TABLE 4.2   Bivariate Regression Analysis of Percent Urban and the Total
              Number of Incidents

	Gang violence	Assaults teachers	Assaults students	Firearms confiscated	Other weapons confiscated
Percent urban	1.23	9.14	.75	.09	1.23
Constant	−26.34	−165.28	−15.23	−1.72	−23.97
R^2	.11	.12	.10	.07	.09
F	33.41	34.84	28.63	20.27	25.91
$N = 254$					

surprising. To further address this issue, three indicators of school-based violent crime were examined as a function of the percentage of urban residents in a county in 1990 (see Table 4.3): the crime rate in 1991, the percentage of residents in poverty in 1990, and the percent of the population over 25 with a high school diploma in 1990. Given the higher rates of gang participation among young Latino students, the percentage of Latino residents in 1990 is also included in the regression analysis. In this regression, each of the school violence indicators is examined as a ratio per 1,000 school-age residents in the county.

TABLE 4.3   Multiple Regression Analysis of County-Level Predictors
              of School Violence and Weapons in Texas Schools (per 1,000
              student-age residents)

	Gang violence	Assaults students	Assaults teachers	Firearms confiscated	Other weapons confiscated
Percent Hispanic	.009	.26	−.002	−.005	.02
Crime rate	.0004	−.0001	.00007	−.000002	.0002
Percent poverty	.02	−.52	−.008	.008	.02
High school graduation	.006	−.18	.02	.01	.05
Percent urban	−.0005	−.04	.002	.0009	−.003
Constant	−1.38	25.59	.147	−.160	−.828
Adj R^2	.27	−.05	.01	.01	.14
F	6.31	.324	1.21	1.17	3.33
$N = 254$					

Table 4.3 presents the multiple regression analysis for each of the dependent variables. The only statistically significant variable is the crime rate, which is found to be a predictor of the number of gang incidents and the number of weapons confiscated. In other words, as the crime rate in the county increases, so do the number of gang incidents and weapons confiscations in the county. No other statistically significant relationships are found between percent Hispanic, the poverty rate, the percent of high school graduates, and the percent urban residents and the different measures of violence and weapons in Texas schools. In other words, variables that should logically account for levels of school-based violence in Texas counties do not.

The findings reinforce the importance of not allowing stereotypes to define our understanding of violent school-based crime. This analysis indicates that when violent crime rates in schools are examined, broad generalizations about where and in what types of schools crime is more likely are nearly impossible to make. The sole generalization that can be advanced with some degree of certainty is that in a county in which there is more crime, there tends to be more crime in the schools in that county.

AT THE SCHOOL DISTRICT LEVEL

While aggregate statistics and quantitative analysis are important, the experiences and perspectives of students, parents, and administrators in individual school districts provide additional insight into the dilemma of solving the problem of school crime. This section summarizes articles published from 1995 to 2001 that were found in a Lexis/Nexis search using the key words "Texas school crime." The search provided a cross section of school policies, activities, and programs that school districts have established to fight all levels of crime and violence in schools.

One interesting finding gleaned from a recently published study of school crime in the United States is that a majority of students believe they are relatively safe in their schools. For example, a survey of students ages 13 to 18, commissioned by the Horatio Alger Association and conducted by Peter Hart and Associates in May 2001, suggests that students do not share the angst that their parents and other adults feel concerning school violence (CNN.com, August 7, 2001).

Three-quarters of the students surveyed said teachers and administrators have already taken measures that are essential to making them feel secure at school. When queried about their level of fear at school, almost two-thirds of those surveyed said they did not worry at all or worried only a little bit about school safety.

Many Texas school district administrators would agree with the students and are confident that policies and programs they have instituted provide their pupils with peace of mind when it comes to school safety. In 1999, a Houston Independent School District (HISD) spokeswoman declared Houston schools to be well protected (*Houston Chronicle*, May 3, 1999). She pointed to the presence of police officers, metal detectors, school uniforms, and alternative schools for students with histories of violent behavior as examples of the HISD's commitment to student safety. These methods of contending with school crime are just a small sampling of policies and techniques that Texas communities and their school districts have undertaken. What is remarkable is the breadth and depth of the various programs begun by school districts around the state. The sheer variety of programs instituted in the last decade mirrors the ongoing debate in the academic and policy communities regarding the best way to combat both mild and more severe forms of school delinquency. Some of the programs are specific to individual school districts whereas others are practiced more generally around the state. Here are just a few examples of the efforts school systems are making to directly attack the problem of school crime in Texas.

Policies to Strengthen School Discipline

1. *Dress code policies*—School districts all around the state have changed their policies on school dress by moving to school uniforms or enforcing codes on clothing style. Noncompliance often results in a student being sent home from school for the day or at least until the offending clothes have been changed.

Intervention by Students

1. *Peer-mediation classes*—Students are taught to solve problems with dialogue and not violence (*Houston Chronicle,* May 3, 1999).

Teacher Training

1. *Violence prevention*—Through a program called Project SOS (Save Our Schools), teachers and administrators are instructed on how to detect nonverbal cues in students that suggest inappropriate activity may be occurring on school grounds (*Houston Chronicle*, May 3, 1999).

2. *Gang awareness*—The city of Houston and the HISD teamed up to present the Gang Educational Awareness and Resistance (GEAR) program. The program provides information concerning gang issues and behavior and trains participants about intervention procedures that can be used to head off gang activity at schools (*Houston Chronicle*, January 29, 1997).

Parental Involvement

1. *Character education programs*—Parents are given information on how to recognize potential problems their children may be having at school, getting their children to open up to them about their experiences, and help build their self-esteem (*Houston Chronicle*, May 3, 1999).

2. *Community monitoring*—Seminars are conducted in various Texas school districts to encourage parents and other members of the community to look out for gang activity in and around schools. Parents are asked to volunteer during the school day and in after-school programs, and report all gang activity to police, including spray-painted graffiti (*Houston Chronicle*, November 5, 1995).

3. *Court-ordered truancy classes for parents*—Judges in Galena Park, Pasadena, and Fort Bend County have sentenced parents of truants, vandals, and curfew violators to 18 hours of instruction on the local educational system, student

codes of conduct, the juvenile justice system, parent–child decision making, and other topics. While the focus of the program is to urge parents to be more attentive to their children's behavior in and out of school, some parents have moved beyond the classes to studying for their GED or other certification (*Houston Chronicle*, March 19, 1995).

Extracurricular Activities

1. *Anti-violence clubs*—At Milby High School in Houston, students formed the "Peace Club," in which over 100 students have promoted school and community unity through problem sharing among members and conducting service projects in their neighborhoods (*Houston Chronicle*, May 3, 1999).

2. *"Good Gang" chapters*—Developed in Houston, the HISD worked in concert with Reverend James Dixon to introduce this program to Houston middle and high schools. According to Dixon, the goal of the organization is to keep students off the streets while promoting growth in five areas—morals, academics, social interactions, artistic endeavors, and health (*Houston Chronicle*, November 21, 1996).

Classroom Instruction

1. *Diversity classes*—In these classes, students are taught to accept the ethnic diversity that surrounds them as well as understanding the social "cliques" that often develop in schools (*Houston Chronicle*, May 3, 1999).

2. *Alternative schooling*—At Sanchez Charter High School in Houston, the Association for the Advancement of Mexican Americans (AAMA) built a large state-of-the-art addition on to the school that has a library, computer lab, science lab, gymnasium, and cafeteria. Both at-risk teenagers and adults use these facilities to further their educations and perhaps improve their skill levels and prospects for employment. Similar facilities have been built in Edinburg, San Antonio, Laredo, and Weslaco (*Houston Chronicle*, July 31, 1999).

Increased Police

1. *Growth in campus police*—Police officers stationed in Arlington schools have been credited with deterring crime and providing a safe environment for students, teachers, and administrative staffs. School officials are hoping to expand their campus police force by hiring three new police officers through a U.S. Justice Department grant. The money, distributed through the Community Oriented Policing Services (COPS) in Schools program, pays for the salary and benefits of a school police officer for three years. After the third year, the school system is responsible for the employment costs of the officer (*Fort Worth Star-Telegram*, June 12, 2001).

2. *School-based "Crime Stoppers" programs*—Some school systems in Harris County have programs whereby students are offered rewards that range from

$50 to $5,000 for tipping off the police about crimes such as alcohol consumption, vandalism, false bomb threats, arson, and weapons possession on campus. Arlington has a similar program in which payments of up to $100 are handed out for those who report similar criminal activities. In both instances, the money is paid once an arrest has been made and charges have been filed (*Houston Chronicle*, October 9, 2000; *Fort-Worth Star Telegram*, February 29, 2000).

One piece of school crime information that is not receiving much attention in either the compilation of state crime statistics or academic studies is the incidence of confirmed and alleged teacher and administrator crimes *against students*. A controversy over the hiring of a baseball coach at Johnson City High School who was accused of sexual harassment by a female student at his previous school, Mathis High School, is a recent example (*Fort Worth Star-Telegram*, April 22, 2001). The allegation that a secret agreement was signed between the Mathis Independent School District (ISD) and the coach not to reveal the accusation to potential new employers set off a firestorm about whether such agreements are improper and keep vital information from superintendents that is necessary to make well-informed hiring decisions.

Other newspaper reports reveal that teacher and administrator criminal conduct against students, although not seemingly widespread, is frequent enough to consider collecting statistics in this area. For instance, a Fort Worth middle school assistant principal pleaded guilty in 1996 to indecent exposure in a city park (*Fort Worth Star-Telegram*, November 14, 1996). School trustees were concerned that the principal had been allowed to stay on the job for 11 days after his arrest, and demands for more stringent background checks were made. In Port Isabel, school trustees in 1995 were forced to address separate controversies involving the high school's band director and assistant band director (*Houston Chronicle*, October 11, 1995). The band director was accused of secretly videotaping the school's cheerleaders as they were changing out of their uniforms in the equipment room of the band hall. The assistant director was seen on the same videotape going through the cheerleaders' purses during their practice.

If it is true that written agreements of the kind approved by the Mathis ISD and its former baseball coach are common (*Houston Chronicle*, April 22, 2001), then the occurrences of teacher/administrator crimes against students are most likely underreported. Just as schools have to be prodded to be more diligent about reporting and recording student crime statistics, similar pressure may have to be exerted for them to earnestly provide information on teacher/administrator crime within the halls of their own schools. This will give parents, local school administrators, communities, and state government officials a more complete picture of school crime in Texas intermediate education.

TEXAS SCHOOL SAFETY CENTER NEEDS ASSESSMENT

The previous section presented some school crime-fighting initiatives adopted in Texas schools and their perceived efficacy. In 1999 study was conducted to examine this issue further. The perceived level of school crime and the support of strategies for addressing existing levels of crime are also relevant for evaluating existing violence prevention and enforcement programs and for program development and modification.

When asked what training is needed, students, parents, and staff demonstrate significant differences regarding which types of training are necessary. For example, 92% of staff members believe that more training in crisis management and response procedures is required, compared to 66% of students and 64% of parents. In this case, different perspectives can account for the differences. However, certain differences are notable. For example, 78% of staff and 77% of parents agree that more training is required in areas of gang awareness, compared to only 53% of students. Parents and staff are more likely to overestimate the amount of violence and could be more influenced by media accounts of gang activity. Meanwhile, students may not feel as threatened by gangs. Perhaps because they are around gang members more often and may know gang members personally, they may feel gangs are not as much of a problem.

On the other hand, students are much more likely to support additional training in anger management (89%) compared to only 67% of staff and 66% percent of parents. Students and staff agree at levels of 77% and 78%, respectively, that training in mediation and conflict resolution is beneficial, compared to only 56% of parents. Again, different perspectives of students, staff, and parents are a likely factor. On one issue, the level of consensus is strong. Students, parents, and staff all agree overwhelmingly (73, 71, and 68%, respectively) that more training in drug and alcohol awareness is required.

Other summary statistics indicate that school staffs are generally confident in the security measures and community support found in their schools. Sixty-two percent of respondents believe that parental support for the school's discipline policy is very strong or strong. Forty-nine percent of respondents feel that they know the legal rights of potentially violent juveniles either very well or pretty well. Eighty-six percent of respondents believe that security measures at their school are highly effective or somewhat effective. Fifty-two percent of respondents believe that community agencies work either very well or well in their school. So, school officials believe they are doing all they can to make schools safer for their communities and are relatively effective in controlling school crime.

DISCUSSION

This consideration of school-based crime and violence in Texas schools reveals several important findings that merit further discussion. In general, we can conclude that violent crime in Texas schools is not as bad as perceived. In many Texas counties, there are no incidents of violent crime. Of course, perceptions drive public policy in many cases, and dramatic incidents, while few in number, color those perceptions. Reflecting the broader political climate that advocates a tough-on-crime perspective (e.g., three strikes and you're out, truth in sentencing), there have been a number of specific initiatives such as zero tolerance and programs designed to better create a climate of order. The ultimate question of whether these initiatives are effective requires further program evaluation analysis.

The commonly held belief that there are higher rates of violent school-based crime in urban areas is supported on one level. For example, the analysis revealed that as the percentage of urban residents increases, the number of incidents also increases. However, when the number of incidents is considered, controlling for the number of students in the county, there are no statistically significant relationships between poverty, adult education levels, percent urban residents, and percent Hispanic. Only the crime rate in the county is a predictor (and only in the cases of assaults against student and confiscated weapons) of school-based violent crime. This finding suggests that any efforts to reduce school-based violent crime should be conducted in partnership with local police, focusing on making the areas surrounding schools safer as well as the community as a whole.

When the five largest urban counties in Texas are considered, no consistent patterns emerge. While this chapter is not challenging the utility of collecting data on school-based violence, the fact that school districts that should exhibit similar rates and consistency across categories, do not present an important paradox that bears additional analysis. Standardized reporting procedures would enhance the confidence and therefore the utility of the data.

There is broad support in Texas for the plans and procedures in place to address school crime and violence. At the same time, there is considerable demand for more training and more programs to address these issues. While the support of teachers, administrators, students, and parents is a positive sign, it is common for surveys to produce high levels of "customer" satisfaction. Solid public policy analysis should be used to justify and direct the future of school-based crime reduction strategies.

REFERENCES

Brooks, A. Phillips (1995). Legislature zeroes in on zero tolerance; State may push school-crime policy, but verdict is still out on its effectiveness. *Austin-American Statesman*, March 7.

Bryant, Salatheia (1999). Violent school crime drops, HISD reports. *Houston Chronicle*, January 12.

Bryant, Salatheia (1996). "Good gang" formed as positive alternative; Program starts at Third Ward school. *Houston Chronicle*, November 21.

Center for Policy Priorities (2001) "For Kids, Everything's Bigger in Texas." *www.cppp.org/kidscount/press/01natl.html.*

Cisneros-Lunsford, Anastasia (1998). Schools, city seek ideas on crime reports. *San Antonio Express-News*, April 14.

Hanson, Eric (1997). School employees told gang problem "manageable." *Houston Chronicle*, January 29.

Hewitt, Paige (2000). Innovative program gives students cash for anonymous tips. *Houston Chronicle*, October 9.

Lam-Yip, Pamela (2000). *Youth violence in the United States and in Texas.* Texas Legislative Council, April. Austin, TX.

Markley, Melanie (1998). Violent crime in Houston schools down. *Houston Chronicle*, June 26.

Markley, Melanie (1995). School crime survey results disputed; Higher figures for midsize districts. *Houston Chronicle*, April 18.

Packer, Jennifer, & Hollace, Weiner (1996). Exposure case upsets school trustees; A former assistant principal who pleaded guilty to indecent exposure was allowed to keep his job for 11 days. *Fort Worth Star-Telegram*, November 14.

Pesquera, Adolfo (1998). Campus crime stats said to be incomplete. *San Antonio Express-News*, April 13.

Pinkerton, James (1995). Secret video upsets parents at high school; Cheerleaders taped while undressing in supply room. *Houston Chronicle*, October 11.

Robbins, Danny (2001). Out of bounds: Deal hid sex charges against coach from district. *Houston Chronicle*, April 22.

Saucier, Heather (1999). Local students and parents working on ways to reduce, prevent violence on campus. *Houston Chronicle*, May 3.

Spangler, Anthony (2001). Police seeking funds to add school officers; District officials say presence helps deter crime. *Fort Worth Star-Telegram*, June 12.

Teens support smaller classes. (2001). Associated Press. *fyi.cnn.com/2001/fyi/teachers.ednews/ 08/07/teen.survey.ap.*

Texas School Safety Center Needs Assessment (1999). Texas School Safety Center–Southwest Texas State University. *www.txssc.swt.edu/schoolsurvey99_results.html.*

Tharp, Robert (2000). Youth drug arrests jump almost sevenfold in decade. *Fort Worth Star-Telegram*, September 4.

Toeing the (hem)line. (1995). Wire service reports. *Houston Chronicle*, August 20.

Tolson, Mike (1995). Anti-gang leaders take prevention message to Spring Branch. *Houston Chronicle*, November 5.

Villafranca, Armando (1999). Nonprofit fights hard for at-risk Hispanics; AAMA works on schooling, drugs, crime. *Houston Chronicle*, July 31.

Violence and Weapons in Texas Schools (1999). Center for Public Policy Priorities. May 18. *www.cppp.org/kidscount/education/schoolsnv.html.*

Zuniga, Jo Ann (1995). Parents attend truancy classes; New program explores education system, gangs and cults. *Houston Chronicle*, March 19.

5

Preparing for Safe Schools

Ronald D. Stephens

The "problem" of school crime has now been sufficiently identified. The scope, amount, and detail of the problem is now known. The next critical question is, "What is to be done?"

Ronald Stephens has been involved with this problem for over 20 years. This chapter is a specific, pragmatic hands-on guide for all of those directly involved in school safety. The first line of defense in the fight against school crime is creating a definite plan of action. Dr. Stephens gives his views here on the specifics of such a plan. The final paragraph of this chapter sums up the author's feelings about safe schools and the part planning can play in its achievement.

Maintaining and managing safe schools is everyone's responsibility. Students, teachers, staff, administrators, parents, police, and all youth-serving professionals must cooperatively and collaboratively work together. Communities get the kinds of campuses they deserve because school safety, more than anything else, is a matter of team commitment and community will. The most exciting thing about safe school planning is that each community has the opportunity to create the type of educational atmosphere and learning climate that it wishes to enjoy. Communities that have placed school safety on the educational agenda are beginning to see positive change. You can, too!

Learning Objectives

This chapter is designed to empower the school peace officer and educator with:

- The skills necessary to cooperatively develop, implement, and evaluate a comprehensive and systematic safe school plan
- An understanding of the changing climate of public education

- A vision of what it means to create a safe, secure, and welcoming educational climate
- The key elements involved in the safe school planning process
- A knowledge of the key players and policy shapers who should be involved in the process
- A working knowledge of promising safe school strategies
- The knowledge and skills to conduct a school site assessment
- The knowledge to prevent, prepare, manage, and resolve a school crisis
- The knowledge to create an attitude of hope and confidence that our nation's schools can be safe havens for children and those professionals who serve them

MAKING EVERY CAMPUS SAFE

Introduction

In the wake of violent school tragedies in Colorado, Oregon, Pennsylvania, Arkansas, Mississippi, Kentucky, Alaska, and recently California that have taken the lives of 30 students and educators and wounded more than 75 others, the school resource officer is being looked to as the newest player to re-create in our schools a perception of safety and well-being. Since the Columbine tragedy, educators have become increasingly motivated to forge new partnerships with policing. Although the expectations are enormously high, the officer represents one of many key components necessary to creating safe and welcoming schools. Police strategies often represent a short-term, quick-fix approach. However, the community-oriented policing concepts of the school resource officer program are about to change that concept. The school resource officer is coming to the campus not merely to arrest students, but first to be present as a problem solver, next to serve as a mentor and motivator, and third to serve as a protector of both students and staff.

A 13-year-old was given a rifle by her parents for her birthday. She practiced with it in her backyard and became a very good shot. She had been frustrated over some bullying and intimidation that had been going on at her school. She became so frustrated that she took the rifle to school and began shooting her classmates on the school grounds. First she shot a young boy in the leg. Next she shot a girl in the wrist. As they called for help, the vice-principal came over to assist. (Keep in mind the 13-year-old had become a very good shot.) She took aim at the vice-principal and hit him directly in the heart. He fell down and died on the spot. Another adult came over to assist. She took aim at him. He was shot in the heart and died on the spot. You are the principal. What are you going to do?

While most of U.S. schools are safe, violent incidents continue to plague them. There are two types of school administrators: those who have faced a crisis and those who are about to. Creating a safe school plan is essential. A school administrator or school resource officer without a safe school plan is like a pilot without a flight plan. The changing climate of public education and the needs that children bring to school reflect the cumulative impact of social issues facing this generation. The school resource officer has become one of the most preeminent players in this process. Educators have felt overwhelmed by student needs. They have sought partnerships and alliances with a variety of youth-serving professionals. At the top of the list is the school peace officer. These new relationships also include probation officers, the courts, psychologists, social workers, and other adult service providers and mentors who are willing to invest time in children.

Inasmuch as young people are required to attend school, it is incumbent upon adults to provide an environment that is safe, secure, and peaceful. Several states, such as South Carolina, California, Florida, Ohio, Kentucky, North Carolina, and Texas, now require comprehensive plans for school safety, discipline, and attendance for every public school in the state. These plans should be part of ongoing district efforts that need to be reviewed and updated on a regular basis. Plans should be developed cooperatively by parents, students, teachers, administrators, counselors, and community agencies, and approved by the local school district governing board. Increasingly, school districts are establishing working relationships with police agencies, service agencies, and parents to provide safe and orderly schools, improve attendance, and expand services to students and parents.

Changing Climate for Public Education

The climate for public education has experienced dramatic changes in recent years. School classrooms include more children of teenage parents and more special education students than ever before. A few years ago approximately 10% of students enrolled were identified as special education; today that number is closer to 15%. Some parents now want their children classified as special education because they perceive that such children have increased rights and benefits. Latchkey children also represent an ever-increasing portion of the student population. Their potential lack of supervision suggests the need for developing several programs and strategies to serve these young people, particularly with before- and after-school activities.

Schools can no longer be seen as "islands of safety" within troubled communities. Crime and violence have invaded far too many of our nation's schools. Former fistfights are being replaced by gunfights; former fire drills are being augmented by crisis drills. Nationally, one out of twelve kids who stay away from school stay away because of fear. School safety has become the latest bargaining chip for teachers; they, too, are demanding a safer working environment. A safe community is a prerequisite for safe schools.

The demographic makeup of student populations has created a greater need for teachers to become more culturally competent to meet diverse student needs. Such a change has occurred within the context of an increasingly violent society with seemingly fewer economic resources facilitating responses to related issues. Personal safety looms large among students, parents, and teachers alike as a top educational concern. Drugs, alcohol, other substance abuse, and gangs also affect school climate. Moreover, society has redefined deviancy in such a way that former types of misconduct that were once considered disruptive may no longer appear on school crime reports. Students and staff must feel safe and secure going to and coming from school. These feelings of safety and security affect attendance and the attrition of staff as well as the continuity of the programs that serve young people. If a school safety plan is to assist in creating an environment that allows students to achieve at optimum levels, then school safety must also include plans for eliminating violence in neighborhoods.

Community violence, underfunding, and politics also contribute collectively and individually to creating a special challenge for administrators. For the most part, school administrators do not design the facilities in which they work; they do not choose the students whom they serve, nor do they control the communities that often surround their campuses with a 360-degree perimeter of community crime. All of these factors are inherited. The cumulative effect often results in a heightened challenge for today's school administrators and communities, unparalleled in any previous generation.

Making a Difference

Perhaps there is no greater challenge today than creating safe schools. Restoring our schools to tranquil and safe places of learning requires a major strategic commitment. It involves placing school safety at the top of the educational agenda. Without safe schools, teachers cannot teach and students cannot learn. Developing and implementing safe school plans is a critical and essential part of this process. School administrators are now recognizing safe school planning as an essential first step in making schools safe.

What Is a Safe School?   A safe school is in place when students can learn and teachers can teach in a warm and welcoming environment free of intimidation, violence, and fear. Such a setting provides an educational climate that fosters a spirit of acceptance and care for every child. It is a place where behavior expectations are clearly communicated, consistently enforced, and fairly applied.

Safe school planning is all about the "art of the possible." It is not limited by special restraints or a set of guidelines. Each community has the opportunity to shape the type of school climate it wishes to create. More than anything else, a safe school plan is a function of community will, priorities, and interests. Only the imagination, creativity, energy, and commitment of the local community limit the components. The key questions to ask are "What is it we want to accomplish?" and "How do we want to make it happen?" Also, if I were the student, how would I want to be treated? When these questions can be asked and answered, a community is then well on the way to creating a comprehensive and systematic safe school plan.

While state and federal policy makers are beginning to recognize the need and require schools to design safe school plans, many educators and community leaders are at a loss as to where to begin such a process. The strategies and concepts included here are designed to help schools and communities to work together cooperatively to reduce the opportunities for crime and violence by promoting positive learning climates.

Why Plan?   The courts have placed school boards on notice either to create safe school campuses or to be prepared to compensate victims for their losses. By developing an effective safe school plan, administrators can prevent many crises and preclude a series of successive crises. Creating safe schools is not simply about avoiding liability; it is about doing the right thing. Children deserve safe schools. An effective safe school plan will reduce school violence and promote a positive educational climate to support the educational success and well-being of every student.

There are only three categories of individuals who are expected to be somewhere against their will. The first group is prisoners. They are protected against cruel and unusual punishment. The second is the mentally ill. They, too, have similar protection. The third category is schoolchildren. Oftentimes we do not afford them the same protection. If young people are required to attend school, then the community must come up with a plan to provide a safe and secure environment there.

Creating this plan must be preceded by creating a climate of trust and cooperation among the stakeholders who serve young people and the students themselves. This compelling duty of care defines the special relationship that exists between the student and school.

Getting Started

An effective school safety plan should include a site assessment, which reviews the facilities and analyzes them from the standpoint of crime prevention through environmental design. The first step involves looking at what facilities exist, how they are laid out and maintained, and the potential problems they may create. This means conducting a facility site assessment. The second step is articulating what changes or modifications need to be made in terms of maintenance, management, or design. The third step is developing a plan for dealing with the difference. Many environmental strategy changes can be made that do not cost money. Other changes, which may cost money, will preserve scarce resources and in some cases may reduce operational costs.

Safe School Planning Defined.   A safe school plan is an ongoing, broad-based, systematic, and comprehensive process designed to create and maintain a positive and welcoming school climate, free of drugs, violence, intimidation, and fear, in which the success and development of all children is nurtured. A safe school plan includes behavioral aspects as well as property aspects of crime prevention. It seeks to create an environment in which teachers can teach and students can learn.

Effective safe school planning involves three key components: (1) It identifies where the school is in the district and in the community, specifying top concerns and/or issues; (2) it asks where the school wants to be; and (3) it calls for the development of a plan to deal with the difference between where the school is and where the school wants to be.

Establishing a Framework for Developing the Safe School Plan.   Safe school planning is an inclusive and cooperative activity that integrally involves the entire community. The safe schools team is the driving force behind the safe school planning process. This group should involve a wide variety of key individuals within the community who touch the lives of children. Examples of essential team players include the superintendent of schools, chief of police, presiding juvenile judge, chief probation officer, prosecutor, health and welfare providers, parents, business leaders, mayor, city manager, church and community leaders, representatives from neighborhood service organizations and from mental health, corrections, parks and recreation, and emergency response teams, among others. Students should be at the heart of the process. They will provide tremendous insight and direction to the safe school planning process.

Before effective safe school plans can be created, the architects of those plans must have a vision and understanding of the forces that provide for safe schools and communities. Achieving envisioned goals begins with the cooperative conduct of those individuals who will lead the effort. There must be a firm understanding that laws and rules alone cannot address all of the issues. Adults have a special duty of care and obligation to protect and serve young people.

Developing the Mission Statement.   A beginning point for safe school planning is the development of the educational mission. School safety should be incorporated into the educational goals. This can be accomplished by adding a phrase to the mission statement stating that "it is the goal of the school to provide a quality education in a *safe and secure environment free of intimidation and fear.*" Such language allows the school district then to create a series of supporting policies that keep students and staff safe while complementing the educational mission.

The following mission statement of James B. Castle High School offers some unique insights into this process:

> We envision James B. Castle High School to be a place where: All students can learn to their highest potential. The promotion of life-long learning is essential. All students, as individuals, can become responsible citizens who think critically, creatively and positively. The environment is safe, fun, secure and conducive to learning. Students will have equal access to, and be taught in, an environment where progressive methods of learning correspond to current technology. As a result of the educational process, students will contribute their talents to the betterment of our global society.

Essential Components of a Safe School Plan.   Safe school plans should be customized to meet the needs of each community. A comprehensive safe school plan includes, but is not necessarily limited to, the following components:

School crime reporting and tracking

Public awareness and the community's perception of violence

Curriculum focusing on prosocial skills and conflict resolution

Behavior/conduct/discipline code

Supervision (formal and natural)

Crisis management and emergency evacuation

Attendance and truancy prevention

Drug prevention

Interagency partnerships

Staff training

Cultural and social awareness

Student leadership and involvement

Parent participation

Involvement of senior citizens

Special event management

Crime prevention through environmental design

Extracurricular activities and recreation

Restitution plan

Nuisance abatement

School/police partnership

Screening and selection of staff

Violence prevention

School security

Community service/outreach

Corporate/business partnerships

Protection of assets

Media and public relations

Health services

Transportation

Legislative outreach and contact

Evaluation and monitoring

As school safety plans and issues are considered, several additional components may also emerge. Safe school planning affords each community a unique opportunity to customize its own strategies and priorities for each program component chosen for examination. Limitless opportunities and strategies exist.

Are Separate Models Necessary for Urban, Rural, and Suburban Schools?

Separate school safety models are not necessarily required for each type of school—rural, suburban, or urban. However, probably no two school safety plans will be exactly the same. Each school should collaboratively and cooperatively develop a safe school plan that is consistent with its unique needs and circumstances. Every school should develop a series of safe school strategies that focus on education, supervision, and crime prevention through environmental design. Many schools promote crime based on the way they are constructed and maintained. Safe school plans become particularly customized when they respond to the unique needs of the school community. For instance, one community may have a serious gang problem. Consequently, its plan should include a substantial component on gang prevention, gang intervention, and gang suppression. Another school may have a particular problem with weapons or drugs. For others it may simply be a matter of dealing with bully prevention strategies. The point is, a safe school plan is a function of the specific and unique issues the local school is facing. Consequently, every safe school plan is likely to have some variation that reflects the local community and its concerns.

Legal Aspects of Safe School Planning.   The first step in safe school planning is to conduct a legal review of federal, state, and local statutes pertaining to student management and school order. This review should include relevant court cases, district policies, and operations manuals, along with labor contracts. The legal review reveals two major themes: First, it identifies what the law requires, and second, it shapes the parameters of what the law allows. Nearly every major school safety issue is embedded in existing law. Consequently, examination of the law is a necessary beginning point in safe school planning. Each school district should ask its legal counsel to develop a summary of laws pertaining to school safety and student management issues. Not only will this document provide an excellent guide for the educator and the school peace officer; it will also educate the school's attorney regarding current laws.

First, it is important to look at federal laws such as the Federal Gun-Free School Zone Act of 1994, which requires school officials who wish to receive federal funds to expel for a minimum of one year any student who brings, possesses, or uses a firearm on a public school campus; the Federal Constitution and the Federal Civil Rights Act, among others; and the Drug-Free Schools and Communities Act of 1986, which requires schools to provide alcohol, tobacco, and other drug prevention programs to all students. A variety of other laws pertaining to Americans with disabilities, special education, and relevant U.S. Supreme Court cases should also be reviewed.

Next, it is necessary to consider state and local laws pertaining to school disorder. There will probably be several of them. At a minimum, the following codes should be checked:

State constitution

Education code

Health and safety code

Penal code

Vehicle code

Child welfare and institutions code

Fire code

Municipal code

School district code

Recent local court decisions

Once all of these laws and court decisions are reviewed, it is important to recognize that some laws or policies that grow out of the laws may be inconsistent with one another. For instance, although it may be tempting to control campus access by chaining closed certain doors, such action may create a fire code violation, setting the stage for a serious liability problem. It is essential that new conflicts or legal problems not be created through establishing incompatible policies or issuing contradictory legal and procedural directives.

District policy and procedure manuals will also provide further insight as to what each local school board may require. Planners should make certain to have the school attorney review all federal, state, county, local, and other municipal ordinances before they develop a safe school plan. Once the plan is developed, the attorney should then provide a complete legal review to ensure that the components of the plan are fair, reasonable, and consistent with other policies, and that they do not promise more than they can deliver.

CREATE A COMMUNITY COALITION

For any plan to succeed, the safe schools team must draw upon the cultural diversity of the community it represents. When the opportunity for including diversity is overlooked, the opportunity for developing wide-ranging solutions can be severely limited. Safe school planning initiatives are best established by community coalitions of school, police, and community leaders.

Who Should Lead the Team?

The safe schools team may be led by anyone in the community. In some communities, the presiding juvenile judge may be the key leader. In other areas, it may be the chief of police or a school board member. Most generally, it will be the superintendent of schools. The safe schools team provides an excellent opportunity for the chief school officer to take an active leadership role in the community. At the site level, the school principal should take this leading role.

Identifying who should lead the team is easy; however, making the team work effectively is a bit more difficult. Each community should capitalize on the people, the resources, and the levels of commitment that are present at the planning table. As a first-tier priority, it is desirable to have agency heads, such as the police chief, the superintendent of schools, or the presiding juvenile judge to lead, empower, and support the safe schools team on an as-needed basis. A second-tier component would include agency and organization representatives who meet on a regular basis to discuss issues and develop solutions. A third tier might be a broader advisory committee composed of community/school representatives who would meet on a regular basis, perhaps monthly or quarterly. They would provide input and direction to the various agencies and organizations that serve young people. By establishing a multilevel/multifaceted network, the safe school planning process can be enhanced. Such options increase participation and can improve the quality and quantity of good ideas. Most importantly, such diverse efforts send a message to the community that school safety is not merely a school problem. It is a community problem—a problem that affirms not only that the school expects and needs the community's full support but also that the problem requires a broad-based community response.

Preliminary Planning Steps for the Safe Schools Task Force

The following steps can facilitate the establishment of a safe school planning task force:

- Identify key players in the community who are willing and committed to serving on the team.

- Hold a community-wide meeting on school safety. All interested parties, including students and parents, should be invited to attend.
- In planning a community meeting, choose a date four weeks in advance. The letter of invitation to persons within the community should state the purpose, date, time, and place of the meeting.

Before the meeting, do your homework:

- Identify the need for safe school planning.
- Approach local police, juvenile justice, and community leaders to solicit their support.
- Review news clips, local crime reports, and current literature in the area of school safety.
- Enlist community support to create a climate of action.

Once the team is formed, members need to educate themselves and the community about school crime and violence prevention. It is a good idea to choose two or three talented people from the team to undergo specialized training in violence prevention. They can then train other team members as well as members of the community.

Creating a Timetable

Making the timetable and process work requires creating an agenda specifying benchmarks and guidelines. Short of developing an individual schedule, the following meeting and task sequence can help a team get started. The safe school planning process will require several meetings and multiple levels of collaboration. A reasonable schedule may include the following expectations:

First Meeting:

Bring together key participants.
Establish the mission and purpose.
Set the framework for developing the safe schools plan.

Second Meeting:

Develop group processes for problem solving and program development.
Identify specific issues and problems.
Ascertain the services and talents each member brings to the group.
Identify local, state, and federal resources.

Third Meeting:

Determine how the site assessment will be conducted.
Develop a list of preliminary information to be considered before the review.

Analyze the needs and issues of each campus.
Identify the needs and issues of the surrounding community.

Fourth Meeting:

Develop the action plan.
Identify constraints and opportunities.
Make assignments and obtain commitments.

Fifth Meeting:

Develop an evaluation and monitoring mechanism.
Determine how to and who will evaluate the program.
Establish an evaluation schedule.

Sixth Meeting:

Announce the program to the public.
Provide training and support to each site.
Implement the plan.

Subsequent Meetings:

Monitor and evaluate the program.
Make changes to program refinements as necessary.
Provide members with updated information.
Develop new and relevant program strategies.
Educate and train new members of the team.
Continue to innovate and evaluate. (Modified from Cities in Schools Plan)

Challenges and Obstacles to Plan Implementation

Although the meeting process is laid out in menu form, it is unrealistic to think that creating a safe school plan is like baking a cake. Certainly there are specific ingredients that are needed in the successful development of such a plan. However, politics creates some unusual, unexpected, and challenging situations that cannot be consistently predicted in all circumstances. One of the biggest challenges involves dealing with big egos and strained relationships. There frequently seems to be a certain contingent of players who are uncooperative, incompetent, or simply difficult to work with. Some individuals or groups simply feel threatened by the new relationships. They may feel threatened when they have to share ownership or information; they may be threatened when they are required to relinquish control; they may be threatened when they are asked to do anything differently. Those age-old questions still linger: What's in it for me? How will the change affect me? How seriously should I take the communication? Some individuals simply do not like change.

To counter these problems, it is important for the team to provide opportunities for developing positive working relationships. Team-building strategies may involve more than simply meeting on a regular basis. Work with those team members who can help create a cooperative momentum. When "foot draggers" and recalcitrants see signs of energy and success in the program, they are much more likely to get on board. Although scheduling regular meetings with the chairpersonship rotated among safe school team members is one option, another useful option is the periodic scheduling of management retreats at which team-building opportunities are provided. It is difficult to create a "recipe" that will ensure positive human behavior, but the process should be placed on the safe school team's agenda. Each team should develop its own plan for building cooperation and support. In the last analysis, no one should have to tolerate unreasonable team members. If someone is too problematic, he or she should be replaced with a new team member or removed from the team. Safe school planning is about options, and it may be necessary to exercise some here.

CONDUCTING A SITE ASSESSMENT

Every school should conduct an annual school safety assessment. This assessment is a strategic evaluation and planning tool used to determine the extent of a school safety problem. It may also focus on a much broader or comprehensive area of school safety or on other school climate issues. Such an assessment could address gangs, weapons in school, drug or alcohol abuse, schoolyard bullying, site evaluation of facilities including hardscape and softscape, policies and procedures, compliance with local and state laws, community support, parent attitudes, student attitudes and motivation, or a variety of other emerging school climate trends and concerns.

A school safety assessment, in broadest terms, is a comprehensive review and evaluation of the educational program of a school or school district. Various issues are examined to ascertain how they affect school climate, school attendance, personal safety, and overall school security. The safety assessment includes:

- A review of student discipline problems, policies, procedures, and practices at both the school site and district level
- An evaluation of the school safety plan and the planning process
- An assessment of the school/police partnership and the relationship with local community leaders and resources
- A review of crime prevention efforts with regard to environmental design
- A review of employee recruiting, selection, supervision, and training criteria as they pertain to school safety
- An assessment of student activities and extracurricular programs
- A review of the crisis response plan
- An assessment of the educational plan and its support for a positive school climate

- A review of the health and medical services provided on campus, by the school nurse or health center, and the local emergency medical facility serving the geographic area of the school
- A review of other areas that may be deemed necessary in the evaluation of the district or site

Before the Assessment Process

In preparation for the assessment process, several resources should be gathered for the assessment team to review. These materials include:

- All security- and safety-related policies of the district
- A floor plan of school buildings
- A site plan showing the campus boundaries and access points
- School crime reports for the previous year
- Known safety and security concerns of the staff and students
- The school's media file of previous news coverage
- Log of police "calls for service" generated from the school or dispatched to the school
- Risk management reports identifying insurance claims
- Maintenance/work orders related to vandalism or graffiti
- Student handbook
- Teacher handbook
- Disciplinary files
- List of students who have been sent to school as a condition of probation
- The terms of probation for students sent to school by the courts
- PTA newsletters that address safety and security
- Labor contracts for classified and certified staff

Collecting Data

There are at least four components of the data collection process. The first involves reviewing school crime reports. Every school should have a comprehensive and systematic school crime reporting process by which written records about school crime incidents are maintained and analyzed. The report should provide for some means of crime analysis to determine what incidents may be linked to other incidents and situations that may be occurring on the campus. Maintaining such records can serve as a valuable student management tool. These reports should be complemented by community crime data obtained from local police officials.

A second component involves a site review. Sample questions that might be used in an assessment process include the following 20 questions. Each question has a specific point value as well as strategic response implications pertaining to the issue identified. These questions are designed to get the evaluation process started. They are by no means comprehensive. The questions were empirically developed over time. They reflect key issues or concerns that should be considered in evaluating school safety. They serve as indicators of critical campus management issues. They are designed to heighten awareness as to how the campus is managed and to help identify community factors that influence the daily management of the school. Local school administrators will likely wish to develop their own evaluation tool customized to their specific needs. Until that is done, the responses to these questions will give the safe school planning team a lot to think about.

School Crime Assessment Tool

1. Has your community crime rate increased over the past 12 months?
2. Are more than 15% of your work orders vandalism related?
3. Do you have an open campus?
4. Has there been an emergence of an underground student newspaper?
5. Is your community transiency rate increasing?
6. Do you have an increasing presence of graffiti in your community?
7. Do you have an increasing presence of gangs in your community?
8. Is your truancy rate increasing?
9. Are your suspension and expulsion rates increasing?
10. Have you had increased conflicts relative to dress styles, food services, or types of music played at special events?
11. Do you have an increasing number of students on probation at your school?
12. Have you had isolated racial fights?
13. Have you reduced the number of extracurricular programs and sports at your school?
14. Are parents withdrawing students from your school because of fear?
15. Has your professional development budget for staff been reduced or eliminated?
16. Are you discovering more weapons on your campus?
17. Do you lack written screening and selection guidelines for new staff at your school?
18. Are drugs easily available in or around your school?
19. Does your annual staff turnover rate exceed 25%?
20. Have you had a student demonstration or other signs of unrest within the past 12 months?

Scoring and Interpretation.   Multiply each affirmative answer by 5 and add the total. Scores of 0 to 20 indicate that there is no significant school safety problem at your school. If you have scores ranging from 25 to 45, you have an emerging school safety problem and should develop a safe school plan. Scores of 50 to 70 indicate that there is a significant potential for school violence. A safe school plan should be a top priority. If your score is over 70, you are sitting on a ticking time bomb. Begin working on your safe school plan immediately. Get some outside help.

A third component in collecting data involves surveying teachers, students, parents, staff, and community members regarding their perceptions of behavior and safety issues. The survey document should not only ask specific questions but also provide for some open-ended input. Several questionnaire models are available from various state departments of education in Texas, California, South Carolina, and Florida.

The fourth and perhaps most important data collection component is to talk with students individually and in focus groups. Typically students will not report their victimization or feelings about school safety to teachers, school administrators, law enforcers, or parents. If adults want to find out what is going on, they must ask. Talking with students is much like a "Pocahontas adventure"—you learn things you never knew you never knew. Good information and insights improve the quality of our decisions about student management. The following questions are excellent icebreakers: Are there areas of the campus you avoid? What types of initiation rites exist for incoming students? Are drugs easily available on your campus? Have you ever seen a weapon at school? The important thing is to get some dialogue going and establish a climate of trust. Students will offer some incredible insights—not only into the problems but also into their recommended solutions.

CONTENT ELEMENTS OF THE SAFE SCHOOL PLAN

The substantive scope of the safe school plan can be as broad as the creativity and commitment of the safe schools team. Generally though, there are at least six overall categories or basic elements of the safe school plan that should be incorporated into the strategic plan. These elements include the physical environment, the social environment, the cultural environment, the economic environment, the personal characteristics of each student and staff member, and the local political atmosphere. A seventh factor—"community will"—may sometimes transcend all of these issues.

The personal characteristics of students and staff, the school's physical environment, and the community's economic conditions are the "givens" that influence the school. In contrast, school social environment, school cultural characteristics, and political components are more "malleable," meaning that they can be changed and improved through planning and action.

School culture is the collection of assumptions, expectations, and knowledge that students, parents, and staff have about how a school should function and how individuals in the school should act. The perception of belonging and commitment to the school that is felt by students and staff is an essential factor for school safety. A safe school plan could have a variety of program components or elements to support these belongingness factors. Safe school plans should be designed to empower communities and schools with strategies and techniques that honor and recognize the value of every person.

Practical Considerations in Policy Development

The National School Boards Association, in a report titled *Violence in the Schools*, recommends that the following questions should be considered as school districts develop violence prevention policies:

Is the content of the policy within the scope of the board's authority?

Is it consistent with local, state, and federal laws?

Have legal references been included?

Does it reflect good educational practice?

Is it reasonable?

Does it adequately cover the issue?

Is it limited to one policy topic?

Is it cross-referenced to other relevant policy topics?

Is it consistent with the board's existing policies?

Can it be administered?

Is it practical in terms of administrative enforcement and budget?

Asking these questions will save school administrators and their boards a lot of grief as well as liability.

Follow up with examples of other policy statements pertaining to:

Reasonable use of force

Threat assessment protocols

Internet use policy

Conflict resolution

CRIME PREVENTION THROUGH DESIGN

Crime prevention through environmental design, or CPTED, is based upon the concept that the proper design and effective use of the environment can reduce the incidence and fear of crime. The underlying objective is to help schools attain their primary goal of educating children in a positive environment free of violence and fear. Reduced crime and vandalism translate to more resources for learning, in not only economic but also educational terms. A safe school campus creates a psychological advantage for learning and positive behavior. CPTED has seven key components: access control, natural surveillance, formal surveillance, territoriality, defensible space, target hardening, and program interaction. When these seven components work together, campus crime and violence can be significantly reduced.

Access Control.   A basic concept of creating a safe school climate centers on controlling campus access. This means that either natural or formal components of access control must be in place. Many school administrators feel they can adequately control the students who are enrolled in their school; however, a major problem arises when "nonstudents" come to the campus.

Addressing the nonstudent issue has several implications. First, the campus perimeter needs to be controlled. Second, the number of entrances and exits should be minimized. Direction flow needs to be consistent with intended traffic design purposes. The campus should be designed so that visitors and guests must pass through a supervised access point. If the campus has several parking areas, those areas should be carefully controlled with limited access capability. Visitor parking must be easily identified with proper signage and control. Pedestrian and vehicular traffic should be designed in such a way to provide natural supervision from the main office or by security personnel.

Uniform screening procedures should be in place on each campus. All visitors should be referred to the front office where they can be screened to ensure that they have legitimate business and that they are in fact custodial parents or guardians who have access to their children. Visitors should be asked such questions as: Who are you here to see? Do you have an appointment? Are you the authorized custodial parent?

Natural Surveillance.   School facilities should be designed in ways that afford natural surveillance. Architectural barriers, overgrown shrubbery, and posters on window glass tend to impede natural supervision. Managing students is difficult at best. The administrator's job should not be made more difficult through poor designs and thoughtless maintenance. Student gathering areas, including student lockers, should be located in areas that provide natural supervision. When formal areas are established, informal areas tend to become off limits. Would-be offenders tend to stand out. Anyone observed in places that are not designated as formal gathering areas automatically will be subject to scrutiny. Illegitimate users will feel at greater risk and will have fewer excuses for being in the wrong places. Teachers and administrators will assume greater challenging powers through clear spatial definition.

Formal Surveillance.   After everything has been done to enhance natural supervision by removing architectural barriers and by keeping sight lines open through proper landscape maintenance, building, design, lighting, and access control, the next major environmental factor includes formal supervision. It is important to create a high-visibility profile of administrators, faculty, students, and staff. However, before school administrators make duty personnel assignments, respective union rules and contractual agreements should be reviewed.

Duty personnel should be assigned to supervise those high-incident areas. This is where the school crime report is critical. The report will suggest areas that need special supervision. Those areas may include the main entrance or campus perimeter, particularly if a school is having problems with intruders. Restrooms, hallways, stairwells, locker clusters, and commons areas frequently experience problems. Student parking areas or other remote locations may generate additional risks. The main point is to identify high-incident locations and provide appropriate supervision.

When staff members cannot be everywhere at once, school administrators may need to look at other more formal surveillance options. When the Las Vegas Unified School

District realized it needed enhanced student supervision in specific campus areas, administrators went to the local casinos for advice. Casino officials advised the school on security equipment specifications, location, placement, management, and system operation. The Las Vegas Unified School District now has one of the most sophisticated and best-managed surveillance programs of any public school system in the United States.

Territoriality.   A specific objective of crime prevention is to personalize space assigned to each person in order to emphasize the perception of ownership. This principle translates to the identification of territories within the school campus. Hallways, classrooms, and foyers are assigned to the "proprietors" of adjacent internal spaces—classrooms and offices. Responsibility for the general supervision and care of these territories goes with the ownership of the internal space. There should be a clear delineation of space as one moves through various areas of the campus. For instance, it should be evident when one is moving from the science wing to the fine arts wing or to the mathematics department. When space is clearly differentiated, it tends to be territorialized and better controlled.

Defensible Space.   Numerous opportunities are available for environmental concepts to contribute to the productive management of schools; for example, simply providing clearly marked transitional zones that indicate movement from public to semipublic to private space. Multiple access points increase the perception that the school parking area is public and provide many escape routes for potential offenders. The use of barricades to close unnecessary entrances during low-use time controls access and reinforces the perception that the parking area is private. As privacy expectations are enhanced, the space is perceived as more defensible by the regular users and is perceived as increasingly risky by the potential intruders.

Target Hardening.   Target hardening helps prevent crime. Target hardening asks the question, "What can be done to reasonably minimize the potential for campus crime without making the school appear to be a prison or fortress?" Effective target hardening maintains a balance between the development and implementation of appropriate security measures without being too draconian. Careful planning should be devoted to identifying unacceptable risks and determining what degree of risk is acceptable. The objectives of target hardening include preventing the crime by making the criminal's objective difficult to attain, controlling the crime by slowing the criminal's progress and thereby increasing the chances of apprehension, and finally, precluding additional crimes against the district. Once the word gets out that criminals will be caught, apprehended, and aggressively prosecuted, they will tend to look elsewhere for entertainment and challenge.

Program Interaction.   Effective program interaction implies that the facilities will be properly designed to enhance natural supervision. Problem areas will be supported by formal supervision. A close partnership will be developed among police and emergency service personnel. The staff and students will work together in creating defensible space and territoriality. The school's administration will take adequate steps to harden the target by minimizing criminal opportunities.

Assigned spaces should be designated and used for the type of activities expected. Effective crime prevention can be achieved by placing safe activities in unsafe locations or placing unsafe activities in safe locations. This will enhance the natural surveillance of these activities by increasing the perception of safety for legitimate users and risk for potential offenders. For example, student parking is an unsafe activity that is often located on the periphery of the campus and obscured by landscaping that minimizes natural surveillance. By locating student parking in an area that has a direct line of sight from the office windows, or removing unnecessary block walls, trees, or landscaping barriers that obscure natural surveillance, student safety can be enhanced.

Improve scheduling of space to allow for the most effective use of facilities. For instance, at lunchtime, conflict often occurs as groups attempt to go to the cafeteria while others are returning to class. It takes longer to get groups through the lunch line because of this congestion. Classroom and locker thefts often occur during this period. Separating the cafeteria entrance and exit by space can help to define movement in and out of the area. Each group will arrive faster and with fewer struggles. Illegitimate users also will feel at greater risk of detection. Adjusting the class change schedule to allow for nonconflicting movement of personnel could also minimize these potentially disruptive circumstances.

The successful application of these seven principles supports the concept that the proper design and use of physical space affects human decision and behavior, leading to improved productivity and profit, with the by-product of loss prevention in a welcoming education setting. Other strategies include overcoming distance and isolation through more efficient communication and design; redesignating the use of space to provide natural barriers for conflicting activities; providing clear borders for controlled space; and redesigning or revamping space to increase the perception or reality of natural surveillance. Observation has shown that the design and use of school facilities have a direct relationship to code of conduct violations and criminal behaviors.

MONITORING AND EVALUATING THE SAFE SCHOOL PLAN

The burden of evaluation analyzes what has been done and suggests what remains to be accomplished. Measuring and evaluating has never been easy. Clearly there are some specific needs for developing effective evaluation techniques and measures. Program effectiveness can be evaluated on the basis of inputs, outputs, or impacts. Inputs and outputs may be the easiest to evaluate. Impacts are the most difficult. For instance, how does one measure the effectiveness of the safe school plan in terms of crime prevention? Can you attribute crime reduction to the implementation of specific program components you have implemented? Is it good enough simply to know that the campus is safer? Whenever one has to measure something that does not exist, the task becomes more difficult. Such circumstances suggest a need to develop a set of objective measures and a complementary set of subjective measures. Together, such measures are more likely to constitute a fuller evaluation of program effectiveness. An initial step might be to determine what criteria will be used to evaluate program effectiveness. Will the criteria include favorable crime statistics, good feelings from students and staff, the percentage of the annual budget devoted to safe school activities, the number of sponsored programs, or some other measures?

To be effective, there is a compelling need to identify what does and does not work so that limited resources can be applied with a maximum return. Here are some examples of questions to use to measure a school's effectiveness:

- Is school crime decreasing or increasing in terms of assaults, thefts, and burglaries?
- Are student attendance rates improving?
- Are staff turnover rates increasing or decreasing?
- Is the number and percentage of your orders related to vandalism and graffiti increasing or decreasing?
- Are academic test scores improving?
- Have police calls for service to the school been increasing or decreasing?
- How do students, staff, and parents perceive school safety?
- Are student transiency rates increasing or decreasing?
- Is community crime increasing or decreasing?
- Is the number of weapons incidents increasing or decreasing?

Unfortunately, there are no nationally mandated crime reporting standards or mechanisms for evaluating the effectiveness of safe school plans. Furthermore, not all school crime is reported because some school administrators believe that reporting the crime will make them look bad. To evaluate school safety and school safety plans, there first must be an adequate database so that progress can be measured. The greatest impediment to a good evaluation program is often the lack of good school crime data followed closely by general resistance issues related to evaluation. Generally, each community or school has been left to its own devices regarding reporting crime and/or developing effective evaluative measures of safe school plans.

Another challenge involves finding schools that have implemented a comprehensive safety plan addressing all components. This is difficult because the nature of safe school planning suggests that each setting is unique. School safety is about identifying specific security issues and then creating a response/prevention plan. With this scenario in mind and these descriptors in place, data have begun to emerge from school systems that have implemented specific safe school components.

For instance, in Long Beach, California, the school district implemented a mandatory school uniform policy. Since its implementation, student assaults have decreased by 34%, assaults with a deadly weapon are down by 50%, sex offenses are down by 74%, and extortion is down by 60% from the previous year. After five years into the program, in 1999 Long Beach reported that assaults had been reduced by 91% from its levels of five years ago. In Houston, Texas, where local police officials worked with the schools to address truancy concerns, school attendance is up and daytime burglaries are down by 70%. When young people are not in school, they are often committing acts of crime and violence in the community. In Washington, Connecticut, where a character education curriculum was implemented at Devereaux Glenholme School, student behavioral problems were reduced by 50%. In Fresno, California, local probation officials and police officers joined in partnership with the schools to provide on-campus services to young people in need of supervision. As a result of their efforts, student assaults were reduced by nearly 50%. These changes have taken place with respect to specific program components. A comprehensive program of prevention activities that focuses on education strategies, supervision strategies, mentoring, and motivating programs could have even greater results.

Evaluation and monitoring should not be left to chance. It should be determined up front what will be measured, how it will be measured, who will perform the evaluation, and where and how the results will be disseminated. After data have been collected and reviewed, it is essential to keep parents, students, and staff informed as to how things are going. Keeping in mind that safe school planning is an ongoing process, school administrators should ultimately incorporate results of the monitoring and evaluation process in the ongoing safe school plan.

6

Recommended Practices for Safe Schools

Ronald D. Stephens

Ronald Stephens continues with his excellent guidance for schools wishing to improve their abilities to react to and be proactive toward school crime. This chapter provides some general and specific recommendations for safe schools. Appendix A in this chapter contains a checklist of specific questions to be asked of any school being evaluated; Appendix B includes examples of a "Memorandum of Understanding," which can be entered into by a public school and local police department.

The chapter ends with this thought: "These guidelines represent the beginning of a continuing collaborative and cooperative process to create safe schools for all U.S. children. Making schools safe requires a total community effort within the context of a broad spectrum of opportunities."

Serve as a consultant to your district and conduct your own site assessment by using the site assessment check sheets provided in Appendix A. In addition to these assessment materials, here are several promising strategies you can advise your district to consider. The following list of general recommendations serves as a menu of potential program elements that contribute to safe, welcoming, and drug-free schools.

CAMPUS ACCESS AND CONTROL

Control campus access.   Continuing efforts should be made to minimize the number of campus entrance and exit points used daily. Access points to school grounds must be limited and supervised on a regular basis by individuals who are familiar with the student body. Campus traffic, both pedestrian and vehicular, should flow through areas that can be easily and naturally supervised. Delivery entrances used by vendors also need to be checked regularly. Parking lots often have multiple entrances and exits, which contribute to the vandalism and defacement of vehicles and school property. Vehicular and pedestrian access should be carefully controlled. Perimeter fencing needs to be considered.

Define campus perimeters with appropriate landscaping and fencing. School campuses should lend themselves to natural supervision. Access points and campus buildings should be easily supervisable. Avoid solid block walls or other architectural barriers that obscure the playgrounds, gathering areas, or structures. Landscaped areas must be maintained in ways that promote observation and supervision. Consider decorative wrought iron rather than chain link fencing, which does little more than provide a ladder anywhere the fence is located on the campus.

Establish uniform visitor screening procedures. Specific procedures need to be established to screen and monitor visitors and potential campus intruders. Signs directing persons to the office should be placed in strategic, easily visible locations and be large enough to attract visitors' notice. Visitors must be required to sign in at the school office, state their specific business, and wear or visibly display a visitor's badge. All school employees should be advised to greet visitors or any unidentified persons and direct them to the main office to ensure that these persons have legitimate business at the school. Teachers and staff need to be trained to courteously challenge all visitors. "May I help you?" is a kind, nonthreatening way to begin.

Post appropriate directional signs on the campus. These are to advise students, visitors, or other nonstudents of the conditions they agree to accept upon entering the campus, including any applicable trespassing statutes, drug-free school zones, weapons prevention notices, or other pertinent statutes requiring public notice. A comprehensive signage program should also be created that clearly designates building names, purposes, and directional flow. Good signage minimizes confusion and provides fewer excuses for unauthorized users to trespass on the campus.

Require picture identification cards for each student and staff member. A school administrator is responsible not only for keeping kids away from trouble but also for keeping trouble away from kids. Being able to differentiate enrolled students from nonstudents and guests is critical. An effective picture identification system will enhance the control and management of the campus. Authorized parent volunteers and school visitors should also display clearly identifiable badges or name tags.

Hall passes should be carefully managed and appropriately monitored. Consider developing a single hall pass form to be utilized by each teacher that provides the student's name, date, time out, time in, destination, and purpose. At the end of the day, the pass would be signed by the teacher and turned in to the office. The information contained on the form could be extremely helpful in solving campus crimes during the day because the report summarizes who was where and when. When hall pass data are combined with school crime data, the opportunity exists to leverage data in ways that enhance problem solving.

Clearly separate and segregate mixed vehicular and pedestrian functions.   For instance, bus loading and unloading should be separated from parent drop-off and pickup points. Deliveries, loading docks, and vendor access points need to be clearly delineated, and visitor, staff, and student parking visibly defined. Pedestrian traffic must be clearly separated from all vehicular access. It is important to ensure that none of these functions conflicts with another.

ADMINISTRATIVE LEADERSHIP

Mandate crime reporting and tracking.   A uniform school crime reporting and record-keeping system is critical to maintaining a safe and secure campus. When school administrators know what crimes are being committed on their campus, when they are committed, and where and who is involved, it speaks volumes about the types of strategies and supervision that should be implemented. In addition, it is important to conduct some level of crime analysis to determine what, if any, linkages exist among various aspects of criminal activity on the campus.

Place school safety on the educational agenda.   School administrators tend to get not only what they expect and deserve but also what they measure. When the district makes a conscious decision that safe and welcoming schools are a high priority, that commitment provides the basis for the development of plans and strategies to achieve this goal. Placing school safety on the educational agenda is a mandatory first step toward safer and better schools.

Mission statement.   The school's mission statement should include a phrase that reflects the context in which the school and district wish the academic learning to take place. For instance, the phrase "to learn in a safe and secure environment free of violence, drugs and fear . . . " enhances the school's legal position to create and enforce policies that promote a safe, caring, and disciplined school climate. A statement of this nature can have a powerful effect upon validity and credibility of the school district's efforts to create and preserve a safe environment.

The Virginia Association of School Superintendents has articulated an excellent statement to assist school administrators in developing their safe school plans. Its position statement states:

> It is the responsibility of schools and their governing authorities to provide safe schools for the children and communities that they serve. The establishment of safe schools is inseparable from the issues of violence and crime in the larger community. Safe school solutions must ultimately be pursued in the context of a commitment to create safe communities, not just safe schools. The broadest possible coordinated response of parents, educators, students, community leaders, and public and private agencies will be sought.

Develop a comprehensive system-wide safe schools plan.   School safety must be placed at the top of the educational agenda on each campus and within the community. A district-wide plan should be established, complemented by a safe schools plan for each school site. Programs need to be developed collaboratively with parents; students; educators; law enforcers; the courts; probation and social service personnel; and religious, corporate, and other community leaders who represent the racial and ethnic balance of the community. Safe school planning is an ongoing process that must be interactively supported by pursuing vigorous interagency courses of action. Strategies must be established that focus not only on security and supervision options but also on educational options, including community and corporate partnerships. Plans should be reviewed, updated, and broadly disseminated annually to students, parents, and staff. As the planning process continues, a series of other positive suggestions and strategies will emerge. Begin the process now so that positive change can occur.

Disseminate a summary of laws pertaining to school disorder. The summary should be drafted and developed by the district's legal counsel and disseminated through the director of security to all site administrators and security personnel to ensure uniformity and consistency of student supervision and management.

Establish a state-of-the-art "Emergency Operation Communications Center." This utilizes the latest technology and allows site administrators to make immediate contact with district school safety personnel. A school communications network should be established that links classrooms and schoolyard supervisors with the front office or security staff, as well as with local police and fire departments. An 800-megahertz, fully computerized public safety emergency frequency is recommended to complement this system.

Develop a clear job description of duties and responsibilities for school peace officers. A set of general orders and standard operating procedures must also be developed. The director of security should develop and distribute an operations manual among all district security personnel.

Establish a crisis response plan. Through responsible planning, many potential problems can be avoided. However, there are times when a crisis is unavoidable. A good crisis plan focuses on crisis prevention, preparation, management, and resolution. It will also identify community resources and agencies that serve students. The crisis response plan should include step-by-step procedures for the following types of crisis situations:

Campus unrest	Utility failure	Assault and battery
Chemical spills	Weapons possession	Suicide
Drive-by shootings	Hostage/terrorist	Rape
Kidnapping/abduction	Bomb threats	Molestation
Natural disasters	Child abuse	Child neglect
Earthquake	Homicide	Unauthorized vendors
Flood	Intruders	Search and seizure
Tornado	Sit-ins	Fire
Hurricane	Extortion	Falling aircraft
Tsunami	Vehicle accident	Illness/injury
Threat assessment		

The crisis plan should include a series of potential evacuation plans, lockdown procedures, emergency kits, and backup communication plans.

Identify specifically assigned roles and responsibilities.   Specific policies and procedures that detail staff members' responsibilities for security should be developed. These responsibilities may include monitoring hallways and restrooms, patrolling parking lots, and providing supervision at before-school and after-school activities.

Work with the central administration to expand the network of alternative placement options for troubled youth.   Weapon-using or weapon-toting youngsters should be removed from the mainstream educational setting and relocated at alternate sites that provide increased supervision and structure.

Establish a community service and restitution program at district schools. Work with the presiding juvenile judge and the chief probation officer to establish a series of community service and restitution programs at the school. Individuals involved in vandalism and acts of malicious mischief must have some positive means of making amends to society for their infractions and offenses. Opportunities for service should be developed with the help of appropriate governmental and community agencies.

Recognize the politics of safe schools.   The politics of school safety can be very delicate and yet turbulent. As widely diverse team members come together, each person and the groups he or she represents must be made to feel equally important. The safe schools team will be no better than the example set by its chair. The following ideas can help the school administrator rise above the politics:

- Emphasize a safe and welcoming environment for all children.
- Set goals in positive terms rather than simply zeroing in on combating violence. Focus on developing safe schools.
- Be aware of special-interest groups. They need to be fairly represented and their views heard, yet their influence must be balanced within the larger group structure.
- Recognize that safe school planning is like a marriage—it requires a lot of cooperation.
- Do not underestimate the value or influence of any member of the school safety task force. Make a special effort to accept, appreciate, and work with each participant.
- Determine in advance the amount of decision-making authority to be held by the safe school planning team. Do members have the authority to make recommendations or decisions? Communicate responsibilities to team members before they decide to serve.
- Do not attempt to force particular decisions upon the group.
- Do not have hidden agendas that require the committee's rubber stamp of approval.
- Realize that most issues being considered do not require immediate decision. Invest the necessary time to consider each issue carefully and develop a positive decision.

It is extremely important to continue to build and develop coalitions throughout the safe school planning process. Students may be the most important group to include in this process. The second most underutilized resource, next to students, is parents. Every campus should establish a parents' center where parents are encouraged to participate in the educational activities of their children. States such as California have even passed laws requiring employers to release parents from their jobs for up to 40 hours per year per child, so parents can participate in school activities or meetings. The California law allows the employee to utilize vacation time, sick time, or compensable time for the site visits. Such law is a remarkable legislative tool; it acknowledges the importance of parent involvement in the education process.

Conduct an annual review.   Every school should conduct an annual school safety assessment and review of its safe school plan because safe school planning must be an ongoing process. The evaluation component is a continuing reality check and refinement of the safe school actions and attitudes that the team wishes to create. The assessment may reveal that additional steps need to be taken to improve adult supervision, revise curricula, pass legislation, redesign facilities, or establish new programs.

The safe school planning team and the community should be involved in the evaluation process on a regular basis. It is important to refer to the original safe school plan, review each component, and ask the following questions:

- Is this priority on task?
- What could we do better?
- Do other options or strategies exist that we should try?
- How can we be more effective?
- How can we combine other efforts or strategies to produce better results?

At least once a year, administrators should review the school's mission statement to remain focused on the school's top priority of serving and preparing young people for productive and responsible citizenship. The bottom line is, an evaluation is never done; the evaluation process needs to continue on a regular basis.

Promote crime prevention through environmental design.   Good facility designs cannot overcome bad management. However, outstanding management can overcome bad designs. Several things can often be done to improve campus management:

- Trim or remove shrubbery that interferes with natural surveillance.
- Provide maximum supervision in heavy traffic areas.
- Provide strategically located public telephones with dial-free connections to emergency services.
- Relocate safe activities near typical trouble spots. For instance, consider relocating a counselor's office next to a corridor or locker bay where problems have occurred. Conduct ticket sales or concession activities in or near problem areas.

- Eliminate obstacles such as trash cans and architectural barriers that block or impede traffic flow as well as supervision and surveillance.

- Use parabolic/convex mirrors in stairwells and other locations that require improved supervision.

- Replace double-entry restroom doors with an open zigzag design to better monitor behavior in restroom areas.

- Utilize automatic flush valves and automatic water faucets to reduce vandalism and control water consumption.

- Ensure that hallways and stairwells are large enough to handle the flow of foot traffic adequately.

- Colors and lighting also affect attitudes and behavior.

Establish two-way communication between the front office and each classroom. Campus communications systems should include two-way communication capability between each classroom and the office. Teachers need to be able to contact the front office from any classroom. Many schools do not have this capability. Campus supervisors, assistant principals, and principals must also have two-way radios. The campus should have at least one radio with cellular phone capability for use in emergency situations. Detention classrooms or facilities for behaviorally disruptive students also need to have emergency buzzers or call buttons.

Identify and track repeat offenders.   The majority of school crime problems are caused by a small percentage of students. It is essential to track, monitor, and closely supervise disruptive youngsters to discourage their continued involvement in misbehavior and crime. The following actions should be considered when planning such close supervision: Place such students with experienced teachers; develop individual behavior and education plans; assign a specific counselor to each student; and assign students lockers located in areas that are visible and easily supervised.

Carefully screen and select new employees.   One of the most important decisions that parents and communities make involves deciding who will teach, train, coach, counsel, and lead their children. Keeping child molesters and pedophiles out of classrooms, schools, and youth-serving organizations is a major task. Responsible parenting and thoughtful leadership on the part of schools and other youth-serving agencies should provide sufficient rationale for establishing appropriate safeguards for keeping child molesters away from children.

Increasing litigation against school systems and child-care providers has created a compelling financial reason for conducting appropriate employee background checks to protect the safety of children. Many school systems and youth-service organizations have already faced multimillion-dollar lawsuits for their failure to appropriately screen, supervise, and/or remove employees who represent risks to children.

Every school system and youth-serving organization needs to have clear policy guidelines and procedures to weed out individuals having criminal backgrounds of misbehavior involving children. Any record-screening program must consider individual rights of privacy and due process as well as the right to a hearing when employee disqualification is involved. However, the screening program must also balance these rights with the rights of the individuals who will be assisted by the youth-serving professional.

Conduct periodic joint meetings of all staff and faculty.   Discuss strategies and procedures to make the campus safer and more welcoming for everyone. This effort can serve as the beginning for a broader and more comprehensive safe school planning effort.

Utilize existing technologies that promote crime prevention.   A host of options exist relative to access control, property identification, and ongoing supervision. For example, consider installing electromagnetic door locking systems and using property control strategies such as microdot systems, surveillance cameras for difficult-to-supervise public areas, and other such high-tech strategies that may also be appropriate to the educational setting.

SCHOOL CLIMATE

Make the campus safe and welcoming, beginning early in the morning.   School safety leadership begins at the top. There is no question that the best principals spend the majority of their time outside their offices. Staying in touch cannot be accomplished behind office walls. Begin the day by greeting students at the front door when they first arrive. Be present in the hall during class changes. Visit classrooms and attend special events. The way the day begins affects the climate of the entire day and has a significant impact on how it is concluded.

Develop a graffiti abatement and community clean up program.   School officials must work closely with police and community leaders to shut down drug houses and stop illegal group activities in the neighborhoods of schools. The local U.S. attorney along with city and county officials represent some excellent resources to cultivate. Their support is critical as local and regional gang, drug, and graffiti abatement strategies are developed. School officials should work with the local community in seeking cooperative solutions to nuisance abatement problems, including protecting the school site and ensuring that the walk to school is crime free and nonthreatening.

Create a climate of ownership and school pride.   Every student and staff member needs to feel like a key part of the school community. Such empowerment can be accomplished by involving every person in the safe school planning process, including students, parents, teachers, and community leaders. Establish homeroom areas for faculty and students. Encourage school-sponsored groups and clubs to take ownership of specific hallways, display areas, or other locations.

Provide close supervision, remedial training, and restitution for the serious habitual offender.   Where feasible, require restitution and community service from all juvenile offenders. Create a special supervision program for the repeat offender. Such a program could include in-school suspension or alternative education offered within the district.

Troublemakers should not be rewarded with time off from school or reduced class schedules. Instead, such students' training and supervision should be intensified.

Remove posters from all window glass.   Posters and construction paper covering windows block natural supervision. Unless glaring sun or the need for privacy mandates the covering of windows, they should be left clear or uncovered to enhance natural supervision.

Enhance multicultural understanding.   Focus on stressing the unique worth of every person. Gang activity and the polarization of student groups indicate a need to develop educational programs and activities that bring students together. Such a desirable result might be brought about by using a multicultural curriculum or by instituting a process of cooperative learning. Bringing students together to work collaboratively on specific projects can also pay great dividends.

Establish a vibrant system of extracurricular programs.   School children need positive things to do. Without interesting, positive, or challenging activities, students tend to fill the void with negative activities. A safe school provides students with several options before, after, and during school.

Enhance interagency cooperation by creating a partnership among youth-serving professionals.   Creating safe schools is a community function. Schools alone cannot accomplish such a feat. Safe schools actively cooperate with community agencies. Campus security operations should be coordinated with local police agencies. Community support agencies such as county mental health, child protective services, department of parks and recreation, juvenile probation, and the courts must actively work together to identify students who are potentially dangerous, provide services to preclude them from causing further problems, and assist them in their educational and personal development. By working together, community agencies and schools can develop effective education and behavior plans to better protect the rights of students and staff while rehabilitating juvenile offenders.

Nuisance abatement.   Work with local city and county officials to develop ordinances and regulations that deal with trash disposal, graffiti abatement, and elimination of drug and gang houses or other unsafe or unsightly neighborhood conditions that negatively affect school climate.

STUDENT BEHAVIOR, SUPERVISION, AND MANAGEMENT

Review the student handbook.   Ensure that behavior expectations are clearly communicated, consistently enforced, and fairly applied. School policies should reflect behavior expectations outlined in federal, state, county, and local statutes or ordinances.

Articulate a clearly defined locker policy.   The locker policy at each school should appropriately reflect the district's custodial interest. Students and parents need to be notified that the lockers are school property. Students should be advised in the student handbook that lockers and their contents may be searched at any time for reasons of health and safety. The student handbook must reflect this expectation. Distributing district-owned locks to students or requiring that students use only locks for which the school has combinations will further enhance the school's custodial position in conducting routine locker checks.

Develop and enforce a school dress code.   Students and staff tend to behave the way they are allowed to dress. Establish a district-wide uniform dress code policy that establishes clear appearance standards for both students and staff. Gang attire should be prohibited and dress code expectations consistently enforced. Contradictory policies and procedures and inconsistent enforcement by staff send mixed messages to students. Involve students and parents in developing appearance standards. Students and parents will support and preserve what they help create.

Review discipline and weapons possession policies.   This is to ensure that the policies attack the problem and not simply the symptoms. Clearly distinguish between disciplinary matters and criminal offenses. Identify top discipline problems and then establish a task force consisting of students, teachers, administrators, and parents to review and/or develop effective strategies and programs. The weapons policy should reflect the new Federal Gun-Free School Zone Act of 1994, which mandates a 12-month minimum suspension for the possession of firearms. The student handbook also needs to reflect compliance with this 1994 law. Failure to comply may result in the loss of federal funds to the district.

Place students and parents on notice.   At the beginning of each school year, all students and their parents or guardians should be provided with written codes of conduct outlining behavior expectations and their sanctions. In addition to providing students and parents with the comprehensive guidelines that establish discipline procedures and due process considerations, consider developing a one-page summary of the school rules, which can be posted in strategic locations throughout the campus.

Provide adequate adult supervision.   Young people need continuous responsible supervision. This may include teachers, administrators, parents, campus supervisors, or police officers. By all means, do not forget the option of utilizing assistance from senior citizens. Just as there are many young people looking for something to do, there are also many senior citizens whose talents and resources have yet to be tapped. For the most part, recent studies have shown that the majority of young people feel that there is a major role for adults to play in counseling and encouraging kids toward nonviolence.

Limit opportunities to transport and store contraband.   School systems around the country have implemented a variety of school crime prevention policies that do the following:

- Allow only clear plastic or mesh book bags or no book bags at all.
- Eliminate lockers completely.
- Establish a coat and jacket checking area requiring large articles of clothing capable of shielding weapons to be left there rather than worn or carried into other areas.
- Provide students with two sets of textbooks, one for home and one at school, to eliminate the need for book bags at school. Eliminating the potential costs of

a full-scale, five-day-a-week/every-student-search would save enough money to justify using this approach.

- Reducing the amount of time between class changes as well as extending the length of class instructional periods so that students will not have to make so many class changes is another promising strategy.

Automobile and parking policies should state that campus parking is a privilege, not a right.   The parking policy also needs to place students on notice that when they drive their vehicles onto school property, they agree to abide by campus rules and agree to have their vehicles searched. Diminishing the privacy expectation can serve as a deterrent to the presence of contraband or weapons. Such a policy will also enhance the district's position for any legal action relative to search and seizure issues.

"Hard looks."   "Stare downs," "mad dogging," "mean-mugging," or whatever name it is called, should be added as actionable offenses to the student code of conduct. Such behavior must not be tolerated.

Train students to take responsibility for their own safety.   Encourage students to report suspicious individuals present on school grounds. Provide students and staff with a toll-free, anonymous hotline for reporting weapons offenses and other criminal activity.

Closely supervise troublemakers.   A small percentage of young people create most of the school problems. There is a growing trend among schools and juvenile-serving agencies/professionals to begin sharing information about the serious misbehavior of juveniles. Such information sharing allows educators, law enforcers, and the courts to work together more effectively in creating appropriate educational and behavioral plans for this small but disruptive group of serious habitual offenders. Youngsters who commit campus and off-campus crimes must be carefully monitored. Students should be provided with special counseling, support, and referral to appropriate community resources, including alternative schools when justified. Organizations that serve these youngsters, including the courts and probation, police, and social service agencies, need to coordinate their activities through appropriate information sharing on a need-to-know basis.

Establish a parent/volunteer center on each campus.   This center recruits, coordinates, and encourages parents to participate in the educational process. Possible activities include helping supervise hallways, playgrounds, restrooms, or other trouble spots. Classroom visitation and participation in special events are encouraged. A special training program that outlines expectations and responsibilities for parents in volunteer roles can be particularly helpful. School crime decreases when responsible adult supervision is present.

STAFF TRAINING

Conduct annual school safety training programs.   Prior to the start of each school year, training sessions should be held for all site administrators and security personnel to review school safety procedures and strategies. School staff need to be informed and regularly updated on safety plans through in-service training. The training should include not only certified staff but also classified staff, as well as part-time and substitute employees.

Establish a vibrant school peace officer training program.   School peace officers should be academy trained and/or "POST" (Police Officer Standards Training) certified. Their training and their compensation should be commensurate with their responsibilities and consistent with the local police agencies. This will increase the preparation and capability of school personnel to meet the specific needs demanded by their position. The professional training required of school security officers today is dramatically different from that of 25 years ago. School security officers must continually take part in special services and in-service training programs to stay abreast of innovative methods and techniques. Officers can also enhance their professional status by participating in such professional organizations as the National Association of School Resource Officers or the International Association of School Safety Professionals.

Provide teacher-training programs.   Special in-house training programs in the area of student behavior management should be offered for teachers and administrators. Strategies that worked 20 years ago may no longer be effective. Teachers must develop coping skills and techniques for controlling classroom behavior and dealing with disruptive youth and angry parents. Such skill building and training is necessary to ensure educational effectiveness and personal safety and survival.

Establish an ongoing professional development and in-service training program for campus supervisors and student personnel workers.   Such programs can include training techniques in classroom management, breaking up fights, and handling disruptive parents and campus intruders. School site administrators must acquire "crime-resistance savvy" and take greater responsibility in working with the school board and district to implement site security programs.

Physical restraint policy.   The school district should establish a physical restraint policy stating that an employee may use "reasonable physical force" to maintain discipline when the employee reasonably believes there is a danger to him or herself or others.

STUDENT INVOLVEMENT

Create an active student component.   Students need to be actively involved in their own safety and in safety planning, including learning conflict-resolution techniques. Involve students in planning and managing student events and programs. Student participation promotes responsible student development and maturity, enabling students to be a part of the solution versus being a part of the problem.

Implement a peer-counseling and peer-mediation program at every school site. Students represent some of the best agents for promoting and maintaining a safe and secure campus. An effective peer-counseling program can head off many problems before they reach explosive and violent levels. In addition, students trained as peer counselors become wonderfully influential resources for nonviolent problem solving.

Incorporate life skills curricula.   These focus on good decision making, responsible citizenship, and conflict resolution. Young people need to learn how to deal with conflict in nonviolent ways. School violence is the tangible expression of unresolved conflict. In helping children identify and implement constructive conflict-resolution techniques, our campuses can be made much safer. A curriculum that emphasizes courtesy and thoughtfulness will go a long way toward creating a more positive and effective campus life. In recent years, schools have forgotten about the other side of the report card—the behavior side. Clearly, success requires more than just academic talent; it also requires the ability to get along well with others. A number of promising conflict-resolution programs are available. Schools that have implemented such programs have seen fewer problems among students as well as reduced tensions among staff members who have served as program instructors.

Create a student advisory council.   A school administrator in south Florida who had been experiencing significant behavior problems on his campus brought together his twelve worst-behaved students, commissioning them the "Council of Twelve." Their role was to advise and assist the principal in developing reasonable behavior standards for the most disruptive students. He pointed out to them that they had two things in common: First, they did not want to be there, and second, he did not want them there either. But the law says they must attend school and that he must provide a free public education for them. So they had to figure out a way to work together. By year's end the campus climate had improved dramatically. These difficult students were now part of the solution and not simply viewed as part of the problem. Students can be a powerful resource.

Develop a student crime prevention program.

- Establish a school crime watch program including such groups as Crimestoppers International, the National Crime Prevention Council's Youth Crime Watch, Neighborhood Crime Watch, Block Watch, and other related programs.
- Establish financial incentives for individuals who report crime.
- Involve students in campus maintenance and beautification projects.

Consider teen court as an option.   Several schools around the United States are establishing teen courts to assist administrators in the daily management and governance of the school campus. The role of teen courts is generally not to determine innocence or guilt, but rather to ascertain the appropriate level of sanctions or restitution to employ in cases involving student misbehavior. Former offenders must also agree to serve as participants in developing fair and meaningful consequences for misbehavior.

BUILDING COMMUNITY PARTNERSHIPS

Identify community resources.   School officials cannot make their schools and communities safe by their exclusive efforts. Every school district must prepare an inventory of youth-serving organizations within its jurisdiction and make this list available at each school site.

Seek intensive community support and involvement in making the journey to and from school a safe one.   Model programs include Safe Corridors, Neighborhood Watch, and Parent Patrol. The Crimestoppers program is another excellent way to involve the community.

Establish a close police partnership.   Include law enforcers in your curriculum, supervision, and crisis planning. Some of the most effective school peace officer programs bring officers in contact with children in the early grades and allow officers to follow the students through elementary, middle, and high school. School peace officers can do some of their best work once they get to know the children.

Create a "Joint Power Agreement" between police and the schools.   A Joint Power Agreement or Memorandum of Understanding between the public schools and the local police department should be created to ensure a clear understanding as to how the two departments will work together in managing serious juvenile misbehavior, crisis incidents, information sharing, and special events. Such an agreement would spell out officer qualifications and assignments, the expectations of the school with regard to student interactions, and the role of the police department in handling criminal offenses. Specific components should include information sharing between the two entities; crisis response procedures; how School Resource Officers (SROs) will be assigned and removed, if necessary; violence prevention at special events; investigation procedures; and other such matters as may be relevant to the current working relationship. Determination of future assignments and specific responsibilities must be worked out between police and school officials. In practical terms, police officers should deal with the enforcement of district policies, disciplinary matters, and "house rules" in terms of student and staff behavior expectations. Any criminal infractions must be referred to the police for appropriate action. Sample agreements are included in Appendix B.

Capitalize upon the school's ability as an organizational vehicle to provide comprehensive student services.   Many schools are leveraging their strategic position to serve as a comprehensive one-stop service center for young people. Young people bring so many problems with them to school, that often education cannot take place until other needs are met, including physical, social, and personal needs. Clearly, schools should not have to provide all of these services on top of their educational mission. But sometimes, for the educational mission to be effective, these other services are required. Consequently, a trend of this decade has been the evolving of public schools into full student service agencies. This includes making the school a health center, a recreation center, and providing social services, counseling, probation, police, banking, and a variety of other services limited only by the imagination and creativity of the local site administrator.

Consistently enforce the information-sharing agreements. At least once annually, school administrators should review their information-sharing agreements to ensure that they are in compliance with federal and state laws and to verify that school administrators and education staff are doing everything possible to share such information with those who have a legitimate need to know. Special follow-up needs to be given by the court to ensure that court orders and other information-sharing agreements among agencies are in compliance with court guidelines so that children can be better served. The student record policy needs to state that student records may be shared with any relevant teacher or staff member or other youth-serving professional with a legitimate need to know.

Consider placing a probation officer on campus. This is to provide increased, intensive supervision for students on probation who attend school. Exercising such an option can complement the efforts of student personnel staff, who can then invest more time reinforcing positive behavior of other students rather than simply disciplining troublemakers. Some schools have gone so far as to bring both police officers and probation officers together. They are each "cross-sworn," which means police can perform the functions of a probation officer and a probation officer can perform the duties of a police officer. In Fresno, California, where this program has been piloted, campus disruptions and assaults have been significantly reduced.

ESSENTIAL INGREDIENTS FOR A SAFE SCHOOL PLAN

Creating safe and orderly schools is about commitment and community will. It requires school and community leaders to articulate the quality of educational climate and learning environment they want to provide for their children and then to collaboratively and cooperatively develop the strategies that will produce the desired results. It is about evaluating where they are, planning where they want to be, and then implementing a series of comprehensive strategies to deal with the difference.

Essential ingredients for creating a safe school plan include the following:

- **Placing school safety on the educational agenda.** This involves making a personal and collective commitment toward creating a safe and welcoming school climate.
- **Building and developing the team.** Making schools safe is a joint responsibility, requiring a broad-based team and working attitudes that complement a collaborative and cooperative spirit.
- **Conducting a site assessment.** Determine the specific issues and concerns that the local community believes are most important. This step begins the process of customizing a relevant and meaningful safe school plan, which as a result of its pertinence will foster an increased level of community commitment.
- **Developing a plan of where you want to be.** Such a determination not only includes the substance of what you want to accomplish but also indicates additional processes by which those goals will be achieved. Articulating the goals and processes for achieving them is an important part of team building, an essential component in creating a cooperative spirit. It is most important for team members to believe

that they can individually and collectively make a positive difference in the quality of life for themselves, their community, and all the children they serve.

- **Involving students and parents.** No plan can succeed without the integral participation of students and parents. Planners must make certain to bring these participants to the table often to collaboratively shape strategies and programs. For the most part, people do not like to have things "done to them." However, they do enjoy being a part of planning, carrying out, and evaluating programs in which they have invested concern and time. Those affected by safe school plans should be involved throughout the creative process.

- **Reviewing the law.** The law defines what is required and what is allowed in safe school planning.

- **Formulating a contingency plan.** Having a backup plan simply makes good sense. Such foresight can save time and energy and can maintain commitment when unforeseen problems arise.

- **Asking for help.** No one can be expert in all areas of safe school planning. Many of the chapters on creating safe schools have yet to be written. Consequently, strategies must be developed even while progress is being made. Who better to develop these strategies than those individuals who will be most affected by them: students, parents, school staff members, and community leaders?

- **Doing the work.** It does not take a rocket scientist to create a safe school. It does require, however, a firm commitment to school safety and believing that a positive difference can be made. Everyone must work together to ensure the success of the planning efforts.

- **Conducting a continuing evaluation.** Safe school planning is like raising children. The job is not done until they become independent. Like raising children, safe school planning requires continuing attention and reevaluation of strategies and new stages that children experience. In a phrase, evaluation is about making continuing improvements and enhancements to a school environment that is designed to serve and support the success of all children. Clearly, each generation gets the children it deserves. The quality of our future will be dependent upon how well we train and how much care we inculcate into those young people who will one day care for us. Safe school planning produces immediate and long-term benefits. It is about the investment theory of work.

These guidelines represent the beginning of a continuing collaborative and cooperative process to create safe schools for all U.S. children. Making schools safe requires a total community effort within the context of a broad spectrum of opportunities.

APPENDIX A

School Crime Assessment Survey

ASSESSMENT SURVEY SECURITY CHECKLIST

Give your school a thorough crime prevention inspection now. Use this checklist as a guideline to determine your school's strengths and weaknesses.

Organization	Yes	No
1. Is there a policy for dealing with violence and vandalism in your school? (The reporting policy must be realistic and strictly enforced.)		
2. Is there an incident-reporting system?		
3. Is the incident-reporting system available to all staff?		
4. Is there statistical information available as to the scope of the problems at your school and in the community?		
5. Have the school, school board, and administrators taken steps or anticipated any problems through dialogue?		
6. Does security fit into the organization of the school? (Security must be designed to fit the needs of the administration and made part of the site management.)		
7. Are the teachers and administrators aware of laws that pertain to them? To their rights? To students' rights? Of their responsibility as to the enforcement of and respect for rules, regulations, policies, and the law?		
8. Is there a working relationship with your local police agency?		
9. Are students aware of expectations and school discipline codes? Are parents aware?		
10. Are there written contingency action plans developed to deal with student disruptions and vandalism?		
11. Is there a policy as to restitution from or prosecution of perpetrators of violence and vandalism?		
12. Is there any in-service training available for teachers in the areas of violence and vandalism and other required reporting procedures? (There must be training at all levels.)		
13. Is there a policy for consistent monitoring and evaluation of incident reports?		
14. Is the staff trained in standard crime prevention behavior?		

Existing security system	Yes	No
1. Have there been any security problems in the past?	_____	_____
2. Are there specific staff assigned to or trained in security awareness?	_____	_____
3. Is there an existing alarm system?	_____	_____
4. Do you have intrusion-detection equipment? Have you consulted with an expert?	_____	_____
5. If you have an alarm system, do you as an administrator know its capabilities and limitations? Do teachers and staff understand the basic working of the alarm system, so as to prevent leaving the security areas in such a condition as to cause needless false alarms?	_____	_____
6. Do you have an alarm response policy and does everyone involved clearly understand his or her responsibilities?	_____	_____
7. Is the system centrally located?	_____	_____
8. Is it local?	_____	_____
9. Is it a police alarm?	_____	_____
10. Is there a policy for consistent maintenance and testing of the system?	_____	_____
11. Do some members of the custodial staff work nights and weekends?	_____	_____
12. Are valuable items of property identified?	_____	_____
13. Are valuables properly stored?	_____	_____
14. Are high-target areas properly secured?	_____	_____
15. Is there a key control system?	_____	_____
16. Are there visitor screening or control procedures?	_____	_____
17. Do students have ID cards or other identification?	_____	_____
18. Do all employees have ID cards?	_____	_____
19. Is there a policy for intruders, those who loiter, or nonstudents on campus? (To ensure a safe campus, violators should be arrested.)	_____	_____
20. Is there proper visibility of parking areas?	_____	_____
21. Is there supervision in hallways, corridors, and other congregating places for students between classes, at lunch, and before and after school? (Teachers and staff must participate in supervision.)	_____	_____
22. Is the school designed with crime prevention in mind (landscaping, fencing, parking, and exterior lighting)?	_____	_____

	Yes	No

23. Is there a light/no-light policy for after-school hours? _____ _____
24. Whenever possible, is vandal damage repaired immediately? _____ _____

Target hardware/perimeter

1. Is there proper fencing around adjacent areas and target areas? _____ _____
2. Are gates properly secured with working locks? _____ _____
3. Is the perimeter free of rocks or gravel? _____ _____
4. Are signs properly posted as to rules and enforcement? _____ _____
5. Are signs properly designed for crime prevention? _____ _____
6. If there is exterior lighting, is it properly directed? Is there proper intensity? Are target areas well lighted? Are there shadows? _____ _____
7. Are all grips, window ledges, roof accesses, and other equipment that could be used for climbing properly secured? _____ _____
8. Are all items removed from the building area that could be used to break in or stand and climb on? (Examples: lumber, ladders) _____ _____
9. Is the school designed with vandal-resistant walls? _____ _____
10. Do the texture, color, and so on act to deter vandal activity? _____ _____

Target hardware/exterior

1. Is there a key control system? _____ _____
2. Are outside handles removed from doors used primarily as exits? _____ _____
3. Are first-floor windows nonexistent or properly secured? _____ _____
4. Is broken window glass replaced with Plexiglas or other break-resistant material? _____ _____
5. Are school facilities kept neat and in good repair? _____ _____
6. Are school facilities sectioned off to limit access by evening users? _____ _____
7. Is after-hours use of playground facilities consistently and closely monitored? _____ _____
8. Are protective screens or window guards used? _____ _____
9. Can any door locks be reached by breaking out glass? _____ _____
10. Are your locks in good condition? _____ _____
11. Are doors equipped with security locks in mind? _____ _____
12. Are locks maintained regularly and changed when necessary? _____ _____

	Yes	No

13. Are doors constructed properly? _____ _____
14. Are door frames pry-proof? _____ _____
15. Are high-target areas (such as the computer center, shop, administrative offices, etc.) sufficiently secured? _____ _____

Target hardware/interior

1. Is school property permanently and distinctly marked? _____ _____
2. Has an inventory been made recently of school property? _____ _____
3. Are school files locked in vandal-proof containers? _____ _____
4. Are valuable items thieves can easily fence (such as computers, printers, copiers, etc.) properly locked or secured when not in use? (Valuable items should be stored in a secure room or bolted down.) _____ _____
5. Is all money removed from cash registers? _____ _____
6. Are cabinets properly secured? _____ _____

Security system

1. Are there specific persons designated to secure buildings following after-hours activity? _____ _____
2. Is someone responsible for overall school security procedures?_____ _____
3. Do job descriptions include vandalism prevention duties? _____ _____
4. Are security checklists used by school employees? _____ _____
5. Through as many channels as possible, are vandalism costs made known to taxpayers? _____ _____
6. Do local police agencies help and advise on vandalism prevention? _____ _____
7. Are administrators, teachers, and students urged to cooperate with police? _____ _____
8. Is evening and weekend use of school facilities encouraged? _____ _____
9. Do police or security personnel monitor school facilities during school hours? _____ _____
10. Do police personnel, parents, or students patrol the grounds after school hours? _____ _____
11. Are local residents encouraged to report suspicious activity to school officials or police? _____ _____
12. Do students get actively involved in security efforts? _____ _____

	Yes	No

13. Are there emergency procedures for incidents, including fire and bombing? _____ _____

14. Is there a joint power agreement or memorandum of understanding between educators and police officials? _____ _____

Alarms

1. Is the entire system checked regularly, or at least every six months? _____ _____

2. Is the number of false alarms kept down to below two for any six-month period? _____ _____

3. Can selected areas of the school be "zoned" by an alarm system that will indicate which area is being entered by the intruder? _____ _____

4. If public utility power fails, is there backup power to keep the system operating without generating an alarm signal? _____ _____

5. Are suitable procedures established for response and turning on and off the system? _____ _____

6. Are the alarms the self-resetting type? _____ _____

Source: School Safety Checkbook, National School Safety Center, Westlake Village, California, adapted from Department of Justice, School Safety Center, Sacramento, California 1990.

APPENDIX B

Sample Memorandum of Understanding (MOU)

May 22, 1998

Superintendent
Jamestown City School District
200 East Fourth Street
Jamestown, NY 14701

Dear _____:

The City of Jamestown Police Department looks forward to collaborating with the Jamestown City School District in delivering the Appalachian Region Commission Area Development grant program to city high school students. The following is our Memorandum of Understanding with the Jamestown City School District.

School Resource Officers will conduct counseling sessions and workshops geared toward making students aware of the effects and career implications of a felony conviction. Activities will be implemented that will help students acknowledge, analyze, and cope with frustrations, stress, and anxiety.

School Resource Officers, with the project counselor, will meet students on an individual and group basis to discuss concerns pertaining to violent crime and its consequences. Issues such as assault, date rape, domestic violence, weapons charges, and controlled substance abuse/sale will be dealt with in a thorough and comprehensive manner so that students may come to recognize and understand the personal significance of these crimes.

Through the proposed program, the City of Jamestown Police Department will provide two School Resource Officers in the schools to help dissuade students from carrying, selling, and using weapons and/or illegal substances on school grounds. Officers will increase safety in the schools and will substantially decrease incidences of violence.

The Jamestown City School District will administer the overall program and will receive and disburse all grant funds per a prearranged schedule.

When signed and dated, this letter will serve as our Memorandum of Understanding.

Sincerely,

_____   _____
Chief of Police   Superintendent
City of Jamestown Police Department   Jamestown City School District

Sample MOU

JAMESTOWN POLICE DEPARTMENT
SCHOOL RESOURCE OFFICER

DEFINITION

The role of the School Resource Officer is to promote rapport with students, which results in strong relationships among the school, the police department, and the community. The School Resource Officer will work in a preventative manner with the students as well as provide intervention strategies for troubled youth and their parents. This officer should provide additional resources to the school in relation to his or her knowledge of the law and specialized training.

DUTY STATEMENT

1. Performs police duties as assigned by the police department during the periods when school is in session while attempting to ensure that such activities do not dramatically interfere with the student curriculum schedule.
2. Works with and remains under the general direction of the staff at the school to which the officer is assigned, establishing and operating such programs and activities in the school as may be consistent with the intent of the School Resource Officer program.
3. Performs duties and assignments in the school as a member of the school's guidance team during the course of the regular school year.
4. Attends specific extracurricular activities of the school, including but not limited to athletic events and school-sponsored dances.
5. During regular school day, conducts activities of the school, including but not limited to athletic events and school-sponsored dances.
6. Conducts follow-up investigations on cases as assigned through the Investigative Division.
7. Promotes working relationships with school counselors and other police and school officials.
8. Promotes rapport between police officers and students in the school.
9. Meets periodically with the building and district administration to discuss and evaluate the School Resource Officer activities.
10. Makes presentations to students, parents, and staff members on law, police topics, safety, and good citizenship.
11. Refers troubled students to proper professional help within the guidance department.
12. Works with parents/guardians of runaway students as much as possible within the school environment.
13. Counsels students who are established juvenile offenders.

14. Assists school officials in the enforcement of the truancy law.

15. Represents the school, along with the assistant principal, in any criminal, misdemeanor, or traffic court action involving students.

16. Provides assistance in conducting routine searches of students or lockers when appropriate, or when requested by the principal or assistant principal.

17. Works beyond regular scheduled hours when required to successfully complete an assignment or case.

18. Files appropriate case reports according to established police department directives.

19. Protects school, staff, and students from violations of the law.

20. Checks unauthorized personnel in and around the school.

21. Assists the administration with crowd and vehicle control and coordinates help if necessary.

22. Performs such other duties as required by state law, city ordinance, or department rule as assigned by a superior officer.

23. Performs specialized assignments as assigned by the chief of police.

24. Performs the duties and responsibilities of a police officer as described in the Duty Statement for Police Officer.

25. During extended school breaks and during the summer months when school is not in session, assumes assigned position in the Community Services Unit or Juvenile Bureau.

26. Performs other duties as assigned by the principal, assistant principal, or superior officer.

Sample MOU
School Resource Officer Program Partnership Agreement

This partnership agreement is entered into this 26th day of July 1999, between the City of Jamestown, hereinafter referred to as the "City." For and in consideration of the mutual promises, terms, and conditions set forth herein, the parties agree as follows:

1. PURPOSE OF AGREEMENT

The purpose of this agreement is for the city to assign one uniformed police officer each to Jamestown High School, Washington Middle School, Jefferson Middle School, and Persell Middle School for the School Resource Officer program. The School Resource Officer, hereinafter referred to as "SRO," will work with the school principal to provide alcohol and drug education, maintain a peaceful campus environment, and take appropriate action regarding on-campus or school-related criminal activity.

2. TERM

2.1   This Agreement shall be effective on July 26, 1999, and shall continue until one party gives the other party thirty (30) days' written notice of intent to terminate.

2.2   City shall provide an SRO to each school on all days that school is in session. District shall provide the City a school calendar on or before June 1 of each year.

2.3   District may request, and City shall provide, an SRO for fall orientation.

2.4   District may request, and City shall provide, one SRO for summer school program, which shall not exceed 35 summer school days.

2.5   During days that school is not in session, an SRO is subject to other assignments as determined by the City.

3. RELATIONSHIP OF PARTIES

3.1   City shall have the status of an independent contractor for the purposes of this agreement. The SRO assigned to the District is an employee of the City and shall be subject to departmental control, supervision, policies, procedures, and General Orders.

3.2   The SRO will be subject to current procedures in effect for City police officers, including attendance at all mandated training. This training takes place throughout the year and will necessitate the absence of the SRO.

4. SCHOOL RESOURCE OFFICER SELECTION, TRANSFER, AND REMOVAL

Selection

4.1   The District and the City will participate in the selection of SROs. The District and the City will each appoint two members to a screening panel whose sole function will be to interview and recommend applicants for the position of School Resource Officer. All appointments will be made by the Chief of Police.

4.2   SRO applicants must be a certified police officer with a minimum of two years' service or experience. Among additional criteria for consideration by the panel are job knowledge, experience, training, education, appearance, attitude, and communication skill and bearing.

Transfer

4.3   An SRO may transfer to another school when a vacancy occurs provided:

1.   The principals of each school agree with the transfer;

2.   The SRO supervisor, the Unit Commander of the Police Department's Community Services Unit, agrees with the transfer; and

3.   Approval by the Chief of Police.

Removal

4.4 In the event the principal of the school to which the SRO is assigned feels that the particular SRO is not effectively performing his or her duties and responsibilities, the principal shall recommend to the District Superintendent that the SRO be removed from the program.

4.5 The Chief of Police may dismiss or reassign an SRO based on Department Rules, Regulations, and/or General Orders, and when it is in the best interest of the City.

4.6 In the event of a resignation, dismissal, or reassignment of an SRO, or in the case of long-term absences by an SRO, the Chief shall provide a temporary replacement for the SRO within thirty (30) school days of receiving notice of such absence, dismissal, resignation, or reassignment. As soon as possible, the Selection Panel shall convene and recommend a permanent replacement for the SRO position.

5. SCHOOL RESOURCE OFFICER RESPONSIBILITIES

5.1 Work in concert with the school principal, meeting with the principal on a weekly basis.

5.2 Provide a program of educational leadership by acting as a guest speaker in addressing tobacco, alcohol, and other drug issues, and in addressing violence diffusion, violence prevention, and safety issues in the school community.

5.3 Act as a communication liaison with police agencies and provide basic information concerning students on the campus served by the officer.

5.4 Present programs to parents on issues related to tobacco, alcohol and other drugs, violence prevention, and safety.

5.5 Provide informational in-services for staff on issues related to alcohol and other drugs and the law, violence, gangs, safety, and security.

5.6 Gather information regarding potential problems such as criminal activity, gang activity and student unrest, and attempt to identify particular individuals who may be a disruptive influence to the school and/or students.

5.7 Assist in maintaining order and enforcing school policies on school property. In conjunction with school officials, the SRO will take the appropriate police action, consistent with a police officer's duty. As soon as practicable, the SRO shall make the principal of the school aware of such action. At the principal's request, the SRO shall take appropriate police action against intruders and unwanted guests who may appear at the school and related school functions, to the extent that the SRO may do so under the authority of law. Whenever practicable, the SRO shall advise the principal before requesting additional police assistance on campus.

5.8 Refer students and/or their families to the appropriate agencies for assistance when need is determined.

5.9 The SRO shall not act as a school disciplinarian. However, if the principal believes an incident is a violation of the law, the principal may contact the SRO and the SRO shall then determine whether police action is appropriate.

5.10 The SRO can perform other duties as may be mutually agreed upon in writing by the City and the District.

Provided further that nothing required herein is intended to or will constitute a relationship of duty for the assigned police officer or the City beyond the general duties that exist for police officers within the state.

6. COSTS

6.1   The District agrees to reimburse City a portion of the matching grant award requirement.

6.2   The City will be responsible for SRO overtime expenses related to or resulting from police work, such as criminal investigations, responses to gang fights, assaults, arson, district disciplinary hearings, counseling sessions, or court appearances resulting from the actions of the SRO at the school.

6.3   The City shall be responsible for the SRO's compensation, including all holidays, vacation days, or sick leave days.

6.4   The City agrees to pay all other costs, including training and equipment.

7. TIME AND PLACE OF PERFORMANCE

7.1   City will assure that the SRO will be on the campus of his or her assigned school each day that school is in session during the regular school year -½ hour prior to the start of classes until ½ hour after classes are dismissed. The SRO's activities will be restricted to the assigned campus, except for:

7.1.a Follow-up home visits when needed as a result of school-related student problems.

7.1.b School-related off-campus activities when officer participation is requested by the principal and approved by City.

7.1.c Responses to off-campus, but school-related criminal activity.

7.1.d Responses to emergency police or court appearances.

7.2   Regular working hours may be adjusted on a situational basis with the consent of the SRO's supervisor. These adjustments should be approved prior to their being required and should be to cover scheduled school-related activity requiring the presence of a police officer.

8. DISTRICT RESPONSIBILITIES

8.1   The District will provide the SRO with access to an office and such equipment as is necessary at his or her assigned school. This equipment shall include a telephone, filing space capable of being secured, and access to a computer and/or secretary assistance.

Signed on the day and year first above written.

CITY OF JAMESTOWN   JAMESTOWN POLICE
SCHOOL DISTRICT   DEPARTMENT

_____   _____

Superintendent   Chief of Police

Sample MOU

AGREEMENT BETWEEN CITY OF GRIFFIN AND THE GRIFFIN/SPALDING COUNTY SCHOOL SYSTEM

This agreement is entered into this 9th day of August 1994, between the City of Griffin (hereinafter referred to as the City) and the Griffin Spalding County School System (hereinafter referred to as the School System) for the purpose of providing a School Resource Officer(s) from the City to the School System and for other purposes.

It is mutually agreed that the City will provide sworn P.O.S.T.-certified police officer(s) to the School System to perform the duties of a School Resource Officer at such school(s) as the superintendent may designate. Said police officer(s) will be jointly responsible to the principal of the assigned school and to the chief of police. The officer(s) assigned may be immediately reassigned upon the request of either the principal or the chief of police. The officer(s) may be required to perform such duties at the assigned school as the principal may designate that are consistent with the job description of a School Resource Officer. Conflict in this area will be resolved by the chief of police and the principal, or if resolution is not possible, by the city manager and the superintendent.

It is further agreed that the designated officer(s) will remain employee(s) of the City with all rights, benefits, and privileges thereto. The costs of the salary and benefits of the designated officer(s) will be shared equally between the City and the School System. The City will bill the School System on a quarterly basis for salary and benefit costs less any cost offset by grant(s). Any overtime costs necessary for the performance of duty at the request of the School System will be reimbursed to the City by the School System. The overtime costs will also be billed on a quarterly basis. Any training costs necessitated by this agreement will be borne by the School System and/or the City as agreed by the city manager and the superintendent on a case by case basis.

This agreement may be canceled by thirty (30) days' written notice of either party.

_____　　　_____
　　　　　(for the City)　　　　　　　　　　　　(for the School System)

Sample MOU

SCHOOL RESOURCE OFFICER QUALIFICATIONS AND DUTIES GRIFFIN/SPALDING COUNTY SCHOOL SYSTEM

Qualifications: Be a P.O.S.T.-certified officer with at least two years' experience as a patrolman with the Griffin Police Department and have demonstrated ability to work with young people. Possess at least an Associate of Arts or Science degree from an accredited college. A Bachelor of Arts or Science degree is preferred. Among the criteria for consideration are job knowledge, experience, appearance, attitude, and bearing.

Duties: The School Resource Officer (SRO) Program has been accepted by the Griffin/Spalding County Board of Education and the City of Griffin. The chief of police and the principal of the assigned school will jointly select the officer(s) for this assignment. Once placed into a school, the officer will be involved in a variety of functions and duties that will include, but not be limited to, the following:

1. As an extension of the principal's office for administrative control and assignment;

2. As a visible, active police figure on campus dealing specifically with police matters originating on the assigned campus;

3. As a classroom source for law education using approved materials;

4. As a resource for students that will enable them to be associated with a police figure in the students' environment;

5. As a resource for teachers, parents, and students for conferences on an individual basis dealing with individual problems or questions, particularly in the area of substance control;

6. In appearances before PTA and other groups associated with the assigned campus and as a speaker on a variety of requested topics, particularly drug and alcohol abuse;

7. As a documenter of activities of all SROs on and off campus and as a compiler of a monthly statistical report to be provided to the police department and to the principal of the assigned school;

8. The SRO is not a school disciplinarian. Disciplining students is a school responsibility, and only when the principal and the SRO believe an incident is a criminal law violation would the principal request police involvement and ask that the SRO take action;

   The SRO will work all cases originating on campus and off campus within the city limits at school-sponsored events. Basic information on cases that are worked off-campus by the police department or other agencies involving students on a campus served by an SRO will be provided to the SRO, but the SRO will not normally be actively involved in the investigation;

   A. The SRO will coordinate his/her actions with the principal's office for police cases of an immediate nature;

   B. All local police and state agencies conducting formal police interviews, interrogations, and arrests should contact the campus SRO when seeking to conduct their business on campus. The SRO will advise on school policy concerning such actions;

9. The SRO will be familiar with all community agencies, such as mental health clinics, drug treatment centers, and so on, that offer assistance to dependency- and delinquency-prone youths and their families. Referrals will be made when necessary;

10. The SRO and the principal will develop plans and strategies to prevent and/or mini- mize dangerous situations that might result in student unrest;

11. The SRO will coordinate all of his or her activities with the principal and staff mem- bers concerned and will seek permission, guidance, and advice prior to enacting any programs within the school;

12. The SRO is first and foremost a police officer. This fact must be constantly reinforced;

13. The SRO may be asked to provide communitywide crime prevention presentations that include, but are not limited to:

    1. Drugs and the law—adult and juvenile;

    2. Alcohol and the law—adult and juvenile;

    3. Sexual assault prevention;

    4. Safety programs—adult and juvenile;

    5. Assistance in other crime prevention programs as assigned;

14. The SRO is a police officer working as an extension of the principal's office; there- fore, the SRO will be attired in the same manner as anyone on the education staff. The SRO gains visibility to students by classroom presentations, conferences, and other activities. When dealing with secondary school students, plainclothes officers have historically been found to have positive effects for all involved. However, the decision for the SRO to shift to plainclothes will be made jointly by the principal and the chief of police;

15. SROs will wear their department issue duty weapons as follows:

    A. Uniform—in accordance with the Police Operations Manual;

    B. Plainclothes—weapon and ASP will be worn concealed.

_____   _____
        (Name)   (Name)
    Chief of Police   Principal, Griffin High School

I have read and understand the duties listed above.

_____   _____
    (Name of SRO)   (Signature of SRO)

7

A Police Officer's Response to School Crime: A Cooperative Venture

Rick SyWassink

This chapter, written from the perspective of a police officer with extensive experience in the field of school safety, focuses on and emphasizes how police, educators, and the community at large need to work together to develop plans for outbreaks of school violence and other disasters. This chapter also touches on possible indicators for potentially violent youth.

Ultimately, it is these police professionals who will deal with the effects of school crime. If they are not on the scene when an incident occurs, they will certainly be called first to respond to any such crime emergency. Reading and listening to their point of view is a must for all school personnel. This chapter deals with "crisis management"—it is simply not enough to have a plan; everyone must understand the plan. The author discusses a chain-of-command structure that serves to answer the question, "Who is in charge?" at a time when everyone must know that answer.

Those first minutes of response time may well be the most critical in the entire episode.

INTRODUCTION

School violence. School crime. Unfortunately, these words and the actions associated with them have become too frequent in today's society. The involvement of police with the educational system is a mixture of professions that were once thought of as never having anything in common. However, with the advent of the problems in today's schools, police have become heavily involved, not only in a reactionary sense but also in a proactive sense.

This chapter will outline the roles of police not only in reacting to school crimes but also in the proactive stages of planning for and reacting to school crimes, especially those of a violent nature. Everyone, not just police, must realize and understand that violent crime in schools is not only a police concern, but that it actually involves and demands the cooperation of the educational system, emergency personnel (police, fire and rescue, and emergency medical responders), and the community at large. This chapter will also outline who is involved in developing a school violence plan, the actual plan and the responsibility of responders, especially police, and lessons learned from incidents that have already occurred.

WHO IS INVOLVED IN THE PLANNING

As was mentioned previously, the concern of school violence and the planning for it do not belong to any one group. An effective plan development process involves not only police but also other emergency responders, school personnel (including maintenance and transportation personnel), parents, students, and the community at large.

It must be recognized that each group not only has specific responsibilities but also must have knowledge of the actions and responsibilities of the other groups involved in the incident. This involves the breaking down of "territorialism" of groups and the recognition that planning is a multifaceted task. In order to facilitate the planning and the implementation, a very important step must take place—the development of a good working relationship between police and the schools.

Each group involved in the development of an incident plan has an important contribution to make not only in the development but also in the implementation of the plan.

MEMORANDUMS OF UNDERSTANDING

The first important step before any planning takes place is the signing of Memorandums of Understanding (MOUs) (Boyd & Harpold, 1999:10). MOUs serve several important functions, including:

- Clearly defining what each organization will do from the beginning to the end of the function
- What resources each participant will provide and what the command structure is
- Recognizing an ongoing liaison among all participants to enhance communications and readiness
- Assigning specific tasks and encouraging agencies to appoint the best employees of the agency to those tasks (Boyd & Harpold, 1999)

Specifically, the MOUs for police should ensure that police agencies consider the need for adequate human resources and technical support (i.e., enough people for the crime scene processing, security, interviews, and computer support for the databases) (Boyd & Harpold, 1999). Additionally, the MOU should specify that all investigators will receive training annually in how to recognize and handle juvenile criminals, especially young mass or spree murderers. Police not only will be responding to the scene of violent school crises and the processing of the scenes, but they will also be involved in such areas as media relations and coordination of the overall management of the scenes. These areas will be addressed later in this chapter. One theme that will be addressed throughout this chapter and throughout the planning for, responding to, and dealing with the school violence incident is that police must work with a large group of other agencies to bring the incident to a successful end.

Before addressing the specific tasks of police in a violent incident at a school, the topic of school violence plans and planning needs to be addressed. Again, police will be extensively involved in the planning process, as will other emergency responders, educators, emergency management, and so on.

THE SCHOOL VIOLENCE PLAN

In developing a school violence plan, it must be remembered that the plan needs to be not only functional but also understood by all entities involved in the situation. A school violence plan cannot address all situations, but it must be flexible enough to be used as a basis for responding to any situation that arises. Several areas are addressed in a school violence plan, including these four items (Federal Emergency Management Agency, 1999a):

1. Identification and mitigation of the problem
2. Preparedness
3. Response
4. Recovery

Part of an effective school violence plan should also include indicators of potential violent juvenile behavior.

Mitigation

Mitigation is the ongoing action that prevents or reduces the effects of a hazardous situation. These can be both short- and long-term activities such as school safety programs, emergency lighting and warnings, and handicap accessibility.

Preparedness

Preparedness activities are those actions that help schools respond effectively and responsibly to any situation. Some of these actions include, but are not limited to, planning and training, which should involve all entities that will respond to the incident. Training, which will vary based on the age of the student, should be expanded to include the community.

Response

This activity includes actions taken during the incident. In addressing the response, it must always be remembered that the protection of life is the first priority. To ensure proper response, drills and exercises to practice and test the plan are essential.

Recovery

Recovery from an incident may take several days, weeks, or even years. Although the physical part of recovery is easier to accomplish, the psychological wounds and scars may last years. Recovery may be defined as short term or long term. Short-term recovery includes restoring of vital services such as power, water, and physical security. Long-term activities include reconstruction, counseling, and reassessing plans and procedures.

Specific Police Responsibilities

Other than the school itself, the police are the agency that is probably involved with dealing with the violent situations for a prolonged period. As society has changed, so have police changed to try to keep up. Police's role in society has primarily been one of responding to a situation and taking action depending on the circumstances, such as arrest, mediation, and so forth. As the violence in schools unfolds at a level never before witnessed in history, police are still thought of primarily as a responding agency, which they are. Very little thought has previously been given to the fact that police's role in the school violence issue should be and is also proactive. However, with the advent of community oriented policing and school resource officers, police's role as a reactive agency is now coupled with the role of a proactive agency. That is to say that police are starting to recognize problems as they develop and are taking action before the problems get bigger or, as in this case, develop into violent situations.

Many programs and ideas have developed over the last several years in the area of police/education partnerships. There are many resources to assist these partnerships in developing programs to fit the particular schools and communities. It needs to be recognized that the schools are a microcosm of the communities that they serve. The problems, hopes, and values of the community are exhibited in the schools, only on a smaller scale. Officers at schools, not necessarily as enforcers but also as helpers and problem solvers, can spot problems and help identify preventive solutions or needed interventions, build positive relationships with students or staff, and offer counseling or access to community resources (National Crime Prevention Council, 1998). These officers, especially if they are regularly at one school, get to know the students' personalities, personal situations, and what their normal behavior patterns are, all of which help in spotting and heading off trouble (National Crime Prevention Council, 1998). Police and school administrators have a wide scope of areas to address regarding the proactive approach to school crimes and violence. Several different approaches can be used in the proactive phase.

It must be noted that although the ideas proffered here come from numerous jurisdictions around the country, there may be ideas or approaches that may not be mentioned in this chapter that have worked for a particular jurisdiction or district. If those approaches have been successful, there is no need to change. In other words, if it is not broken, don't fix it.

One method mentioned earlier in this chapter was developing a good working relationship between educators and police. Once this relationship is established, the first area that police need to address with the school is policies and procedures (National Crime Prevention Council, 1998). An area that has received much national attention is "zero tolerance" toward weapons, alcohol, and drugs. Not only must the school's policies regarding this be enforced, but the local ordinances and the police community need to enforce applicable laws. It should be noted that, unlike officer discretion that is widely exercised "on the street" as to actions to take given a situation, these zero tolerance policies must be firmly enforced. Along these same lines, as policies are developed, reviewed, and implemented, one policy that should always be used is that anything that is illegal off campus is illegal on campus. Students, school personnel, and the public at large need to know that the school will not be a haven for illegal activity or misbehavior.

Another activity that police need to use with cooperation of the schools is the task of intelligence gathering. This must be approached cautiously, as many states, as well as the federal government, have laws that govern it. Not only is gathering this information regulated, but so is the exchange and storage of this information. Confidentiality laws that are in place to protect students, parents, and school districts further cloud this issue. Legal advice and guidance should be obtained before implementing procedures. A form used in the state of Iowa is Appendix A in this chapter. However, whenever information is developed that may indicate the possibility of potential criminal activity, this information needs to be verified or shown to be unfounded. Many times information that is received indicates there is a potential of criminal activity; however, there are officers as well as school administrators who say, "That can't happen here." Unfortunately, these same individuals later realize that "it can happen here."

But again, going to the premise that a good relationship between police and the schools should be cultivated. This relationship would cause the free flow of information between educators and police concerning potential problem students. However, once the information is received, there must be avenues and leads that are followed up to determine whether there is a problem. If so, what options are there to address the problem? Along these same lines of thinking, protocols need to be developed to identify "kids at risk" to commit crimes, especially violent crimes. Some of the traits that are associated with kids at risk will be identified later in this chapter.

So far many of the topics that have been discussed have been in the area of policy and procedure development. Another area that needs to be considered and requires police involvement is the walk-through. Many times police respond to a call without ever having been in the particular business or residence. Schools, however, present a unique problem. Not only are they laid out in many different configurations, which causes response problems in the best of situations, but the layout problems are compounded by the chaos that will be taking place when police arrive on the scene of a violent incident. To avoid this problem, tours of the schools that are served by a particular police agency should be conducted. Depending on the size of the police agency, this may or may not be an easy task. However, any officer working the street should have knowledge of the layout of the schools in the area he or she works. These tours of the buildings should also include personnel from the fire departments and ambulance services. The tours should be conducted with personnel from all of these agencies together, which will enhance the response of the various agencies when the time comes. In some jurisdictions, this may not be possible. However, every attempt should be made to familiarize officers with the school's physical plan. This task may have to be accomplished through the use of video or in-service presentations. In addition to walking through the school, information should be maintained in each patrol unit as to the layout of the facility, building floor plans, and maps. These diagrams need to be reviewed and changes made on at least a yearly basis (International Association of Chiefs of Police, n.d.:34).

Another vital area to be addressed in the proactive stages is that of communications, both within the school and among responding agencies. In instances of school violence response, communication among the responding agencies is crucial. In today's world of changing radio communications, there has been an attempt to develop a system of communication that allows different agencies to be able to exchange information with each other. In some instances, however, this can cause a bottleneck in radio traffic, and consequently, nobody can talk to anybody. Not only does the use of various communication systems cause problems among the responding agencies; specialized units such as SWAT are not able to talk to other teams that are engaged in the same type of specialized operations.

In the Columbine incident, the inability to establish a common frequency had a positive side; keeping communications separate among police, fire, and emergency responders helped minimize the confusion and overload that would have occurred on a single channel (Jefferson County, Colorado, Sheriff's Office, 2000). Each agency communicated predominantly with its own dispatch center. Communications between agencies often had to be relayed through their dispatch centers or through an agency representative at the incident command post (Jefferson County, Colorado, Sheriff's Office, 2000).

Interagency cooperation has been discussed earlier in this chapter; this should include not only networking with the schools but also working with other emergency responders in their in-service training. Remember, police need to understand the duties and responsibilities of other emergency responders, and they in turn need to understand police needs and responsibilities at the crime scene and after the area has been secured. To this end, training should be provided to the other responding agencies as to crime scene security, the recognition of evidence, and how it is to be handled or not handled at the scene. Providing training in the area of reviews of other incidents in the nation and how these incidents were handled may prevent mistakes from occurring again. In addition, the lessons learned by other agencies may assist in the development of the emergency response plan.

What other kinds of training can police provide, and to whom? One other group that benefits from training is the office personnel at the school. Many times, these individuals are the first to observe or come in contact with a suspect. Office personnel are usually the first to receive bomb threats or may even be designated to release the code word to the rest of the school in the event of an incident. Training in receiving threatening phone calls, threats by mail, or threats in person, and in what questions to ask and how to document them, are all a vital part of the responsibility of these critical individuals.

The last area to be addressed in this section is that training and development concerning the Incident Command System, which coordinates supervision and direction of different school authorities, police personnel, and emergency responders from a central command post, needs to be provided (Jefferson County, Colorado, Sheriff's Office, 2000:34). As earlier stated, it is mandatory that "who is in charge" be determined before the incident occurs, so that valuable time is not lost determining the commander of the overall operation at the scene. Developing the Incident Command System (ICS) and having it in place is a good way to break down jurisdictional boundaries. A brief description of the ICS follows. It should be noted that this system is not a new idea. The fire service and emergency management departments have used it for years.

Incident Command System[*]

ICS is a method by which the command structure for a major incident is determined so that when an incident occurs, there is no question as to who is in charge and directing the operation. Although the ideas put forth in the following paragraphs are basic ICS, each district and police jurisdiction may need to change the basics to fit its needs. ICS basically states that emergencies require certain tasks and functions to be performed, and that every incident needs to have a person in charge. Based on these premises, it is easy to see that at the scene of a major incident there are actually two ICS structures that eventually come together.

The first ICS that should be in place at the time of an incident is the ICS for the school. This ICS structure must be addressed in the plan development stages. Within the school itself, the Incident Commander (IC) may in fact be the principal; however, the principal may designate another administrator to be in charge. At any rate, who is in charge and who is in charge in the absence of the IC need to be addressed, as earlier stated, in the planning stages as should the duties of the members of the ICS.

When an incident occurs and the decision is made to implement the emergency plan, the ICS for public safety also is activated. When the school ICS and the public safety ICS are implemented, there evolves a Unified Command System (UCS) of which the school becomes a part. A school site ICS has predetermined divisions, which are Operations, Planning and Intelligence, Logistics, and Finance/Administration. There are also a Public Information Officer, a Safety Officer, and a Liaison Officer. The structures of both the school ICS and the Public Safety ICS may be found in Appendixes B and C, respectively.

RESPONDING TO THE SCENE

When responding to the scene of a violent incident at a school, the police officer will face many challenges. The basic rules of crime scene security and investigation will still be in effect, and as always with these rules, flexibility still needs to be applied. In this section, the crime scene response will be examined as well as lessons learned from incidents that have occurred. A crime scene is defined as any place where a crime has been committed and also any place where evidence might be found. Again, it must be noted that the discussion to follow contains only guidelines, and that jurisdictions must examine their own particular situations and formulate their plans.

When responding to the scene of a violent incident, it must also be remembered that the most important premise is the preservation of life of both the victims and the personnel responding. A violent incident at a school might be looked at as a kind of terrorist attack. When this premise is considered, that also means that the responders must be concerned about the possibility of secondary devices, snipers, and the idea that in a terrorist attack, one of the major objectives is to cause harm or disable the emergency responders.

The first arriving officer will be faced with a scene of chaos, confusion, and carnage. Unlike many scenes that involve injury or death, it must be remembered that the suspect is probably still present, so the officer is faced with an active hostile environment. Responding officers will need to evaluate their situation quickly, and backup units will need to be directed as to where they are to go to set up a perimeter and secure it. Upon arrival and after

[*]Federal Emergency Management Agency, 1999b

the initial assessment, the officer will meet with the school's Incident Commander for an update that can be communicated to responding units and to the communications center. Communication will be a big factor, and getting information to responding units and to the communications center may be impossible. That is why it was referred to earlier that through pre-planning and training, a dedicated communications channel could be used. However, it was also realized that some jurisdictions do not have this luxury, and the first officer(s) will have to work through this.

Securing the scene accomplishes several objectives. It offers containment of the situation, prevents the spread of the incident into the community, and prevents further injury or death to the public at large. In short, it will prevent the escape of the suspect(s) and give victims a safe place until they can be moved to a predetermined safe location for medical treatment and accounting of the individuals. Containment of the scene is also critical to the responding officers in that it prevents them from becoming victims of the suspect(s) who might now be behind them if allowed to escape.

During these first few critical minutes of the incident, the personnel exiting from the school (both students and staff) need to be gathered and moved to a safe, predetermined place. This predetermined location, which should have been planned for in the crisis plan, now needs to be activated and secured by police. The location of the haven should have been unidentified to students, to prevent the possibility of suspects planting bombs, or conducting sniper activities. This location not only will provide a safe location for school personnel but also will offer a location where students may be reunited with their parents or guardians after the initial incident is declared over.

Responding officers need to remember as they arrive at the scene that they must position their vehicles so that they do not block the entry or exit of other responding emergency personnel. Again, this potential problem should have been addressed in the crisis plan and solidified through training.

Entry into the building is a decision that will have to be made. Information should have been provided by the school's incident command as to details outlining the number of suspects, the last known location of the suspects, the location of the injured, and if possible, the types of weapons and the amount of weaponry possessed by the suspects. Entering the building will obviously pose significant risks. In addition to the exposure to this harm, it must also be remembered that officers may be hampered with communication problems because of the structure they are in. Radio signals may not reach outside the building to other units or the communications center, and likewise may not be able to go between officers who are within a few feet of each other. Officers entering the building are also faced with the problem of not knowing where the suspects are or if there are any hostages.

Another problem faced more by the Command Post (CP) but that will have to be addressed by the officers initially on the scene is that of responding news media and parents. Notification of these two entities in many situations has occurred by the initial radio traffic heard over a scanner. As personnel from the school are being evacuated, there is an influx of concerned parents and the media to add to the confusion and traffic problems, possibly preventing the response and entry of further police and medical units.

As was earlier mentioned and referenced, in Appendix C of this chapter, the ICS has a position for Public Information Officer (PIO). In all probability, this person will be the one giving briefings to the news media. The need for the PIO is critical, because this individual not only controls the release of information but also prevents the release by several individuals who may have conflicting information and thus add to the confusion. As the sophistication of the police function has progressed, so has that of the media. In some areas, there will be aircraft used by the media for flyovers of the scene. In some instances, they can be utilized to assist police in checking the roof of the building and also the surrounding area. However, if the media are reporting live from the aircraft or, for that matter, from outside the building, and the suspect(s) is watching TV in the school, the situation could become more problematic than it originally was. It must be realized that very little can be done to prevent the media from "conducting their own investigation" at the scene through interviews of persons from the scene and even attempting to get as close to the scene as possible. That is why the media need to be educated and police need to cultivate a good working relationship with them.

Moving personnel to a central area is one way to manage the media and prevent their interference with the functions at the scene. It is also a method by which a head count of students and personnel can be conducted. In addressing the release of the students to their parents or guardians, it must be remembered that the school is still responsible for the release of each student to the proper person. This is facilitated by having someone from the school present with a roster indicating to whom the student is to be released. Proper identification of the person to whom the student is released is mandatory, and the records indicating to whom the student was released are a must.

Traffic Control

Needless to say, with an incident happening at a school, there is a large amount of traffic converging on the scene. Emergency vehicles, onlookers, conspirators, and parents are all coming into a small area, which could affect the rescue efforts and the police function. Perimeters must be established as soon as possible and the area sealed off. Ambulances should be staged at an area away from the scene in order to minimize the number of vehicles in the immediate area. Once a secured, safe area can be established, ambulances and personnel can be allowed in.

Evidence

Evidence is any item that associates or disassociates a suspect to the crime. Anything can be evidence, and in the instance of a violent school incident, the crime scene is usually very large. Evidence is located throughout the area and could be as small as a shell casing from the suspect's weapon or as large as a car. Care should be taken not to disturb evidence from its original location. However, it is recognized that in the "heat of the battle" items get moved and relocated, usually without any intent to interfere with the investigation.

Once the entire incident is secured and brought to an end, the task of reconstructing the scene begins. Before any crime scene processing takes place, however, it should be remembered that by following the definition of a crime scene that was provided earlier, the residence and vehicles of the suspect(s) need to be secured until a processing of those locations is completed. There are many obstacles to overcome in processing the scene of violence. Because of the victims (students and teachers), the location of the crime, which is meant to be a safe haven in the community, and the fact that the proper processing will take days at the minimum, police are faced with a burden heavier than is experienced in "normal" violent crime scenes.

Probably the biggest obstacle that police face is the fact that in order to process the scene properly, evidence, including the bodies of victims, must be left as it is found, if they are deceased. There is a large amount of public outcry about this practice, and if the bodies are located outside, immediate attention should be given to that location to complete the process as meticulously but expediently as possible. There can be no hurrying the processing of the crime scene.

Once the processing is completed and the bodies are removed for autopsy, the scene should remain secured in the event that the pathologists or investigators must return to it to complete the investigation. The crime scene should not be released until completion of the autopsy. Not only will there be physical scars to heal, but the psychological trauma to the victims and their families and friends, as well as to the emergency responders causes scarring that might take years to heal, if ever.

AFTER THE CRISIS (INTERNATIONAL ASSOCIATION OF CHIEFS OF POLICE, N.D.:42)

The actions taken after the violent acts at school may affect not only the students, staff, and emergency responders as to how long recovery will take, but they also affect the community as to its recovery and the resuming of "normal" living. Police must take immediate action for their personnel (preferably within 72 hours) to help them cope with what they have just been involved in. For many years, police felt that letting an incident affect them psychologically was a sign of weakness. Many of the feelings affecting an officer as a result of being involved in a critical incident were internalized. These ideas have slowly changed, with administrators establishing Critical Incident Stress Debrief Teams to give their personnel involved in the incident an outlet for their feelings and reservations that have developed as a result of the incident. There are still macho men and some women who never admit to their real feelings. This eventually manifests itself as physical and psychological problems for many years to come. It might in fact cause an agency to lose a good officer.

Through all of this, officers must still continue their duties, unless policy or debilitating actions prevent it. Police need to assist at the scene with helping parents or guardians to find their children. It must be remembered that some families will not be as fortunate to find survivors. They may be the parents of a victim, and at the discovery that their child has been taken to a hospital, or is a deceased victim still at the scene, police need to assist in getting these parents to the proper location where the parents can be assisted.

Other areas that police can assist in the aftermath of a school crisis may include:

- Providing a central point of contact in the agency to answer questions of students, staff, and parents
- Facilitating meetings wherein people from the school can express their thoughts as to how police handled the situation
- Facilitating critiques of the incident, identifying areas in need of improvement
- Encouraging the schools and police to coordinate the press releases

CHILDREN AT RISK

As mentioned earlier in this chapter, a complete crisis plan will have a section devoted to characteristics of children at risk to commit violent crimes. With the wave of school violence that has been occurring in the United States, there have been attempts to understand why the suspects committed the acts that they did. Juvenile crime in this country has seen very little study until recently. Studies have been undertaken of the suspects involved in these crimes, as well as of adult criminals who have been involved in violent crime, to ascertain if there is a correlation between these two supposedly diverse groups.

Some studies have indicated that serial killers have exhibited some of the traits that children at risk exhibit. What implications does that have for the police? Police have the ability to interact with these youth and observe patterns or characteristics of children at risk, and with this ability comes the opportunity for police to channel the child into intervention programs that may reduce the risk associated with the characteristics. Police and school officials need to remember that even though the student in question exhibits one or two of the listed traits, that does not necessarily mean he or she is going to commit a violent crime, but that the child needs to be examined further. Additionally, background checks need to be conducted of the suspect's family and friends to ascertain if there are problems. In short, a complete psychological autopsy needs to be done.

Dr. Reid Kimbrough of the Justice Group in his book *Pathological Maturity,* cites some critical warning signs of children at risk. It should be remembered that just because a child exhibits one or two of these traits does not indicate that the child is going to commit a violent act, but there needs to be closer examination of the child and his or her background.

The traits include but are not limited to the following:

- No remorse for their actions
- Violence seen as being acceptable
- Elevated anger
- Emotionally distant from others/impairment in sharing love or affection
- Substance abuse
- Cruelty to others or animals
- Fire setting
- Brooding
- Making threats
- Self-inflicted wounds
- Collecting weapons
- Chronic lack of respect for others
- High levels of irresponsibility
- Chronic theft or stealing
- Out-of-control behaviors
- Aggressive sexual behaviors
- Chronic deception

The primary role of the police is not that of a psychologist or social worker. They are, however, in contact with youth on a day-to-day basis and are in the position to observe these traits and channel the child to the proper agencies for intervention. This is because without intervention, either through the school or other agencies, studies show a child exhibiting these traits is more likely to be involved in violent crime.

SUMMARY

Throughout this chapter it has been emphasized that addressing the school crime problem is not just a police problem or concern, but one that is a community concern and needs the cooperation of the entire community. Also discussed was the method of developing a crisis plan for the school to enact in the event of a violent incident. This planning is also a cooperative effort utilizing all facets of the education system; the planning is also a task that needs to be reviewed at least once a year. It is simply not enough to develop a plan, because the plan must be understood by everyone and practiced often.

If an actual crisis takes place, the most efficient method of management is the Incident Command System (ICS), which has been utilized by the fire service for many years. In order for the ICS to work properly, it must combine with the ICS that the schools have for each building. Responding to a crisis creates many different problems, recognizing, of course, that each district and, in fact, each school in the district has different needs. It must also be remembered in the responding phase that the primary goal is the preservation of life. Other concerns in the response phase are the processing of the scene, security of the scene, and media relations.

Finally, there are children who exhibit warning signs of violent behavior. Police are in contact with these at-risk children on a daily basis and must be able to recognize the signs and understand what resources are available to intervene in these children's lives.

REFERENCES

Boyd, Stephen, & Harpold, Joseph (1999). School violence lessons learned. Federal Bureau of Investigation. Washington, DC: U.S. Government Printing Office, September.

Federal Emergency Management Agency (1999a). Multi hazard program for schools. Washington, DC: U.S. Government Printing Office.

Federal Emergency Management Agency (1999b). Planning to respond. Washington, DC: U.S. Government Printing Office.

International Association of Chiefs of Police (n.d.). Guide for preventing and responding to school violence. Alexandria, VA: International Association of Chiefs of Police.

Iowa Safe Schools Task Force (1999). A plan for keeping our schools and communities safe. March.

Jefferson County, Colorado, Sheriff's Office (2000). Final report on Columbine. Jefferson County, CO: County Sheriff's Office.

National Crime Prevention Council (1998). Safer schools: Strategies for educators and law enforcement seeking to prevent violence in schools. Washington, DC: National Crime Prevention Council.

APPENDIX A

Code No. 506.1E8

JUVENILE JUSTICE AGENCY INFORMATION-SHARING AGREEMENT

Statement of Purpose: The purpose of this Agreement is to allow for the sharing of information among the School District and the Agencies prior to a student's adjudication in order to promote and collaborate to improve school safety, reduce alcohol and illegal drug use, reduce truancy, reduce in-school and out-of-school suspensions, and to support alternatives to in-school and out-of-school suspensions and expulsions which provide structured and well-supervised educational programs supplemented by coordinated and appropriate services designed to correct behaviors that lead to truancy, suspension, and expulsions and to support students in successfully completing their education.

Identification of Agencies: This agreement is between the Community School District (hereinafter "School District") and (agencies listed) (hereinafter "Agencies").

Statutory Authority: This agreement implements Iowa Code § 280.25 (1997 Session Laws) and is consistent with 34 C.F.R. 99.38 (1997).

Parameters of Information Exchange:

1. The School District may share any information with the Agencies contained in a student's permanent record which is directly related to the juvenile justice system's ability to effectively serve the student.

2. Prior to adjudication, information contained in the permanent record may be disclosed by the school district to the Agencies without parental consent or court order.

3. Information contained in a student's permanent record may be disclosed by the School District to the Agencies after adjudication only with parental consent or a court order.

4. Information shared pursuant to the agreement shall be used solely for determining the programs and services appropriate to the needs of the student or student's family, or for coordinating the delivery of programs and services to the student or student's family.

5. Information shared under the agreement is not admissible in any court proceedings which take place prior to a disposition hearing, unless written consent is obtained from a student's parent, guardian, or legal or actual custodian.

Code No. 506.1E8

6. This agreement only governs a school district's ability to share information and the purposes for which that information can be used. Other agencies are bound by their own respective confidentiality policies.

   Records' Transmission: The individual requesting the information should contact the principal of the building in which the student is currently enrolled or was enrolled. The principal will forward the records within 10 business days of the request.

Confidentiality: Confidential information shared between the Agencies and the school district shall remain confidential and shall not be shared with any other person, unless otherwise provided by law. Information shared under the agreement is not admissible in any court proceedings which take place prior to a disposition hearing, unless written consent is obtained from a student's parent. Agencies or individuals violating the terms of this agreement subject their entity represented and themselves personally to legal action pursuant to federal and state law.

Code No. 506.1E8

JUVENILE JUSTICE AGENCY INFORMATION-SHARING AGREEMENT

Amendments: This agreement constitutes the entire agreement among the agencies with respect to information sharing. Agencies may be added to this agreement at the discretion of the school district.

Term: This agreement is effective from (September 1, 200X or other date).

APPROVED:

Signature: _____   Address: _____
Title: _____   City: _____
Agency: _____   State: _____ ZIP _____
Dated: _____   Phone Number: _____

Signature: _____   Address: _____
Title: _____   City: _____
Agency: _____   State: _____ ZIP _____
Dated: _____   Phone Number: _____

Signature: _____   Address: _____
Title: _____   City: _____
Agency: _____   State: _____ ZIP _____
Dated: _____   Phone Number: _____

Signature: _____   Address: _____
Title: _____   City: _____
Agency: _____   State: _____ ZIP _____
Dated: _____   Phone Number: _____

This agreement is optional and can only be used if the board has adopted a policy approving of its use.

APPENDIX B

SCHOOL ORGANIZATIONAL SYSTEM

```
              ┌─────────────┐
              │  PRINCIPAL  │
              └─────────────┘
        ┌───────────┼───────────┐
┌───────────────┐ ┌─────────────┐ ┌──────────────┐
│ ADMINISTRATION│ │ INSTRUCTION │ │ MAINTENANCE  │
└───────────────┘ └─────────────┘ └──────────────┘
```

APPENDIX C

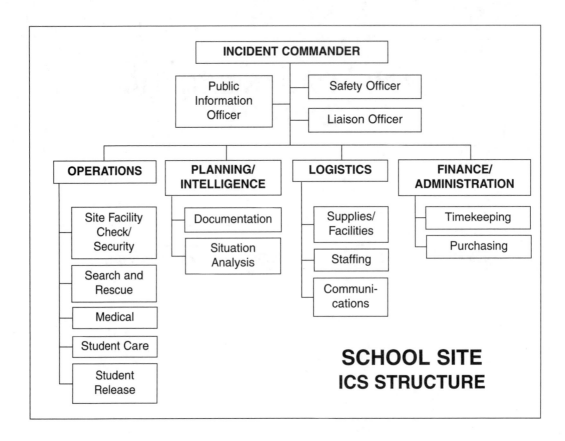

SCHOOL SITE
ICS STRUCTURE

8

School Violence from the Classroom Teacher's Perspective

Chris Ardis

Greatly overlooked in the macro-discussion of school crime and violence, in this editor's opinion, is the view from the front of the classroom. Ground zero, the front line, "where the rubber meets the road," are apt phrases to describe the position of the classroom teacher in any consideration of the issue of school crime or violence. Eight hours (or more) a day for 180 (or more) days every academic year finds this group of professionals in the most immediate proximity of whatever crime or violence is likely to occur in any school in the United States.

This chapter comes from such a classroom teacher. Ms. Ardis cannot be referred to as "the average teacher." In fact, the modifier "average" somehow does not seem appropriate for any teacher, in any classroom, in any school district in the U.S. She is a certified, special education teacher with almost 20 years of experience in an average-sized district, in an average-sized city, in the southernmost tip of the continental United States. Chris Ardis no longer teaches hearing-impaired students, but rather has been in a regular classroom teaching American Sign Language as a foreign language for the past few years. Her editorial instructions for this chapter were brief: "Tell the story of school crime/violence from the teacher's point of view." That story follows. It is a personal story, which is compelling and instructive.

Ms. Ardis tells the story as she sees it—what it was like in schools 20 years ago, what it is like today, and what, in her opinion, happened to make it change. Of all the chapters in this book, of all the chapters in other books of a similar type, of all the data, of all the footnotes, and of the entire debate—every parent, every administrator, and every taxpayer should be required to read and remember what this teacher has to say.

The message is clear and unmistakable. What happens at school is only symbiotic of what is happening in the community at large. Much of what is wrong with schools is also wrong with the society within which they exist. At some point, each school district in each community is going to have to make some hard decisions. Permissiveness with children at home and at school has limits. Schools and communities must look within themselves to see if those limits have been reached. This teacher thinks they have, and that some boundaries need to be established.

Stated again: This chapter is required reading!

Joshua, Christina, Ronald, Cassie, Paige, Ben, Isaiah, Dave, Shannon, and Rachel. Their stories, along with the stories of so many others, will be engraved in our minds and hearts forever. They died because they were students or teachers who made the decision to go to school one day, never imagining their names would be added to the growing list of victims of school shootings. A few short years ago, we could not have fathomed that our nation would witness the deaths of children and their teachers at school. All of those who died had their lives cut short in the most inconceivable fashion. All of them had so much of life left to live.

Who would have guessed that we would reach a point in time when students, teachers, and administrators would fear going to school? How can we come to terms with the fact that children and adults are killed in a place that once was synonymous with safety? When is it all going to end?

One only has to look at the numbers to see that we are in a crisis. According to the web site of the National Home Education Research Institute, there were between 1,300,000 and 1,700,000 children in grades K-12 being homeschooled in the United States during the 1999–2000 school year (National Home Education Research Institute, 1998). According to Jim and Lorena Nutting, members of the Rio Grande Valley Chapter of the Texas Home School Coalition, each time a school shooting occurs, those numbers grow (Jim and Lorena Nutting, 2001). In a June 2002 edition of *The Monitor,* McAllen's daily newspaper, an article read: " . . . there is a teacher shortage in Texas of between 37,000 and 40,000, said Ed Fuller, co-director of research at the State Board for Educator Certification." According to Fuller, there are plenty of certified teachers in Texas; however, "There is a shortage of certified teachers who are willing to teach in Texas public schools given the current working conditions." (Mabin, 2002) It is a nationwide trend, and although most analysts seem to attribute this disturbing statistic to low pay, it is time we openly admit that school violence and the deterioration of conditions within our school system are major contributing factors to this nationwide teacher shortage.

When a school shooting occurs, the news spreads rapidly throughout the school. Students, teachers, administrators, and parents alike shake their heads in disbelief that it has happened yet again. More schools develop safety plans, psychologists meet to discuss the whys of students shooting their classmates and teachers, and the media play the horrifying scenes over and over again. But within weeks, the shooting becomes a sad memory that we store in the back of our minds. And then the next shooting is reported, the scene repeats itself, and visions of the last school shooting that we hoped were tucked away forever are once again revisited.

Meanwhile, those of us still employed in schools throughout the country feel what boils down to a false sense of security. We know that our school could be the next one on the evening news and that our own students could be the ones running for their lives.

How did we get to this point?

A Brief Background

On February 19, 1997, a school shooting in Bethel, Alaska, left the principal and one student dead.

On October 1, 1997, a school shooting in Pearl, Mississippi, left two students dead.

On December 1, 1997, three students were killed at a school in Paducah, Kentucky.

On March 24, 1998, four young girls and a teacher were killed during a school shooting in Jonesboro, Arkansas.

On April 20, 1999, 12 students and 1 teacher in Littleton, Colorado, were killed when two fellow students opened fire at school. The two young men completed their plan by killing themselves.

And on March 5, 2001, two students had their lives cut short during a school shooting in Santee, California.

These are only a few of the school shootings that haunt us all. Some have happened in small towns few people had even heard of until the shootings occurred. Most happened in schools no one dreamed could fall victim to such a horrendous fate. All of them have devastated so many lives.

It Didn't Just Happen

Studies have been conducted, countless interviews have taken place, and professionals from around the world have been consulted, all in an effort to determine why all of these school shootings are taking place. But perhaps it is time to ask the teachers why school violence has become so prevalent.

Most of us who work in the school system, though deeply disturbed by this seemingly endless trend, are not exactly shocked by what has happened. So many of us could see it coming. After all, conditions within our schools and within our society have obviously played a significant role in allowing young people to believe that guns and violence are the answer to troubling circumstances in their lives.

Though it is difficult to pinpoint exactly when things began to change within our schools, it is easy to explain just how much conditions within our schools have deteriorated. One merely has to listen to the local news or read the newspaper to hear stories about yet another school in our country that has installed metal detectors at its front doors. A couple of years ago, many schools stopped allowing students to use school lockers for fear that weapons could be hidden within them. Many schools now require students to carry only see-through backpacks. And a growing number of schools now have a police force specifically assigned to their campuses for safety reasons.

So, how DID we get to this point? And why is it that no one seems to be listening?

That Was Then

When I began teaching in 1983, it was at Brown Junior High School (now Brown Middle School) in McAllen, Texas. At that time, Brown was considered a rough school. Located in one of the poorer areas of town, many of the students who went to Brown came from neighborhoods with known gangs.

I had just moved to the Rio Grande Valley from Peoria, Illinois. Although many people told me right away that Brown was "rough," the students there were actually relatively harmless. There were occasional fights and a lot of threats, but I never feared for my life or for the lives of the students in our school. While there was talk among fellow faculty members and students about impending major fights, the brawls that did occur were more like big fistfights, not scenes from *West Side Story* in which opposing gangs brought weapons in to fight their battles.

At that time, there was definitely foul language in our schools, but it was much different than it is today. Students walking down the hall would occasionally slip and utter a four-letter word, but they would immediately apologize to any adult within earshot. Often, those students would be taken to the office and were dealt swift punishment. Though students surely cursed, they knew it was inappropriate to use that type of language in front of teachers and administrators within the school.

Even then, there were dress codes. At the junior high, students were not allowed to leave their shirttails out. Teachers were required to stop students in the hall and in the classroom and require them to tuck their shirts in. While there were definitely students who complained and even at times who argued about this, without much of an ordeal, they would end up tucking their shirts in and be on their way. I don't remember ever having a parent come to school to ask why the students had to tuck their shirts in. Nor do I ever recall a student coming to school and telling the teacher or administrator that his mom or dad thought this rule was "dumb" and to leave it out if he wanted to.

And back in 1983, if teachers sent a progress report home or called a parent about misbehavior, chances were very high that the parents would come to school to make sure the matter was taken care of and to assure the teacher that this would not happen again. Often students would come to school the next day and discuss how they had been punished for their disregard for their grades or their manners.

This Is Now

My, how things have changed since those days. Conditions inside schools across the nation today definitely tell a very different story. At first the changes were rather subtle. In 1983, it was common for teachers to be called into the office to witness a student receiving corporal punishment for a serious or repeated offense. Corporal punishment consisted of a principal or assistant principal using a long wooden paddle to give the offending student three "swats" on the buttocks. McAllen district policy demanded that a witness be present. Whether one supports or opposes corporal punishment, it was a common practice and was very effective in many cases. Many students who received this punishment did not want it again and thus refrained from repeating the behavior that had resulted in their being paddled.

Parents were required to sign a form giving permission for the school to use corporal punishment on their child, and most parents at the time signed it. When the parents were called to inform them that their child was to be paddled at school, it was common for the parent to tell the administrator who had called to let the student know that he or she would be getting further punishment for that transgression upon arrival at home that day.

Suddenly, corporal punishment ceased to exist in our school. I do not remember discussing it at the start of the school year or ever hearing much about it, but suddenly the paddle was merely put in some closet somewhere to collect dust. Interestingly enough, in the 2000–2001 McAllen Independent School District Student Code of Conduct, there is a section entitled Corporal Punishment. The same rules apply now as in the past, according to this booklet that every student in the district receives. However, in talking to teachers at various levels from throughout the district, it seems quite clear that none of the schools choose to use corporal punishment.

This brings us to another major change in our schools: lawsuits and the threat of lawsuits. Whereas back in the 1980s I cannot recall a parent ever threatening to sue one of my fellow teachers or me, today it is common for a teacher to be threatened with such proceedings. Most schools would surely prefer to ignore the fact that corporal punishment is still considered an acceptable punishment in the district than to follow the guidelines for its use and be stuck in court defending their decision.

It is not only parents who threaten teachers and administrators with lawsuits. Many students have become adept at demanding various things and threatening a suit if their wishes are not met. One only has to talk to teachers across the country to discover how prevalent this threat is. Teachers' and administrators' unions have become a necessity for most school district employees, as they guarantee representation should a lawsuit be filed.

Living under the threat of a lawsuit for the most ludicrous reasons has definitely had an extremely negative impact on our school systems. It has become increasingly clear in many school districts that it is easier to buckle under pressure from parents and give in to their demands than to risk being taken to court. So often it feels as though the students and their parents are controlling our schools today rather than the administrators and teachers. When will we stand up and say, "No more"?

The use of foul language has escalated to unbelievable heights. Walking down the halls of schools today, it is not unusual to hear students saying, "Fu**," "Bit**," "Sh**," and any number of other foul words as if they were saying, "Good morning." Today, most students do not refrain from saying the words if they see teachers or even parents in the hallways. This type of language seems to have become acceptable in many of our nation's schools. In fact, adults often just tune it out rather than go to the trouble of fighting it. In essence, by doing this, we are telling our children that it is okay to use this type of language.

Ask many students today, and they will tell you they are allowed to curse at home, too. Cursing to and at parents, in many homes, is considered a "form of expression." While some students who are allowed to curse at home have nonetheless been taught not to use these words with teachers and other adults, many others will argue that using this type of language around adults is not disrespectful. After all, they will tell you, "They are just words."

Most schools still have some sort of dress code in place, though the enforcement of these codes has a tendency to be quite lax. According to our Student Code of Conduct, "Revealing clothing such as bare midriffs, crop tops, cut-out backs, halter tops, undershirt cut shirts (tank tops, muscle shirts), unbuttoned shirts or blouses, and other items similar to these are not acceptable for school. . . . Any apparel containing obscene slogans or other emblems or writing that may reasonably be expected to cause disruption of or interference with normal school operations shall not be permitted." (McAllen Independent School District, 2000–2001) When it comes to footwear, thongs are prohibited.

To most teachers, this dress code is pretty basic. However, walk onto the campus of a school in our district on any given day, and you are sure to find more than a few students who have knowingly and willingly made the decision to come to school in attire that directly defies this dress code. And our district is not alone in this. It seems to be a nation-wide trend. The time that is wasted having students go to lockers to change into appropri-ate attire or to call parents to bring them proper clothing is ludicrous at best. What is more, often parents encourage this behavior because "that rule is stupid." Again, adults on school campuses often choose to ignore the dress code violations rather than waste the time to send the offending student to the office. After all, chances are that same student will be breaking the dress code again the next day. So like the cursing, once more we turn our heads rather than address the problem.

Across the country, it is obvious that our society has reached a point at which students feel they have the right to protest every rule and every demand that comes their way. In most schools, defiance and disrespect are the norm. National media often cover the stories of parents who have filed lawsuits on behalf of their children for violation of First Amendment rights. Parents actually file lawsuits based on a dress code. Why are we teaching our chil-dren to fight even the most simplistic rules? Are we not sending them a message that if you fight hard enough, all rules will disappear?

That is not to say that all of our young people are like this. Fortunately, many stu-dents were obviously raised to respect their teachers and administrators, to treat others with dignity, and to obey rules that are set before them. But with each passing year, the number of students like this seems to get smaller and smaller, and the problems within our schools become greater and greater.

Another major change that has occurred over the last few years is the lack of positive contact with parents. As mentioned earlier, in the past, when students received progress reports or poor report cards, parents would call or come to the school immediately to address the problem. When teachers called home to report a student's misbehavior, parents were quick to respond with support for the teacher, and the following day, it was usually obvious that the child had been dealt with at home and would not be repeating the negative behavior that had resulted in the phone call.

That type of reaction has become a rarity. Today, many parents do not respond at all to progress reports or poor report cards. Teachers often dread calling parents of students who misbehave today. The call is sometimes met with a very positive response from the parents who are grateful for having been informed of their child's misbehavior and who promise to handle the situation that very day. Just as often, however, parents are quick to begin chastising the teacher. In fact, it is not all that rare for parents to go so far as to use extremely foul language to cast guilt on the teacher and away from their child.

So what does all of this have to do with school violence? Plenty! Each year there is a little less respect, a little more bending of the rules, and a much stronger feeling that teachers and administrators are no longer in control of our schools. Now it often seems as if students, and sometimes even their parents, make all of the decisions for the school. And the end result, as we are witnessing across the country, is devastating.

Violence as an Answer

In the January 2000 edition of *Reader's Digest*, a story entitled "Losing It" (Nack & Munson, 2000) began by describing the scene that so many of us have listened to in horror. It was July 5, 2000. Two fathers were at an ice skating rink in Reading, Massachusetts, while their sons practiced their hockey skills. One of the fathers, Thomas Junta, became upset when he saw his 10-year-old son get checked and elbowed in the nose. He began complaining, and the other father, Michael Costin, told him this is what happens when you play hockey.

A small scuffle ensued, and rink employees are said to have asked Junta to leave the arena. Junta left but returned a short time later. The two fathers began to fight, when the 275-pound Junta knocked the 175-pound Costin on the floor and allegedly began beating him in the head and neck with his fists (Federal Trade Commission, 2000). Costin was knocked unconscious, and two days later, this single father of four died. Four children will grow up without a father. All because of a hockey match.

This story is sad enough on its own, but what makes it even sadder is that this is not an isolated case. Although Costin's death was the extreme, violence by parents at sporting events is becoming more and more widespread. In cities across the nation, a person can go to any sporting event involving young children or teenagers, and there will often be at least one adult in the crowd who resorts to name-calling or violence during the event.

The *Reader's Digest* story tells of other situations in which this epidemic of out-of-control adults resulted in violence. For years, T-ball, club swimming, junior football league, high school games, and other youth sporting events were places where young people could play, have fun, and learn all about healthy competition. Not so today. Presently, sporting events intended for our youth are often ruined by irrational adults. When young people see adults respond with name-calling and violence over such simple things as a bad call by an umpire or an elbow jab during a game, instead of learning about healthy competition, what do they learn instead? That violence is acceptable. Do they not get the message that this is how we resolve conflicts, as meaningless as those conflicts may be? They get the message all right. They get it loud and clear.

Other Contributing Factors

On June 1, 1999, following the school shooting in Littleton, Colorado, then-President Bill Clinton requested that the Federal Trade Commission (FTC) and the Department of Justice conduct a study to determine whether the motion picture, music, and electronic game industries were marketing violent products to children and teenagers. This was a direct result of information that had been gathered suggesting that the two perpetrators of the Columbine tragedy were fascinated with violent movies, music, and electronic games. The title of the FTC's study was "Marketing Violent Entertainment to Children: A Review of Self-Regulation and Industry Practices in the Motion Picture, Music Recording, and Electronic Game Industries" (FTC, 2000).

Nationwide concern had been growing over the violent nature of movies, music, and electronic games and the effect this has on children and teenagers. Prior to the study, all three industries adopted self-regulatory systems in an attempt to assuage these concerns.

The motion picture industry has developed a rating system that is used in virtually all movies released in the United States. Most of us are familiar with this rating system that also requires that the established rating for the movie appear in all advertising. This industry also attempts to review movie ads to ensure that they are deemed appropriate.

According to the web site of the FTC, "The music recording industry recommends the use of a general parental advisory label on music with 'explicit content.' The decision to place a parental advisory label on a recording is made by the artist and the music publishing company and involves no independent third-party review" (FTC, 2000). This industry has also taken it a bit further by recommending that recording companies refrain from advertising music that has been given the explicit content label to audiences that consist of mainly children and teens under the age of 17.

"The electronic game industry requires games to be labeled with age- and content-based rating information and requires that the rating information appear in advertising. It also is the only industry that has adopted a rule prohibiting its marketers from targeting advertising for games to children below the age designations indicated by the rating" (FTC, 2000).

The Commission's findings warrant great concern. It learned through its study that all three industries routinely market products they have found to be violent to children under 17. The FTC found that these three industries, though they themselves developed the rating and warning label systems that are in place today, have marketing plans that directly target the very audiences the warnings are designed to protect. These industries go so far as to purposely advertise during television programs they know are primarily viewed by children under the age of 17 as well as in magazines and through other venues that attract young children.

As if these findings were not disturbing enough, the FTC also discovered that retailers often do little to prevent children under 17 from watching movies they should be prohibited from seeing, buying music with warning labels intended to keep children from buying them, or playing electronic games with violent content. Equally disturbing is the fact that the FTC also determined that parents have very little understanding of the rating systems used by these industries. Parents obviously need to be educated about these rating systems.

The results of this study are critical if one is to truly understand school violence. Although students regularly argue that seeing violent movies, listening to violent music, or playing violent electronic games does not lead to their running out to shoot someone, evidence suggests otherwise. According to the Parents Television Council web site, syndicated columnist L. Brent Bozell III, in his article entitled "The Culture Makes a Killing," wrote about Andy Williams, the Santee, California, teen who opened fire on his classmates on March 5, 2001 (Bozell, 2001). Bozell indicates that one of Williams's friends said that a song by the band Linkin Park inspired Williams to commit this act of school violence. In this same article, Bozell goes on to discuss other teens who have committed violent murders, teens who were obsessed with movies like *Scream*, *Natural Born Killers*, and *Menace II Society*.

On May 3, 2001, ABC's *Nightline* aired a similar story of a teenager from California. One evening, this teenage girl was at her home when she received a telephone call from three friends, two 16-year-olds and a 14-year-old. She snuck out of her home to go and meet the boys. She never came home. For eight months, her parents searched for their daughter before finding her body. She had been choked with a belt and stabbed repeatedly.

The boys finally admitted to killing the young girl. One of the boys said they had killed her as a human sacrifice, just like what they had heard in the song "Altar of Sacrifice" by the band Slayer on its *Reign of Blood* album. The boys believed that if they offered her up as a human sacrifice, it would bring good luck to a band they had created.

Here are some of the lyrics of that song:

> *Waiting the hour destined to die, Here on the table of hell, A figure in white unknown by man*
> *Approaching the altar of death, High priest awaiting dagger in hand, Spilling the pure virgin blood, Satan's slaughter (Slayer, 1986)*

Tip of the Iceberg

To say this is disturbing is obviously putting it very mildly. Words cannot describe how incredulous teachers feel today as we hear our students talk about the thrills they get when they go to a violent movie or listen to such heinous music.

Students have such great admiration for musicians like Marilyn Manson and Eminem. In his 1998 album, *Mechanical Animals,* Marilyn Manson sings:

> *And I am resigned to this wicked fuc*ing world, On its way to hell*
> *The living are dead and I hope to join them too*
> *I know what to do and I do it well . . . . When I hate it I know I can feel*
> *But when you love you know it's not real, No*
> *Shoot myself to love you, If I loved myself I'd be shooting you (Manson, 1998)*

Equally disturbing is the music recorded by Eminem. In his 2000 CD, *The Marshall Mathers LP*, in the song "The Way I Am," Eminem sings:

> *And since birth I've been cursed with this curse to just curse*
> *And just blurt this berserk and bizarre sh** that works.*
> *But at least have the decency in you to leave me alone,*
> *When you freaks see me out in the streets . . .*
> *I don't know you and no, I don't owe you a motherfuc** thing . . .*
> *When a dude's getting bullied and shoots up his school and they*
> *Blame it on Marilyn (on Marilyn) . . . Where were the parents at?*
> *(Eminem, 2000)*

We hear lyrics like this and realize we live in a society today that allows children and teens to purchase such music, many times with their parents' permission. Many young people are allowed to watch incredibly violent films and to play violent electronic games. And then, when there are school shootings, everyone asks why.

Parents or Friends

Whether you like Dr. Laura Schlessinger or not, many of the things she says about teenagers today are right on target. Time and again, parents call in to Dr. Laura's radio program to discuss their teenagers. Often the parents tell Dr. Laura that they do not approve of the music their children want to listen to or the movies they want to see. After making this point, they then begin to change their tune and say how they just feel bad because their kids really want that CD or to be able to go to a particular movie, and they know their child is good, and . . . the excuses continue. Dr. Laura can see it coming, and she is prepared to attack. In the very next breath, the parents are saying they will feel so bad if they do not allow their children to have what they want, and their children will get mad at them. And the attack begins.

It is what I call the Parent/Friend Complex. More and more, our schools have become the breeding grounds for young people whose parents are much more concerned with being their child's friend than his or her parent. We see kids talking to their parents using every curse word imaginable and the parent not even flinching. We also see parents hosting parties for their children and other teenagers and serving liquor. When children today do not study for a major test or do not complete a homework assignment, a growing number of parents tell them to stay home that day. Often the parents even call the school making incredible excuses for their children.

In the Spring 2001 edition of *American Educator*, the magazine put out by the American Federation of Teachers, Kay S. Hymowitz discusses this same phenomenon. In her article entitled "Parenting: The Lost Art," Hymowitz calls parents like these "parent-advocates" (2001). She says, "At home, parent-advocates aspire to be friends and equals, hoping to maintain the happy affection they think of as a 'good relationship.' It rarely seems to happen that way. Unable to balance warmth with discipline and affirmation with limit-setting, these parents are puzzled to find their 4-year-old ordering them around like he's Louis XIV or their 8-year-old screaming, 'I hate you!' when they balk at letting her go to a sleepover party for the second night in a row" (Hymowitz, 2001).

Hymowitz goes on to discuss how parents today often refuse to set boundaries for their children. She talks about teenage coed sleepover parties and other such events happening in our nation that would have been unheard of just a few short years ago.

Allowing children to play music of a violent or sexual nature at home. Allowing them to go to movies inappropriate for their ages or to rent such movies. Making excuses for children rather than teaching them that for every choice there is a consequence, and letting them learn this for themselves. Failing to teach right from wrong. Permissiveness is plaguing our young people today.

In years past, parents would set their own curfews for their children. Inside by eight, homework done, bath taken, and to bed by nine. As the child grew older, these curfews would be extended. Going out on a school night was usually prohibited except for very special occasions. Today, however, it is common for students to go out partying with their friends until two or three in the morning, even on a school night. Many teens have jobs where they work on school nights until midnight or even later. The effect this often has on their schoolwork is obvious.

In the 1980s, occasionally parents of a high school student would tell a teacher, "We just don't know what to do with him anymore." Teachers would often just shake their heads in disbelief that parents would admit they had lost control of their own child. This used to be rare, though, and nine times out of ten you could be sure that these parents had not begun by setting limits for their children back when they were toddlers.

It has become progressively worse. Today you will hear elementary teachers talk about the number of parents who come to them and say those same words. "We just don't know what to do with him anymore." In elementary school? Something is very wrong!

In my 19 years of teaching, it has been relatively easy to point out the kids who have had close relationships with their parents from the time they were little. These kids know their boundaries and abide by them. As most young people will do, they test those boundaries from time to time, but deep down they know they are not going anywhere. What is still true is that the children whose parents have set boundaries and lived by them respect their parents tremendously. Most of the time when teenagers have close relationships with their parents and speak about them very highly, it is obvious the parents have truly talked to their children since they were little about the important things in their lives. They have had open communication for years. If parents do not begin that type of relationship with their children at a young age, trying to create it when those children become teenagers almost always results in disaster.

So what is the problem with the Parent/Friend Complex? Dr. Laura recently explained it most adeptly when she said that parents have become kids and kids have become parents. The problem with this, she explains, is that kids do not have the wisdom it takes to be effective parents.

What About Bullies?

Following several of the school shootings, we were inundated with news stories about those who had committed them. We heard about how they were outcasts, how they had been made fun of by athletes and other "popular" students, and again and again, we heard that these shooters were "bullied." The shooters had suffered long enough, it was said, and they saw violence as the only way to make it stop.

So what about bullies? As I recall my own childhood, I can remember being teased because of my weight. When I was little, I was a skinny kid, but when puberty hit in sixth grade, I blossomed too much in all of the wrong places. I was suddenly fat. There were definitely a couple of so-called bullies at my school who got some kind of perverse pleasure out of hurting my feelings and the feelings of many other kids. Bullying has been around for years.

Working in the school system, it seems there is a difference in bullying tactics depending on the grade level. In the elementary schools, taunting seems to be the most common type of bullying. Kids tease each other about height, weight, race, and other such things, but that is about as far as it goes.

In middle school, the taunting tends to get meaner and the rougher form of bullying usually sets in. This is the age level when kids are chased home from school by groups of bullies or when they are confronted during physical education or in the bathroom at school. Middle school students who are the victims of bullying will often begin to beg their parents to let them stay home from school. School is the dreaded place because the student never feels safe or loved. Middle school is also when adolescence really sets in, and this often makes the bullying that much more difficult to handle.

At the high school level, bullying is often almost a cross between elementary and middle school. Some students deemed unworthy by bullies for whatever reason are often taunted mercilessly. Others are bullied with more physical abuse. Either way, the bullying will most likely bring about fear, anger, depression, loneliness, and other painful feelings. Teenagers deal with these feelings in many different ways. Some may quit going to school. Others are able to focus their attention on extracurricular activities that allow them to make friends who help divert these feelings of inadequacy. And still others resort to violence.

One of the most difficult things about teaching is seeing the children who are considered the "outcasts." I will never forget one particular high school student. There was nothing unattractive or strange about his appearance. He was very bright. He had a short temper, but I soon realized that it was most likely developed as a result of the intense taunting he was subjected to on a daily basis. And it was a vicious cycle.

He would come to school, and students would make fun of him. He would become very angry, and then the kids would say that he had a really bad temper. At lunch, while most high school students would eat with groups of friends, he would always be sitting alone, often reading a book. Every time I saw this, it would make me so sad. I spoke to our counselors and suggested they form a group for kids who were treated like this. Perhaps, I thought, they could become involved in the community or with students from other schools. Obviously, these students needed more positive feedback in their lives.

And then one day this student had an outburst in my class. He had become very upset over a grade and blew up. When I spoke to his mother regarding what had happened, she began to cry. She told me she did not know how to help him. She said that for years he had been the victim of abuse by other children, and she really did not understand why.

As a teacher, I felt so helpless. How do you stop bullying? How do you help the kids who are the victims of it? I spoke to all of my students on several occasions about how important it is to treat all other students nicely. I would remind them how much fun high school is and ask them how they would feel if their high school years were filled with loneliness and with put-downs. I still do that now. But I know this is not enough.

Our Schools

So what about our schools? Are they addressing the bullying issue as well as other factors believed to be part of the school violence puzzle of problems? Actually, bullying is being addressed both nationally and internationally.

In *The Monitor*, McAllen's daily newspaper, on April 25, 2001, a writer for *The Associated Press* penned a story about a nationwide survey that had been conducted. The survey was given to 15,686 public and private school students, and it found that nearly one in every three children in grades 6 through 10 in the United States had been affected by bullying (Ever been bullied? 2001).

The story, entitled "Ever Been Bullied?" went on to say that schools across the country have begun to adopt bullying intervention programs. It continued, "Children who said they were bullied reported more loneliness and difficulty making friends, while those who did the bullying were more likely to have poor grades and to smoke and drink alcohol" (Ever been bullied? 2001).

According to the story, studies in England and Norway have shown that when schools implemented intervention programs, this type of behavior can be reduced by 30%

to 50% (Ever been bullied? 2001). The article points out the importance of involving school personnel, parents, and other students in the program.

From a teacher's perspective, one thing that is rather disturbing is that more and more it seems that our society is expecting our schools to teach the very things that for years were taught by parents. Take Texas, for example. In the April 4, 2001, edition of *The Monitor*, we learned that the Texas House passed a bill that could provide additional federal funding to school districts that implement a character education program. The writer notes that "House Bill 946, written by Barry Telford, D-Dekalb, authorizes schools to teach students the values of courage, trustworthiness, honesty, reliability, punctuality and loyalty, as well as integrity, respect and courtesy" (Education legislation; House passes character program bill, 2001).

According to the bill, schools that implement this type of program will receive a "Character Plus" designation from the Texas Education Agency. Federal funding may then be considered for these districts to support such a program. The program recommends involvement by parents and community leaders, too. Just one more thing for school districts to teach.

Lawmakers Gone Crazy

Although character education is definitely important in the upbringing of all children, is school truly the place for the formal teaching of this? It seems our schools have become a fertile ground for every type of program one can imagine.

A week after we learned about House Bill 946 regarding Character Education, editors at *The Monitor* chose this topic as their editorial view for the day. In it they wrote, "It's disturbing that Americans are turning over more and more of their parental duties to the schools. And teachers are hard-pressed to convey everything they're already required to impart to students" (Teaching character; job should fall to parents as well, 2001). They go on to say words that could have easily been said by any number of teachers across the nation: "Educators should weave positive values into everyday subject matter. If teachers convey the values of honesty, hard work and discipline on a daily basis, students will pick that up along with other subject matter. But it's a shame they aren't learning it from their parents in the first place" (Teaching character, 2001).

Most schools today have special pullout programs for students who are habitual troublemakers and who cannot seem to function in the regular school setting. Students are pulled out of their regular classes for a given number of days, often 5 to 10. Sometimes they are removed for even longer. In these programs, students are given very strict rules by which they have to abide. In many of them, students are put on a point system and have to earn a certain number of points in order to return to the regular school setting.

Many of these programs, while conducted on the school campus, are removed in the sense that students who are placed in them are not allowed to socialize with students not in the program. They eat separately and are taken to the restroom during class time so there will not be any interaction with the rest of the student population.

For the past 10 years or so, it seems that every year we learn of one more program our state and national lawmakers have established. Most of them are mandatory. School districts have to set aside funding for these programs, staff them, and practically jump through hoops to abide by all of the requirements of the new programs.

When you work in the school system, you often find yourself wondering if these same lawmakers who are demanding all of these special programs actually visit the schools in our nation on a regular basis. Most lawmakers, it seems, visit our school campuses only when invited as distinguished guests for special ceremonies. But do they have any idea what it is really like day in and day out in our schools?

I have often held that if our lawmakers sent members of their staffs into school districts throughout the country to work as substitute teachers, without the knowledge of anyone in the district to avoid special treatment, these same lawmakers would be passing very different laws. Teachers and administrators recognize that many of the laws that govern the punishment of students for various transgressions instead serve to protect them while often putting the other students and school district personnel at risk. While every effort is being made to "protect the rights" of students who probably have no business being in a regular school system, our schools nationwide have become places where almost anything goes.

We have school shootings? Let's pass a bill that encourages school districts to implement antibullying programs. Children cannot behave in school because they have no discipline? Let's require our schools to establish programs to deal with these children. Students have been arrested on a number of assault charges and other serious crimes? Let's make it so those children are removed for short periods of time but then make sure the schools know they are required to accept the students back regardless of whether or not it is safe to do so. And then, when all of this is said and done, let's sit back and wonder again why we have violence in our schools.

Is There Fear?

I can still remember the Columbine shooting as if it were yesterday. The day after it happened, things were very quiet at school. I was teaching at Memorial High School in McAllen. I was in a portable building, the farthest one from the front office. I remember locking the door for days following the Columbine shooting. It was this fear within me and a need to know my students were safe.

Very soon after the Columbine shooting, a rumor circulated throughout our community that there would be a similar act of school violence on our campus. The rumor was that the shooting was to occur sometime around 11:00 in the morning. Chaos ensued. Everywhere you went, students were crying, many of them hysterically. Parents were coming in droves to pick up their children. Some of the parents were crying. I remember standing there in shock, stunned that something like this could be happening at school. Of course, there were students who were taking advantage of the situation and checking out of school because they knew they could, but there were so many students who were truly terrified that a shooting was going to take place.

The shootings have not stopped, and neither has the fear. In April of 2001, I asked my students to write essays about school violence and to include in them whether they thought a shooting could happen at our school. I also asked them if they ever feared this. I was surprised that most of my students wrote that they really did not think it would ever happen at our school. After all, isn't that what the kids who have been victims of school violence thought?

One common thread in my students' essays was that many felt counselors could make a big difference in school violence. Students wrote that counselors rarely have time to actually counsel students, and they are so right. Years ago, counselors' jobs revolved mainly around talking to students, listening to their problems, offering them advice or other types of help, and really getting to know the students. Today things are much different. Counselors today are given the responsibility of administering tests, registering students for classes, making schedule changes, and, if they have any time left over, counseling students. The frustration they feel is often evident on their faces. It is strange that at a time in our nation when school violence is on the rise and an increasing number of students are faced with problems heretofore faced primarily by adults, counselors rarely have time to address these issues with the children in our schools.

Although many young people will say they do not fear school shootings, one has to wonder if this is actually true. Recently, our school was asked to choose five journalism students to be the featured teens in *The Monitor*'s Saturday "As We See It!" section. Each student was to come up with one question, and then all five students wrote an answer to the five questions. In the May 19, 2001, edition of the paper, the question one of the students wrote was "Do you think a school shooting would ever happen here in the Rio Grande Valley?" (It must be on their minds.) All of the students responded that yes, it could happen here. One of the students wrote, "While the Valley community has done a great job focusing on our children, I believe there are still children who are not raised in the proper environment. Without this, these shootings will continue" (As we see it, 2001). I could not agree more.

It seems adults are much more outwardly concerned about the possibility of a school shooting happening at their own child's school. As previously mentioned, homeschooling is on the rise. In addition, in many states, private school enrollment continues to rise. Many schools have developed emergency action plans to deal with school shootings. Our school recently had a Lock Down Drill, specifically developed to prepare for an act of school violence. Recent history tells us this is definitely needed, but it is nonetheless frightening to actually see it taking shape. It reminds us that any school in our nation could be the next to be featured on the nightly news.

So What Is Being Done?

Antibullying programs, Character Education, Lock Down Plans, new laws, new programs. Are these Band-Aids, or will they alleviate some potentially volatile situations?

More and more people seem to be accepting the fact that our society is very much to blame for the violence we see in our schools today. Obviously not every child who sees a violent movie or listens to a CD about violence will go out and commit a violent crime. However, some do, and young minds are often fertile ground for warped ideas.

On April 26, 2001, Senators Joe Lieberman (D-CT) and Herb Kohl (D-WI) introduced legislation that would prevent the entertainment industry from marketing the products they have deemed to contain adult material to children. Called the Media Marketing Accountability Act, this bill would allow the FTC to bring action against the entertainment industry if it is found to specifically target the marketing of its adult-rated products to children (Media Marketing Accountability Act, 2001). This legislation would apply to movies, music recordings, and video games. The FTC would have the authority to levy civil fines against the companies in violation of this act. They could either choose to issue a cease and desist order or level penalties of up to $11,000 per day per violation (Media Marketing Accountability Act, 2001).

This appears to be a wonderful start. If leaders in these industries were to visit our schools and see the effect their products have on many teens today, they would surely be hard pressed to prove otherwise.

Parent accountability definitely needs to be addressed. While there are many students in our schools with wonderful and responsible parents, a growing number of parents seem to be failing their children.

Discipline should definitely be the top priority for change within our nation's schools. However, it is essential that lawmakers at both the state and national levels be a part of these changes. There should be much less leniency allowed for misbehavior in our schools. School districts should regain control of our schools, many of which now are unofficially controlled by parents, students, and civil rights lawyers. Respect, expectations, and responsibility need to return to our schools. This would definitely contribute to the overall return to safety within them.

A person can prune a tree to try to make that tree look beautiful. However, if the roots of that tree are damaged, all of the pruning in the world will not help that tree. So it is with our schools. Unless we get to the root of the problems in our society that have led to our current out-of-control school system, everything else is just an attempt to try to make our schools look nice and pretty and happy. It is time we, as a nation, say NO MORE. No more children will die in our schools. No more parents will fear sending their children to school. And no more teachers will live the rest of their lives mourning the deaths of their students at school.

The Bad News

Unless some drastic changes are made in our society, in our schools, and in our families, we can expect to see more acts of school violence. More administrators, teachers, and children will die in our schools.

Open the newspaper and evidence of this abounds. Here are some examples from *The Monitor*:

> *April 13, 2001—"Student faces suspension after threat" (Mercedes, TX)*
>
> *April 21, 2001—"Hit list causes stir at school"(McAllen, TX)*
>
> *April 26, 2001—"16-year-old arraigned for high school bomb threat" (Weslaco, TX)*
>
> *May 10, 2001—"Teen says shooting was an accident" (West Palm Beach, FL)*
>
> *May 16, 2001—"Student commits suicide in front of an English teacher" (Ennis, TX)*

All of these incidents occurred in the span of just over a month. All of them involved teens, schools, and violence. It is like never awakening from a nightmare, only much worse. This is all too real.

The Good News

The reward of teaching today is that there are still many wonderful children in our schools whose parents are just that . . . parents. Their job is not easy, especially in light of the fact that the biggest obstacle they face is other parents. Talk about peer pressure.

How do you tell your child no when all of his or her friends' parents are telling their children yes? How do you refuse to allow your child to go to a party where everyone is drinking and the host's parents allow it? How do you maintain your values and standards in a world that has gone crazy?

It is usually easy to pick out the young people whose parents have established ground rules in their homes since their children were mere toddlers. These parents stick to what they believe is right and good and accept the fact that at times they won't be very popular with their children. They realize the payoff will come when their children are adults who work and have their own families instead of wasting away in a prison cell.

Teachers rejoice with parents like Dr. Norman and Julie Ramirez from McAllen. They have a son and a daughter in college. Their youngest daughter entered high school in the fall of 2001. These three young people have a great deal of respect for other people, especially adults. They do not use foul language in front of adults, they strive for good grades, and they have both immediate and long-term goals and know it takes hard work and determination to achieve them. They are the kind of children who allow teachers to teach instead of spending an inordinate amount of class time disciplining.

Raising children has always been difficult, but today, the task is phenomenal. Mrs. Ramirez lists some of the parental choices she and Dr. Ramirez have made that she feels have had a significant impact on their lives:

- Having dinner together every evening as a family and utilizing this time to talk over the day's events.
- Growing up, Mrs. Ramirez cherishes the memories of her parents giving her and her siblings a kiss and sitting on their beds to talk to them. She carries on this tradition with her own children.
- Basing decisions on what they feel is right, not what other parents are allowing their children to do. Their children were prohibited from watching television programs such as Married with Children and The Simpsons.
- Talking, talking, talking to their children from the time they were little and carrying this over into adolescence and young adult life.
- Teaching their children that life is full of choices but that they have to be willing to live with the consequences of the choices they make.
- When their children were small, Mrs. Ramirez would often put notes in their lunch boxes that said such things as "Have a wonderful day. I love you." As the children grew older, the notes would be placed in their bathrooms so they would see them when they got up in the morning.

The Ramirez's daughter, Jessica, came up with her own list of things her parents did that she believes kept her and her siblings on the right path in life:

- Being so close knit, not only with their immediate family but with their extended family as well.
- Sitting with their parents and really talking to them.
- Having their parents always make themselves available to them, despite the fact that their father is a cardiologist and their mother is deeply involved in the community. Family always comes first, and Jessica and her siblings have no doubts about this.

- Learning to always respect their elders. Their parents never cursed at them and this taught them deep respect. There is a time and a place for cursing, and this was clear from the time they were youngsters.

Although the term *communication* is greatly overused, it is obvious from both the parents and their daughter that this is an integral piece of the puzzle. This true communication, as opposed to surface talk about what time dinner will be served or who is going to pick up the kids after the game, must start from the time the children are very little.

We hear so much today about "broken homes." Although it is often said that single-parent homes have produced more than their share of juvenile delinquents, it is obvious in our schools that there are many single parents who are doing an incredible job of raising their children.

The product of one such home is Norma L. Garza, a library assistant at McAllen High School. Norma's mother became a widow at the age of 39 and was left to raise 10 children on her own. While the enormity of this responsibility would frighten many people, Mrs. Garza's mother took her job very seriously.

School was always stressed in their home, and skipping school was not an option. In today's era of judges conducting court on school campuses to deal with the astonishing rise in truancy cases, it is obvious that many parents could learn a great deal from Mrs. Garza's mother. She and her siblings knew that while their punishment at school might have been severe enough had they been caught skipping school, it paled in comparison to the punishment that would be awaiting them when they arrived home that day.

All 10 children were expected to be in the house by 9:00 in the evening, and all homework was to be completed by 10:00. A curfew was set and all of the children knew it was in their best interest to abide by it. Mrs. Garza and her siblings never raised their voices to their mother. From a very young age, they learned the meaning of respect and were expected to exhibit it at all times.

Now a mother of two children, Mrs. Garza and her husband are raising their children with the same values, the same rules, and the same expectations.

What a glorious word . . . expectations.

Expectations

That's what it all boils down to, from a teacher's perspective. It used to be a joke that "Rules are made to be broken." Now we are raising our children to believe this.

Rules need to be established in the home and carried over to school. Parents and teachers need to work together to create a safe and secure environment for our children. It starts out simple, but the implications are far-reaching . . .

- If there is a dress code at school, children should be taught to abide by it. Create consequences that become stiffer with repeated violations and stick with them. Consistency is the key.
- Respect is a basic. It starts in the home from childhood and is extended to the school, the church or synagogue, and all other places. Using foul language with or around adults is disrespectful regardless of how you look at it. They aren't "just words." They are symbols of an attitude of disrespect. Expect respect.

- Parents must talk to their children. Let them know they can come to you with their joys, their sorrows, their celebrations, and their disappointments. Turn off the cell phone and the TV and listen to them. Listening has become a dying art at a time when our young people are screaming to be heard.

- There is a difference between a parent and a parent-friend. There will be time for friendship with your children in years to come. Right now they need the wisdom and guidance from a parent. Sometimes you will not be popular with your children. Deal with it.

- EXPECT children to complete chores at home. EXPECT them to get good grades in school. EXPECT them to treat others with respect. EXPECT them to always do their best.

- Parents, establish and stick to your own censorship. Listen to the music your children are listening to. Watch the movies they are watching. Play the games they are playing. If any of them contradict your own values, prohibit them. Again, popularity is not the goal.

- Administrators and teachers, if you have school rules, enforce them at all times. Children learn quickly that inconsistency means they can do whatever they want. If they are not expected to suffer the consequences of their decisions, they will never learn this important life lesson.

- Stop making excuses for bad behavior, bad grades, and bad habits. Again, consequences are key.

- Demand laws that protect our children and return our schools to safety. Cut programs that perpetuate the myth that has developed that more and more programs will help children who are unable to abide by established school procedures when in actuality, despite the fact that our schools are overflowing with programs, the violence has only gotten worse.

- Children should see the adults in their lives resolving conflicts and struggles through measures other than violence. It has often been said that children learn what they live. They need to learn the skill of confronting difficult issues and dealing with them in a healthy manner.

- The 2 As and the L: Attention, Affection, and Love. These should be constants in our children's lives.

No more Band-Aids, no more psychoanalysis, no more deaths. It is in our power to change what has happened within our schools. It is within our power to say NO MORE. It is within our power to demand and participate in change.

But will we?

REFERENCES

As we see it (2001). *The Monitor*, May 19.

Bozell, L. Brent III (2001). The culture makes a killing. *http://www.parentstv.org/publications/lbbcolumns/2001/col20010320.html.* March.

Education legislation; House passes character program bill (2001). *The Monitor*, April 4.

Eminem (2000). The way I am. *Marshall Mathers LP.* Interscope Records.

Ever been bullied? Nationwide survey shows problem widespread among students (2001). *The Monitor*, April 25.

Federal Trade Commission (2000). Marketing violent entertainment to children: A review of self-regulation and industry practices in the motion picture, music recording, and electronic game industries. *http://www.ftc.gov/os/2000/09/violencerpttest.htm.* September.

Hymowitz, Kay S. (2001). Parenting: The lost art. *American Educator, 25* (Spring), 6.

Mabin, Connie (2002). "Teacher shortage may take years to solve, panel told," *The Monitor*, June 19, 2002.

Manson, Marilyn (1998). Fundamentally loathsome. *Mechanical Animals.* Nothing/Interscope Records.

McAllen Independent School District (2000–2001). *Student Code of Conduct,* 4.

Media Marketing Accountability Act. (2001). *http:www.senate.gov/~lieberman/press/01/04/2001426632.html.* April.

Nack, William, & Munson, Lester (2001). Losing it. *Reader's Digest,* (January), 63.

National Home Education Research Institute (1998). Facts on home schooling. *http://www.nheri.org/98/research/general.html.*

Nutting, Jim, & Nutting, Lorena (2001). Personal interview. McAllen, Texas, May.

Slayer (1986). Altar of sacrifice. *Reign in Blood.* Sony/Columbia.

Teaching character; job should fall to parents as well (2001). *The Monitor*, April 12.

9

School Violence
from the Administrator's
Perspective

This chapter is designed to give the reader samples of concerns coming from the offices of superintendents in school districts. The chapter, organizationally different from the others in this book, presents several topics that come directly under the jurisdiction of the chief administrative officer of the district. These public administrators are responsible for the entire district organization. Their view is holistic. It is their job to contemplate issues and functions that encompass the total school district—all schools, grade schools, mid-level schools, and high schools. These articles are from the pages of the journal of the American Association of School Administrators and reveal some of the complex issues faced by school administrators.

The first article, "Safeguarding Rights, Minimizing Exposure," deals with the subjects of student rights of procedural due process and substantive due process. Both processes are guaranteed by the Fourteenth Amendment of the U.S. Constitution and interpreted by courts nationwide. A wide range of diverse student interests is presented within the context of procedural due process. Public schools, when disciplining a student, are holding an administrative hearing. A full range of protective procedures is not required in these types of hearings. However, the basic necessities to be afforded are a fair hearing, notice of that hearing, and an impartial tribunal. Substantive due process requires that the substance of school rules that place personal restraints on students do not violate constitutional principles. Dean Essex does an excellent job of presenting these subjects in a straightforward and commonsense manner.

"How Safe Are Your Schools?" is the question the second article poses. With these words as a headline, the article almost becomes required reading for all those in the elementary/secondary school community. In the wake of a school shooting tragedy, Superintendent Stetzner lays out the safety team, the causes, and the response. With action, education, and problem solving, her school district has responded to the question with a comprehensive program. This is must reading for those who think, "It can't happen here."

Profiling students to help identify "bad apples" is the subject of "The Perils of Profiling." The authors begin with an objective discussion of profiling, but quickly develop a good deal of negativism about its prospects. This article makes a number of valid points and is worthwhile reading. It is presented as a balance between those who argue for using this tool and those who are afraid of the ramifications related to the typecasting of young people.

Could school violence be reduced and school safety enhanced through the design and construction of a different kind of school building? In "Building Security into Schools," school architectural and design specialists discuss elements necessary in building some safety features into the school building of the future. Concepts such as safer sites, security technology, monitoring equipment, educating students, and cost effectiveness are discussed. The authors conclude that, with a little extra planning and attention to details of safety considerations, it is possible to construct and operate a safer physical structure.

Is a certified, gun-carrying police officer in your school's future? The article "School Security: A Resident Cop Can Improve School Climate," summarizing the experience from one New Hampshire school district, is instructive. The school board goes from minority support for such a concep, to unanimity in a year and a half of experience. Hiring an officer with the "right stuff" was the key for this district. Students, principals, teachers, and staff are greatly satisfied to have this "resource officer" on campus. The good news is that this program is an unqualified success; there is no bad news.

Finally, from rural America, "Rural Schools: Alternative Schooling for Troubled Youth in Rural Communities" shows how the twenty-first century has arrived there. Alternative education for students with discipline problems and those students who need help outside the traditional academic setting are discussed from the most "agricultural county in Ohio." A discussion of problem identification leads to the development of community backing, the organization of a flexible program, and an evaluation of its effectiveness.

Safeguarding Rights, Minimizing Exposure

Nathan L. Essex

How far can school officials go to protect students and others from possible harm when disruptive or violent behavior erupts on school grounds? Can penalties be imposed on students who threaten the safety of others when such penalties might be viewed as a violation of their individual rights?

The School Administrator, June 1999, pp. 18–21.

And what legal consequences might school district face for failure to act when it is foreseeable that injury may result from serious misconduct?

School officials have a moral and legal duty to preserve the safety and well-being of all students, while not trampling on the constitutional rights of students involved in disruptive behavior. When violent acts occur on school campuses nationwide, officials tend to act swiftly and aggressively, sometimes too swiftly and aggressively, without proper consideration regarding the constitutional rights of students.

In light of the recent tragedy in Littleton, Colo., I can provide 10 guidelines to school administrators who wish to provide safe schools without violating the constitutional rights of disruptive students. While courts allow school administrators broad discretion in handling students whose behavior poses a threat to the safety of others, especially in school environments that have been plagued with incidents of violence or serious acts of misconduct, school officials must act responsibly. They must resist the temptation to act too aggressively when the situation does not warrant such a response.

DEFENSIBLE POLICIES

- No. 1: Be certain administrative actions are based on well-developed and legally defensible school district policies.

    The recent federal district court of appeals case, *M.K.V. v. School Board of Brevard County* [sic. The title of this case is *M.K. v. School Board of Brevard County*. It may be found at: 708 So.2d 340, Fla. App. LEXIS 3750; 23 Fla. Law W. D. 935 (1998). It is from the Florida State Court of Appeals, Fifth Circuit; not a federal case.] illustrates what can happen if a policy statement is not explicit and officials attempt to expand the coverage of a policy that lacks sufficient specificity.

    A middle school in Florida enforced a student discipline policy prohibiting students from disrupting classes, distracting others, damaging school property or threatening and endangering the safety of other students. Telephone pagers, firearms and weapons also were banned under this policy. Students were prohibited from carrying dangerous weapons on school property or during school events. Failure to abide by this policy constituted grounds for expulsion. A student was expelled by the school board for possession of eight bullets on the school bus.

    At the hearing, no evidence was presented indicating the student had exhibited disruptive behavior on the bus. He had, based on the assistant principal's testimony, created disruption on school grounds. The student was expelled and later appealed the board's decision to the district court of appeals. Arguing that he should not be found guilty of violating the school's policy because bullets are not deemed weapons, he further claimed that no one had been injured by his conduct.

    The court held for the student in stating that the policy only referred to pagers, weapons and firearms. Moreover, there was no evidence the student had attempted to use the bullets in any manner. The court reversed and remanded the board's expulsion decision.

- No. 2: To the fullest degree possible, make certain that policy statements are as explicit as possible in identifying serious infractions that will result in suspension, expulsion or other forms of punishment.

    Student should know specific infractions that will result in disciplinary action. Consequences should be linked with certain misbehaviors. For example, students should know that fighting will result in suspension.

    It may be helpful to classify the various infractions by categories or levels from less serious to more serious and identify the specific disciplinary action associated with each infraction. This procedure will ensure that students are aware of consequences for violation of school rules. While this approach likely will minimize misunderstandings among students, rule violations should still be carefully explained in instances where students charged with infractions indicate they are unaware of the policy violation in question. Providing information to students in these situations is consistent with fundamental fairness.

PARENT UNDERSTANDING

- No. 3: Take steps to ensure that students and parents are knowledgeable of policies regarding improper student behavior and the consequences of such behavior.

    Students and parents must understand what is expected in the schools. Students should not be expected to conform to rules that are vague or ambiguous in interpretation or meaning. They should not be placed in the position of having to guess at the meaning of these rules.

    School officials should set aside an adequate period of time once or twice a year for teachers to review disciplinary policies with students to increase their understanding of what is expected of them. Opportunities also should be provided for students to seek clarification on any policy, rule or regulation that they do not fully understand.

    Once policies, rules and regulations have been sufficiently reviewed with students, they should be sent to parents for review and verification that they have been read and understood. School officials should be available to clarify any concerns raised by parents during this process.

- No. 4: The gravity of the situation and the immediate need to act should determine appropriate administrative actions in disciplinary matters.

    Obviously, some infractions committed by students are not as serious as others. School officials should resist the tendency to move too quickly in cases involving minor infractions. Officials should ask themselves if the offense is one that is clearly punishable based on policy. Is it a first offense or does it reflect a pattern of misbehavior? Did the infraction create material or substantial disruption or a threat to safety? Did it result in disrespect for authority? These are but a few examples of questions that should be raised as school officials attempt to respond to disciplinary matters.

    If a student's actions create disruption, gross disrespect for authority or a threat to safety, then immediate and swift disciplinary action is warranted. In all cases, officials should rely on approved school policies and procedures for guidance and direction to insure that due process occurs.

- No. 5: Minimal due process should always be provided for students facing short-term suspension.

    Short-term suspension involves suspension of 10 days or less as defined by the U.S. Supreme Court in the landmark *Goss v. Lopez* [419 U.S. 565 (1975)] case. Students facing short-term suspension must be provided a fair and impartial hearing.

    They also must be informed of the charges brought against them and given an opportunity to respond to these charges.

    Officials must be mindful that students have a property interest in attending public schools. The school district may not withdraw this right to attend on grounds of misconduct absent fundamentally fair procedures to determine if misconduct occurred. The court ruled in *Goss* that students facing short-term suspensions from school not exceeding 10 days (thereby facing a loss of protected property interest) must be given some form of notice and afforded some type of hearing.

DUE PROCESS

- No. 6: A violation of either substantive or procedural due process will result in a violation of student's 14th Amendment rights.

    School officials must recognize that due process involves both dimensions mentioned above. Consequently, they must be certain that their actions are not in conflict with either procedural or substantive requirements.

    Officials meet procedural concerns when they follow prescribed constitutional steps in matters involving student discipline to ensure fundamental fairness. Substantive concerns are met when officials can demonstrate that they had a valid reason to take necessary administrative action against the student. They also must demonstrate that the methods they used during disciplinary proceedings were reasonable.

    Many administrative decisions involving student disciplinary matters have been correct in substance but overturned later by the courts based on grounds that procedural requirements were not met. Conversely, procedural requirements have been met in many disciplinary cases while substantive requirements were not. In both instances officials have not been supported by the courts.

- No. 7: In loco parentis is not a license to treat students in an arbitrary and capricious manner. Students are entitled to 14th Amendment protections.

    While in loco parentis gives school officials latitude to exert authority over students under their supervision, it is not a license to act in an arbitrary or capricious manner. The constitutional rights of students must be respected. The exercise of in loco parentis is limited to school matters involving academics and discipline. Areas outside of these two are reserved to parents.

    Neither school officials nor teachers fully occupy the place of parents because they do not have the natural affection that parents hold for their children.

Simply stated, in loco parentis requires prudence on the part of school personnel to ensure their actions are consistent with those that the average parent would exercise under similar circumstances. Usually when administrative actions conform to this standard, they are considered reasonable. Reasonable administrative actions are almost always supported by the courts.

We all are aware that students are subject to reasonable rules governing their behavior. But we also know that they enjoy personal rights and freedoms that must be recognized and respected. Students are entitled to fundamental fairness and equal protection guarantees of the 14th Amendment.

- No. 8: Failure to respond to threats by one student to another may result in liability charges if the student against whom the threat is made received bodily harm.

    Threats made by students to other students always should be taken seriously especially in light of the perception that school violence is increasing. When school officials or teachers are informed of a possible threat, they must take appropriate and immediate steps to prevent the threat from being carried out. Failure to respond to threats that result in injury to another student may create serious personal liability. For example, if a student is injured by another student based on a threat where the evidence reveals that school personnel knew of the threat and failed to act, it may be difficult to escape liability charges based on the fact that the injury was likely foreseeable.

    The recent tragedy in Littleton might have been avoided if school officials had been informed of threats made by troubled students and had taken appropriate steps to investigate the claims.

    School officials and teachers have a duty to foresee that students may be harmed under certain circumstances. Once determined, they must act swiftly to protect students from harm. This action must be taken even if a threatened student is not under the direct supervision of a particular teacher. Knowledge of possible harm to students is the key that should trigger the need for appropriate action by school personnel.

- No. 9: A reasonable exercise of administrative authority will pass court scrutiny.

    School officials who act in a reasonable and prudent manner will receive less scrutiny by the courts. While we all recognize that school officials have broad discretion in establishing rules governing student behavior in school, their powers, however, are not absolute. They are subject to the standard of reasonableness.

    Rules generally are considered reasonable when they are necessary to maintain proper order, decorum and a peaceful school environment so that teaching and learning can occur. The test used by the courts to determine enforceability of school rules is whether there is a sufficient justification by school officials of the need to enforce the policy, rule or regulation in the first place. The reasonableness of a rule cannot be decided in the abstract but rather in the context of application.

- No. 10: School officials always should be guided by fundamental fairness and a regard for the individual rights of all students in disciplinary cases.

Since students are afforded many of the same constitutional rights as adults, it is important that their rights be protected. The Supreme Court's *Tinker v. Des Moines Independent Community* [sic] *School District* [393 U.S. 503] in 1969 reminded all of us that students do not shed their constitutional rights at the schoolhouse door. We should treat students fairly not because the courts mandate it but because it is the right thing to do.

We always must strive to model fairness in our dealing with students in all disciplinary matters. This means that a sufficient effort should be made to gather all facts surrounding each disciplinary case, including the student's side of the issues, and carefully weigh all facts before any punishment is contemplated. The seriousness of the situation, the student's past record of behavior and the urgency to act should be carefully considered prior to taking disciplinary action. When these steps are taken, students are assured of a fair hearing and a fair administrative decision, and school officials will have met their goal of ensuring fundamental fairness to all students, which is what really matters.

How Safe Are Your Schools?

Kate Stetzner

I was the principal of Margaret Leary Elementary School on April 11, 1994, when a 10-year-old brought a .22 semi-automatic handgun to school and killed Jeremy Bullock, a 5th grader. At the time, Jeremy was the youngest student in the United States to be murdered at a school.

The tragedy served as a terrible wake-up call not only to Butte, Montana, but to the rest of the nation. After each subsequent fatal school-based shooting, including the most recent in Littleton, Colorado, communities have issued a common refrain: "We didn't think that could happen here."

In Butte, we were left wondering how a community could be nursed back to health after such a sudden and violent schoolyard calamity. We also needed to learn how secondary victims could receive caring support and long-term rehabilitation for post-traumatic stress.

We looked for solutions that would address the multifaceted problems wrought by the homicide and that would allow students, teachers and the entire school community to move on with their lives.

A SAFETY TEAM

Our school district's initial step was to create a school-based safety team. The team, consisting of individuals from child service agencies, teachers, counselors, parents, law enforcement, the county attorney's office and the faith community, focused on crisis debriefing, children at risk of troubled behavior and restoring the school to some measure of normalcy.

The School Administrator, June 1999, pp. 22–23.

This interagency group continues to meet on a weekly basis to discuss crisis procedures and operational safety.

We discovered immediate crisis debriefing in the hours after a serious act of violence to be an absolute must. Ideally, this debriefing should be conducted by someone who is trained in critical incidence work. In Butte, I filled that role, having been trained years earlier by Community Intervention, a Minnesota-based training organization that deals with crisis management.

I immediately gave notice to fellow team members that I needed assistance and at least 40 counselors, law enforcement officers and school board members responded from throughout the state. Teachers and other school staff needed firsthand information of how to deal with traumatized children and, more importantly, how to get the classroom back to "normal" as quickly as possible.

The tragedy propelled our community into action. Ultimately, these efforts have gained national attention for our district, and I have been privileged to serve on several national school safety committees. In April 1998, I was appointed to a presidential task force to study the causes of youth violence and discuss preventive measures that could be shared with educational leaders and others nationwide. Ironically, the school shooting in Springfield, Oregon, last spring occurred on the first day of the task force's inaugural meeting.

ANALYZING CAUSES

That first meeting of the Presidential Task Force on Youth Violence, hosted by Attorney General Janet Reno and her legal staff, focused on analyzing the causes of violence in the schools. Three key questions were raised:

- Is there a trend between recent school shootings?
- What can the federal government do to help schools deal with gun violence?
- What commonalities were present in the recent school shootings?

As we reviewed the most serious schoolyard shooting incidents of the 1997–98 year, the common factors about the perpetrators emerged rather quickly:

- All were boys;
- Each shooting was over a relationship problem;
- All had experienced childhood depression;
- About 85 percent had been sexually or physically molested.

Subsequently, the task force was invited to the White House to meet with the president and his cabinet for a roundtable discussion on school violence. During a three-hour meeting the president listened intently to the task force's recommendation for federal funding for early prevention and intervention programs in schools.

It was clear to me that our federal leaders are beginning to understand the need for early intervention programs at the local level in our elementary schools, as well as after-school problems and holistic services for students today.

BUTTE'S COMPREHENSIVE TACK ON VIOLENCE PREVENTION

Five years after the fatal shooting of a 5th-grade pupil at school, the Butte Public Schools have not relinquished their violence prevention efforts.

In fact, just a few days before tragedy struck Columbine High School in Littleton, Colorado, Margaret Leary Elementary School in our district was selected as one of 10 schools in the nation for a site visit by the U.S. Department of Education's School Safety Recognition Program. The department is recognizing us for the comprehensive leadership role we have taken, working cooperatively with other community agencies, to deal with childhood depression, the access to weapons by youngsters and creative approaches to keep our children safe.

Many of these initiatives started soon after the tragedy. Others have been added more recently.

The No. 1 target this year in our 5,000-student district is reducing student truancy. The school district attendance officer and the elementary school resource officer make home visits as often as necessary when children are unexcused from school for more than five days. These officers work closely with the county attorney's office, which aggressively pursues fines against parents who fail to send their children to school. We also provide mentors to these families to work on parenting skills.

The key features of school safety in Butte are the following:

- A child study team intervenes with at-risk children, who have been referred by their teachers. The intervention involves the child and the family. This is a critical component of the school safety team.

- Crisis drills, intruder drills and other safety-related exercises are practiced consistently throughout the year.

- All school counselors in Butte now teach the Second Step School Anti-Violence Curriculum to children in grades K–6.

- Conflict resolution groups allow children to be part of the Peer Patrol, and parents conduct schoolyard conflict facilitation groups.

- An after-school daycare program, running from 3 to 6 p.m. daily, has been instituted.

- Bus stop patrollers have received training. Patrollers are women enrolled in the Career Futures Program for welfare recipients who wish to learn job skills.

- A model alternative education program for K–3 is in its second year. This program, funded by the state education agency and the Board of Crime Control, targets children who exhibit severe behavioral problems in the regular classroom setting. The children are taught how to behave properly before they are returned to the regular classroom.

- School resource officers have been hired for the high school and middle school.

- A review panel for our zero tolerance policy for weapons on school grounds was developed. This process allows families to plead on a case-by-case basis, leading to alternative education or early re-entry for students who are expelled for 365 days.

- VISTA volunteers working districtwide in mentoring programs, and volunteers from the Foster Grandparent program and Big Brothers and Big Sisters are paired with at-risk children in grade K–6. These mentors receive training before being matched with a teacher and students.
- Parent Academies and Parent Resource Centers are being opened in the elementary schools. Mothers are being encouraged to learn parenting skills, work with their children, learn how to read and become part of the educational process.
- Legislative lobbying to support the new gun laws, reduce access to guns by children and demand blended sentencing for youth offenders that includes rehabilitation with accountability. We also seek increased funding for school-based services at the local level, for work with at-risk, violent children and for health care for these children.
- Through a partnership with Western Montana College, we make graduate-level college courses available to school administrators, teachers and student teachers through which they can learn how to detect violent behavior, find resources to deal with violent children and learn how to develop conflict resolution skills, classroom management skills and crises planning procedures.

The Perils of Profiling

Gil-Patricia Fey/J. Ron Nelson/Maura L. Roberts

A 1993 report by the American Psychological Association on violent youth cast an enticing initiation to consider the issue of student profiling when it stated: "Our schools and communities can intervene effectively in the lives of children and youth to reduce or prevent their involvement in violence. Violence involving youth is not random, uncontrollable or inevitable."

Today, under considerable pressure to demonstrate they are taking every possible action to ensure safety at schools in their communities, school leaders are turning to what they see as a promising prevention tool formally reserved for criminal investigations—student profiling.

However, identifying students at risk of committing violence through the use of checklists of personal characteristics and behaviors is a strategy accompanied by plenty of unanswered questions, recognized weaknesses and serious implications for implementation. Deciding whether to profile elementary and secondary school students is a decision not to be made lightly.

TWO TYPES

Criminal investigators and criminologists in the United States have used profiling since 1969 when the Federal Bureau of Investigation introduced it as an investigative strategy. Law enforcers view a profile as a "set of behavioral indicators forming a very characteristic pattern of actions or emotions that tend to point to a particular condition," according to Brent Turvey, a criminal profiler and partner in a forensics firm in Corpus Christi, Texas. To arrive at the characteristics that comprise a specific profile, a person's behavior is compared to case studies and evidence from other profiles.

Despite its use over the past several decades, Turvey says criminal profiling is beset by several unresolved issues. These include lack of agreement regarding the basic information that a profile should account for, the appropriate uses of profiling, ethical and unethical conduct by profilers and whether the profiling process should be peer reviewed. These serious questions should give pause to educational leaders considering the use of profiling in schools.

Essentially, two types of profiling exist: inductive and deductive criminal profiling.

In inductive profiling, the profiler looks for patterns in the available data and infers possible outcomes—in the case of schools, possible acts of violence committed by students who fit the pattern. The strategy is used to predict behavior and apprehend potential offenders before they commit a crime. In criminology, inductive profiles include formal and informal studies of incarcerated criminals and public data sources, such as news media reports. General profiles, which can be assembled quickly, include general characteristics on a one- or two-page list.

However, the use of inductive profiling carries serious implications. First, the generalizations that are made to construct the profile stem from limited and often very small population samples. Inductive profiles also only take into account the characteristics of apprehended offenders and neglect offenders who are at large. Characteristics of non-apprehended offenders are likely to be missing from profiles.

Another problem is that behavior and motivations are assumed to be constant over time in inductive profiling. For violence prediction among children, this assumption neglects the very nature of changes in children's behavior during their development process over time.

The second method, deductive profiling, interprets forensic evidence from a crime to reconstruct behavior patterns, deduce offender characteristics, demographics, emotions and motivations.

Anyone who has read Sherlock Holmes stories by Arthur Conan Doyle has encountered deductive profiling. Holmes uses physical evidence, gut feelings and his work experience to deduce profile of the criminal. Deductive profiling requires great skill and considerable effort.

Most FBI profiling is deductive in nature. However, while an offender for a particular crime might be identified successfully, deductive profiling cannot serve as a reliable base for generalizations and identifications of other offenders. Several researchers have pointed out repeatedly that a review of profiling use by the FBI clearly shows it is appropriate only for specific crimes and cases.

DISCOURAGING EVIDENCE

Would either profiling strategy be a useful tool for school leaders to use in identifying students prone to violence? Do we have a reliable knowledge base to apply either inductive or deductive profiling as a strategy in schools?

Could the crimes committed by the youths in Littleton, Jonesboro and Springfield have been predicted with the use of inductive profiling? Did we have previous incidents in other schools that pointed undoubtedly to the occurrence of these tragedies or allowed the construction of a profile that would have identified the students involved in the incidents?

The FBI already has applied deductive profiling to an analysis of the last six multiple-fatality shootings on school grounds to generate a list of common characteristics found among the perpetrators. Yet the federal investigators admit they aren't yet prepared to construct a general behavioral profile that could be used to identify students at risk of committing violent acts.

Evidence about past profiling use in law enforcement is not encouraging. In the 1985 book, *Mass Murder: America's Growing Menace*, authors Jack Levin and James Fox examine a survey of police agencies that had used profiling in traffic violations. The survey found profiles helpful in only 17 percent of the cases that were solved. Even highly regarded criminal profilers admit that profiling can fail miserably when it is done without expertise, facts or caution.

BEHAVIORAL LISTS

Despite the lack of evidence about its efficacy, profiling seems to remain popular with police authorities and more recently has been promoted by the U.S. Department of Education and the National School Safety Center, a resource organization in Westlake Village, Calif., funded partly by the U.S. Department of Justice. [See Chapter 1 of this book.]

Profile lists already exist and are readily accessible to school leaders. In 1998, the U.S. Department of Education published "Early Warning, Timely Response: A Guide to Safe Schools." The guide includes a profile in the form of a checklist of early warning signs to help administrators identify youth at risk for violent behavior and actions. The NSSC published in 1998 its "Checklist of Characteristics of Youth Who Have Caused School-Associated Violent Deaths." [That table is reproduced here.]

Profiling Lists of Violent Student's Characteristics

U.S. Department of Education	*National School Safety Center*
1. Social withdrawal	1. History of tantrums and uncontrollable angry outbursts.
2. Excessive feelings of isolation and being alone	2. Characteristically resorts to name calling, cursing or abusive language
3. Excessive feelings of rejection	3. Habitually makes violent threats when angry
4. Being a victim of violence	4. Previously brought a weapon to school
5. Feelings of being picked on and disciplinary persecuted	5. Background of serious problems at school and in the community
6. Low school interest and poor academic performance	6. Background of drug, alcohol or other substance abuse or dependency

Profiling Lists of Violent Student's Characteristics (continued)

U.S. Department of Education	*National School Safety Center*
7. Expression of violence in writings and drawings	7. On the fringe of his/her peer group with few or no close friends
8. Uncontrolled anger	8. Preoccupied with weapons, explosives or other incendiary devices
9. History of discipline problems	9. Has previously been truant, suspended or expelled from school
10. Past history of violent and aggressive behavior	10. Displays cruelty toward animals
11. Intolerance for differences and prejudicial attitudes	11. Little or no supervision and support from parents and caring adults
12. Drug use and alcohol use	12. Witnessed or been a victim of abuse or neglect in the home
13. Inappropriate access to, possession and use of firearms	13. Has been bullied and/or bullies/intimidates peers of younger children
14. Serious threats of violence	14. Tends to blame others for difficulties and problems s/he causes her/himself
	15. Constantly prefers TV shows, movies or music expressing violent themes and acts
	16. Prefers reading materials dealing with violent themes, rituals and abuse
	17. Reflects anger, frustration and the dark side of life in school essays or writing projects
	18. Involved with a gang or an antisocial group on the fringe of acceptance
	19. Often depressed and/or has signifcant mood swings
	20. Threatened or attempted suicide

Sources: 'Early Warning, Timely Response: A Guide to Safe Schools,' U.S. Department of Education; 'Checklist of Characteristics of Youth Who Have Caused School-Associated Violent Deaths,' National School Safety Center, 1998.

Close inspection reveals the two lists are inconsistent and greatly diverge from one another. A point-by-point comparison shows they have only six points in common and differ on the majority of characteristics. This leaves school administrators with the daunting task of deciding which list to use and suggests little empirical evidence is available to make this task any easier or defensible in a court of law.

Another problem with the lists is the ambiguity of some items. Are such phrases as "excessive feelings of rejection," "tends to blame others" and "is on the fringe" measurable and indeed identifiable? In addition, many characteristics could be detected only in a setting where the teachers know their students as well as their own flesh and blood. How, for instance, does a high school teacher with a student load of 150 or more know the youngster's preferences in TV shows, movies, music and reading materials? How does a teacher know whether the child's experiences outside of school include access to firearms, witnessing of violence and animal cruelty?

In an ideal world teachers would know their students this well. Perhaps the answer for school leaders lies in restructuring large school populations and class sizes to personalize students' experiences rather than turning to profiling.

In addition, both lists include cautionary statements that further underscore their problematic nature and weakness. The Department of Education publication acknowledges as much: "There is a real danger that early warning signs will be misinterpreted." There is a real danger that school professionals using the checklist will wrongfully identify students as potential offenders. Similarly, the National School Safety Center claims: "There is no foolproof system for identifying potentially dangerous students who may harm themselves and/or others." Yet the checklists are described as a promising starting point.

The ambiguity of the checklists is reflected in the lack of specific instructions for their use. For instance, how many of the warning signs and to what degree must a child exhibit them to be conclusively identified as a future violent offender?

Possibly most troubling is the potential to discriminate against certain groups of students and label and alienate children from other children and educators, thus producing consequences that are undesirable and unbearable in many ways. School leaders will have to decide whether they are willing to accept the risks associated with the use of these checklists. They also must decide whether schools are to become places where criminal investigative methods are part of the daily regimen.

POLICY IMPLICATIONS

The implementation of profiling at schools will carry several implications for school policies and practices in three interrelated areas: provision of special services; school suspensions and expulsions; student rights and privacy laws.

- *Special services*

    Special services will be in demand as students are identified through profiling as being at risk for committing violence. Will the children identified as being at risk receive all their instruction apart from the other children or will intervention programs be integrated into the regular school day for these youngsters? What will the interaction between these children and the other children in the school look like? What demands will be placed on school personnel, and will they be given the necessary training?

- *School suspensions and expulsions*

    Suspensions and expulsions will become two more prominent alternative strategies to deal with the students identified to be at risk for violence. School leaders will have to decide whether youngsters who exhibit the behavioral characteristics described in the profile would benefit from the exclusion from the education process or become more likely to commit violent acts if they are excluded from the school.

- *Student rights and privacy laws*

   School leaders are sure to confront questions about rights of individuals under a system of student profiling. Stereotyping, discrimination and the wrongful identification of potential perpetrators are ethically unjustified, even if the intention is to protect children from harm.

   Student privacy rights are likely to be trampled through the use of profiling. School authorities could face legal action, as well as negative media attention, once a student is wrongfully identified as being at risk for committing violence.

   Will the kind of privacy invasion that profiling would bring with it be justifiable? Can we ensure no harm will be inflicted on children who are exposed to these procedures?

BEYOND PRAGMATISM

School leaders face difficult decisions about how best to prevent violence in response to the clamor from parents, politicians and public. With the existence of profiling lists, such as the ones in circulation from the Department of Education and the National School Safety Center, profiling appears to be an easy-to-use strategy that is at the fingertips of school leaders.

   The decision to use profiling reaches beyond pragmatic implementation issues and touches on the very core of what schools should and will look like. Its use carries serious implications. Profiling can be justified neither by deferring to a climate of public pressure nor by employing it as an emergency response to heightened concerns by parents and public about school safety.

   We need to keep searching for strategies that constitute more than a Band-Aid to a deep wound. If profiles were the solution to violence prevention, all prisoners would be guilty, all crimes would be solved and all future crimes would be prevented.

Building Security into Schools

John E. Kosar and S. Faruq Ahmed

   It's a terrible truism today that children in fear cannot learn, and teachers who are on guard against violence in their classrooms cannot impart a love for the lesson at the same time. But how do we ensure safety without turning schools into virtual prisons in the name of security?

   School buildings should provide a warm and inviting environment that stimulates learning and development. However, with school safety concerns intensifying nationwide, architects and school administrators are concluding that while schools should not operate as secure fortresses, school building design must integrate security functions into remodeling and new construction plans.

The School Administrator, February 2000, pp. 24–26.

DESIGNING SAFER SITES

Research on school building design and safety has led to the development of security systems and technologies that not only make schools safe and nurturing places, but also reduce operating costs associated with traditional precautions. For example:

- When planning a school design, exterior doors should be secured with hardware that is unobtrusive and does not affect the aesthetic of the environment. School entrances and doorways must create a positive and welcoming first impression, while at the same time incorporating appropriate and necessary security devices, such as locking mechanisms, intercoms and access-card readers.

- Areas that house computers, other expensive equipment and important records require special safety planning, and designs must allow for additional security equipment on all doors in these areas. Furthermore, a building designed with a proper air-conditioning system ensures that windows and doors are kept shut, thus minimizing the potential for transferring objects through such openings.

- Pay phones, restrooms and stairwells all are potential security problems. Pay phones should be installed sparingly in schools, either within the range of a closed-circuit television camera or in a location where faculty and staff easily can observe them.

No easy answer exists for restroom security, although some school building designers are choosing the more costly approach of small restrooms within each classroom. For traditional restrooms in school hallways, students should be provided with a way to report suspicious activity anonymously. Because stairwells are difficult spaces to observe and can present serious security hazards, we recommend single-floor school buildings where possible.

SECURITY TECHNOLOGY

According to the 1996–97 National Center for Education Statistics report, "Violence and Discipline Problems in U.S. Public Schools," 4 percent of schools perform random metal detector checks on students. While the use of metal detectors may help calm public concerns, a few pieces of security equipment alone will not solve the problem. This equipment is most effective as one element of a broad-based safety and security plan, which would include some or all of the following:

- Closed-circuit television cameras are the most cost-effective form of surveillance for educational facilities. Costs have decreased rapidly in recent years, while capabilities have increased. Although some areas are difficult to monitor, every attempt should be made to use cameras to observe all public corridors, stairwells and exterior doors as well as the cafeteria and gymnasium during school hours and public use in the evening or on weekends.

These cameras are an important addition to security for playgrounds, school bus dropoff areas, parking lots and school grounds. The perimeter of the school property, including the playground, should be posted for no trespassing, and students on the playground should be supervised carefully.

- Door security hardware in school buildings with generators allows doors to be fastened with electromagnetic locks, which require minimal maintenance and hold doors closed with a force of either 600 lbs. or 1,200 lbs.

Schools that do not use emergency generators may want to consider electric strike mechanisms. In the event of a power outage that shuts down an electric door entry system, electric strike mechanisms allow people to exit the building freely, but permit entrance only with a key, thus keeping intruders out even when the electric-door system is not functioning properly.

- Electronic security panels should be installed to monitor doorways. Door hardware is connected to these panels, which are networked and connected to a security control console that records all alarms and is monitored by in-house security personnel or transferred to an off-site monitoring facility after hours.

- ID cards should be issued to all teachers and staff, and access cards should be issued to faculty and staff who require after-hours entrance to certain parts of the building. Access cards, frequently used in hotels and office buildings, are electronically or magnetically encoded to open doors for designated users and can monitor and track who entered which rooms and when the entry took place.

Though inexpensive magnetic-stripe cards are most common, they are easy to duplicate and, therefore, not secure. Weigand Technology cards, however, use fixed-foil patterns in their construction, are inexpensive and are virtually impossible to duplicate.

- Metal detectors, when used in conjunction with a carefully thought-out security plan, can prevent contraband materials from being brought into the building, but each fixed metal detector costs about $4,000 and requires three people to operate it. Detectors at only one entrance are ineffective when there are many other areas where metallic material may pass through. Hand-held metal detectors for case-by-case usage often are a better investment.

- Panic buttons, telephones and intercoms are contingents of many school security systems. Schools have installed inconspicuous panic buttons in teachers' desks and use two-way intercoms connected to the school office.

Panic buttons can be wired into either the security or the phone system. Some schools also provide teachers with an internal "911-only" telephone. Doors equipped with card readers also may include intercoms and video cameras.

MONITORING EQUIPMENT

Security centers should be installed to allow all closed-circuit TV cameras, access systems and door intercoms to terminate in one centralized place. The security center should be a comfortable, adequately staffed room near the school office. Since the purpose of an on-site security center is to investigate all suspicious activities, security personnel must not be responsible for any other duties in the school.

In smaller school buildings, one trained security guard must monitor video cameras and alarms while two more provide routine patrol and incident followup. However, larger schools with many cameras may require a larger monitoring staff.

According to "Indicators of School Crime and Safety," a 1998 study published by the National Center for Education Statistics and the Bureau of Justice Statistics, students in the 12–14 age group are most likely to experience violent crime at school. In addition, a report issued by the North Carolina Department of Public Instruction in 1998 indicated that disproportionately more violent incidents are reported at the state's largest schools, regardless of grade level, and that the incidence was greatest at high schools of 1,500 students or more.

A single person can be expected to effectively monitor no more than eight pictures from closed-circuit cameras at one time on a continuous basis. During after-school hours, the monitoring of building security functions may be transferred to an outside security company.

Video monitoring systems can display camera pictures and record them on a time-lapse recorder. After hours, the system can be programmed to check for changes in the picture. If more than a certain number of pixels change in a picture, an alarm sounds, and the picture can be remotely transmitted to the off-site monitoring facility that dispatches response teams.

EDUCATING STUDENTS

Ideally, students and staff should fully understand the security functions that are in place. It's also important to establish penalties for tampering with security equipment, setting off false alarms and making security threats.

According to the NCES, most schools have zero-tolerance policies toward such serious student offenses. Many also mandate predetermined consequences and penalties against students who make threats or tamper with security equipment.

School districts also are forming security committees of parents, teachers, students and volunteers to discuss security challenges and develop plans of action. Some have established telephone hotlines through which students, parents and faculty can report threats and concerns anonymously.

Teachers and administrators also must be made aware of their legal obligations and liabilities. False security equipment never should be used as a deterrent because it does not deter incidents and is a major liability if something does occur.

COST EFFECTIVENESS

School security has suffered in the past from lack or adequate staffing and inadequate monitoring, lack of oversight, poorly trained security staff, under-reporting of incidents and several other problems. However, incidents can be minimized through the adoption of measures that are parts of a comprehensive security plan. Ideally, careful planning for security should start with the school building design/renovation, when the security considerations can be most cost-effectively incorporated into the buildings.

But the basic point of all this planning is simple yet critical: One student injured or killed in a school is one too many.

School Security: A Resident Cop Can Improve School Climate

Raymond Yeagley

My school board wasn't convinced we needed a police presence in the Rochester, NH schools. When we first took up the idea, only five of the 13 board members supported it, and some of them were rather lukewarm in their support.

Some opponents feared we would turn our schools into a "police state" or "gulag." Others were uncomfortable in thinking that assigning a uniformed officer would represent the first step toward changing the face of our schools when Rochester hadn't been plagued with gang activity or any other significant safety problem.

But after more than six months of emotional debate, the school board established a school resource officer program in partnership with the Rochester Police Department. That was nearly 18 months ago. After successfully sharing a police detective in our high school and middle school in 1998–00, the board unanimously approved adding a second officer this year through funding by the police department.

AN ATYPICAL PRESENCE

The success of the program is due, in large part, to the appointment of a detective skilled in dealing with youngsters. His selection was the result of careful planning by police and school officials.

Meeting Detective Stacy Gilman in the school doesn't create the stereotypical sense of police presence. He dresses casually, always has a smile and friendly word for students and others and seems to know something positive about each student he meets. Although every student and staff member in the building knows he is (unobtrusively) armed and ready to deal with any situation, his emphasis is on, as his job description puts it, "working within the school system to build positive relationships between students, faculty and the police, while enforcing the laws promoting a safe and drug-free environment."

The officer does not serve as the school's disciplinarian, but he serves as a backup to the schools' administrators. Students know that we will call upon his investigative skills to help us determine the truth.

How have students and staff reacted to his presence? The general consensus is that the atmosphere has improved. One high school student summed up the change by stating, "I never felt unsafe at school, but now I feel safe. Somehow it's different."

The School Administrator, February 2000, p. 44.

Principals have praised the school resource officer program for helping to reduce fights, drugs, vandalism and other disciplinary problems at the two schools—1,200-student Rochester Middle School and 1,500-student Spaulding High School. Students also are more willing to confide in him information on problems that may be brewing. In one unusual instance, a student accused of theft was willing to talk to the detective and later surrendered the stolen property in his possession as long as the principal and assistant principal weren't present.

Teachers bring the detective into their classrooms to talk with students about citizenship and careers in law enforcement and to debunk some of the myths about the law. Gilman has been a good resource for strengthening curriculum and instruction in these and other areas.

COMMON USE

The school resource officer program is neither new nor unique. Such programs can be found in schools nationwide. In some places, such as Texas and Florida, state laws permit school districts to form their own police units, and more than 80 districts in Texas have done so. The largest is that of the Houston Independent School District with 177 officers and a $12 million budget.

An Internet search turned up more than 1,000 references to school resource officers, including many Web pages created by students who were working cooperatively with their officers. A common theme they expressed is the positive impact of the school resource officer on school environment, student behavior and overall safety for students, staff and visitors.

One of the most useful Web sites for school leaders looking for more information belongs to the Center for the Prevention of School Violence in Raleigh, N.C. (*www.ncsu. edu/cpsv*). The site includes sample job descriptions, ideas for creating a school resource officer program and other valuable information.

The school resource officer is now an integral part of our school district's safety plan. The good news: It has worked to improve school climate exactly as we envisioned. The bad news: We haven't seen any yet and don't expect to.

Rural Schools: Alternative Schooling for Troubled Youth in Rural Communities

Eugene P. Linton

Try as we might the ability to meet the needs of all students in traditional high schools is becoming more difficult all the time.

Challenges that once faced students in urban and suburban districts now have found their way to rural America, where school administrators are faced with the task of meeting these needs with limited fiscal and support resources.

In Mercer County, Ohio (the leading agricultural county in the state), school districts are experiencing a growing number of students who just don't fit in the traditional school setting. Many of the challenges once viewed as strictly urban problems are becoming increasingly common here. In an environment in which two-parent families are still the norm, teenage pregnancy and alcohol and drug abuse are new to us.

To meet the needs of these students, our schools have joined forces with the entire community, and the beginning results are exciting.

ALTERNATIVE NEEDS

Alternative education can take many forms. Typically, it is geared toward students who are either discipline problems in their traditional high schools or who need specialized academic programs because they are not progressing in the general academic classroom. Both types of programs are needed in many rural communities.

But lasting change doesn't happen quickly. For an alternative-school program to succeed, ample time must be spent assessing the needs of the community. School personnel, law enforcement representatives, child advocacy and mental health agencies, drug and alcohol treatment organizations, churches and temples and the court system must be involved in the process.

We found that using a committee of representatives from these community agencies was effort well spent. In just a couple of months we identified common needs and assessed the effectiveness of programs already established.

The team then formulated a program to address these needs. Although the problems may be most noticeable at school, the resolution of these problems was viewed as the responsibility of more than the educators.

COMMUNITY BACKING

Student truancy often leads to other delinquency and adult literacy problems. Therefore, continuing cooperation of the community agencies is essential, and sharing lessons learned from existing programs can provide direction to the goals that have been identified. For instance, one current program taught us how to individualize instruction, and from another we obtained ideas on how to provide a safe school environment.

If both discipline and academic problems have been identified, two separate learning environments often prove most beneficial. Discipline problems can be addressed in a strict short-term program, while the academic learning problems will need a longer, more concentrated effort. But both programs can operate in the same facility and even share staff to maintain fiscal efficiency, which is the approach we took in my district.

For students with discipline problems, an alternative academic setting is designed first and foremost as a way to avoid out-of-school suspension, a method that has proven to be highly ineffective as a means of punishment. Students often enjoy out-of-school suspension. This fact, coupled with the failing grades often associated with that option, makes a student's success when he or she returns to school highly unlikely.

For a discipline program to be successful, it needs to be strict and offer the student very few freedoms. Students arrive and leave on school-arranged transportation with their assigned work for the day. They are given individual work stations and are not free to move around the room.

Talking to fellow classmates is not permitted and total isolation from peer interaction is essential. Our classrooms are monitored by video cameras, and students who break classroom rules may be removed by law enforcement officers and forced to appear in juvenile court for a probation violation.

ALWAYS FLEXIBLE

Academic-opportunity programs are much more involved and require many more resources. The reasons for lack of academic success vary widely and thus require diverse programs and services. These students have demonstrated a lack of academic advancement at the junior and senior high school levels, and without intervention they are likely to drop out of school. In the two years since we instituted this program, we have seen the dropout rate of these troubled students fall from nearly 100 percent to less than 30 percent.

For these alternative programs to succeed, more than academic intervention must be present. We have found that students who have not been successful in a typical classroom do much better in programs housed away from the traditional school setting.

Cooperation among the various agencies involved with the students is essential for progress to be made. Opportunity students and their parents must agree to abide by the requirements of the program developed for each of them in the admittance conference. Mandatory drug testing, as a case in point, may be required to determine whether such a problem exists with a particular student, so that treatment, if necessary, can be prescribed.

Flexibility in the opportunity program is also essential. The curriculum must allow for the many individual needs of students, including accommodations such as part-time programs for young parents who need to work to provide for their families.

But ensuring this flexibility is undoubtedly our most difficult challenge. Coordinating service-learning activities, class work, job schedules and counseling sessions can be a logistical nightmare. Nonetheless, I believe every staff member of the alternative school would say the rewards are worth it.

10

The Appropriate and Effective Use of Security Technologies in U.S. Schools: A Guide for Schools and Law Enforcement Agencies

Mary W. Green

This chapter contains information to assist school personnel in evaluating and incorporating more extensive security measures into their school safety programs. The following pages are designed to guide school administrators and their school security personnel in an analysis of a school's vulnerability to violence, theft, and vandalism.

The following edited National Institute of Justice research report is based on a 7-year study of more than 100 schools. It offers practical guidance on several aspects of security, including security concepts and operational issues, video surveillance, weapons detection devices, entry controls, and duress alarms.

The full report runs to almost 120 pages and is detailed, comprehensive, and extremely informative. It is highly recommended to access, read, and possibly download the full report at the following location: www.ncjrs.org/school/state.html (January 6, 2003). This site provides free download capabilities, both print and disk. Additionally, the report can be ordered from the National Criminal Justice Reference Service, U.S. Department of Justice, for $3.

NCJ 178265 National Institute of Justice Office of Justice Programs U.S. Department of Justice, September 1999.

FOREWORD

Creating safe schools is the responsibility of the entire community in which a school or school system resides, but responsibility for maintaining them on a day-to-day basis lies principally with school administrators and, to a lesser extent, the local law enforcement agency. To assist schools in this task, the U.S. Department of Education and the U.S. Department of Justice have sponsored, often jointly, both research and demonstration programs to collect data and test useful new ideas that will expand understanding of school violence and disorder and lead to new programs to reduce these problems.

This document provides basic guidelines to law enforcement agencies and school administrators and encourages their collaboration as they decide what, if any, security technologies should be considered as they develop safe school strategies. In the wake of recent high-profile school tragedies with multiple homicides, many of this Nation's communities have urged their school districts to incorporate security technology into their safety programs. This guide should help schools, in concert with their law enforcement partners, analyze their vulnerability to violence, theft, and vandalism, and suggest possible technologies to address these problems in an effective manner. This guide describes existing commercially available technologies and urges thoughtful consideration of not only the potential safety benefits that may accrue from their use but also the costs that schools may incur for capital investments, site modifications, additional staffing, training, and equipment maintenance and repair.

Topic areas included in this guide are security concepts and operational issues, video surveillance, weapons detection devices (walk-through and hand held metal detectors and x-ray baggage scanners), entry controls, and duress alarms. Though this document does not replace the use of appropriate expert advice or provide detailed instructions on installing equipment or making cost estimates, it does offer practical guidance that should enable schools and law enforcement agencies to make better informed decisions on security technology.

Safety and security technology can only be one tool in a comprehensive program that each school must develop to create a safe learning environment that is perceived to be safe by all students and staff.

PREFACE

A team of security specialists from the Security Systems and Technologies Center at Sandia National Laboratories first talked with local schools in 1991. It was our intent to share what we had learned about the strengths and weaknesses of security technologies through our work with the U.S. Department of Energy (DOE) in many public schools.

After visiting some 120-plus schools across the country, completing our DOE-funded work to improve security at Belen High School in New Mexico and performing additional school security work for the National Institute of Justice (NIJ), we have learned that school security, like security for other applications, is not simple and straightforward. We have learned a lot about the unique aspects of school security from the many students, parents, and school and law enforcement personnel we met during the course of our work. At any particular school, security is the product of funding, facilities, building age, building layout, administrators, teachers, parents, kids, personalities, campus order, security personnel, procedures, the neighborhood, policies, the school board, local law enforcement, fire codes, local government, politics, and reputation. No two schools will have identical and successful security programs—hence, a security solution for one school cannot just be replicated at other schools with complete success.

What did become clear after working with more than 100 schools during the past 7 years is that school administrators need a good information resource on technologies for physical security problems. This guidebook, "The Appropriate and Effective Use of Security Technologies in U.S. Schools," is anticipated to be the first in a series of manuals designed and written for use by school administrators and law enforcement agencies. The goals of these documents are to provide nontechnical, nonvendor-specific information on:

- The kinds of security products available on the market.
- The strengths and weaknesses of these products and their expected effectiveness in a school environment.
- The costs of these products, including installation, long-term operational and maintenance expenses, manpower, and training.
- Requirements to include in Requests For Quotes (RFQs) to get a good product for an application.
- Legal issues that may need to be addressed.

Although security products can certainly have many different applications, this document covers products that can be applicable to some of the issues of violence in schools: video surveillance, weapon detection, entry control, and duress alarms. Future volumes are expected to cover issues and products such as bomb threats and explosives detection; drug residue and drug vapor detection; drug use detection; alcohol use detection; interior and exterior intrusion detection sensors; alarm communications; antigraffiti sealers; false fire alarm pulls; glass-break sensors; two-way radios; fencing; antitheft property marking; doors, locks, and key control; Crime Prevention Through Environmental Design (CPTED) principles; and parking lot safety. Most of the issues and philosophies covered in these manuals are geared toward middle schools and high schools, but elementary schools will likely find several of the technologies to have possible applications at their facilities.

Although this document addresses nontechnology measures that we felt were important for the completeness of the topic, there are many good resources and references available that address these people/policy/procedure/program issues much better. See the Resources section at the back of this book. Feedback from law enforcement agencies, schools, and product manufacturers/vendors is welcome, especially regarding any oversights or errors on our part. This guidebook is intended to provide an overview of security technology product areas that might be appropriate and affordable for school applications. Appropriate corrections or additions will be included in future updates. (We apologize if our cost estimates for hardware do not reflect current pricing; this document was written more than a year before actual publication.) I would like to extend our deep appreciation to the many schools who have allowed us to visit them and to assess the security vulnerabilities of their facilities and operations (and to take photos of the good things on their campuses, as well as the bad). I never failed to learn something new at every school we have visited. I found there to be many great schools in this country, with very motivated and hardworking administrators giving 110% of their energies to keep their students safe. I was humbled by the intense and stressful hours they worked and the ultimate importance of their jobs.

My thanks to the National Institute of Justice (NIJ) for providing the funding to conduct the research that allowed me to prepare this guidebook. I hope that we have met the high standards NIJ has set for providing the best that science and technologies have to offer in fighting crime in the United States. Information regarding the availability and ordering process for these manuals and any updates may be obtained at the NIJ Web site: www.ojp.usdoj.gov/nij; the Justice Technology Information Network (Justnet): www.nlectc.org; or by calling 1-800-248-2742.

I would be interested in hearing from readers regarding their successes, as well as their failures, in dealing with school security technology issues.

Mary W. Green

mgreen@sandia.gov

Sandia National Laboratories

Mail Stop 0782

P.O. Box 5800

Albuquerque, NM 87185

[Table of contents for the complete publication is included here to facilitate the reader's ability to understand the comprehensiveness of this publication and its possible utitlity. Editors]

Chapter IV Entry-Control Technologies

    A. Limiting entry/exit points

    B. Entry-control approaches

        1. WHO lets you in

        2. What you HAVE

        3. What you KNOW

        4. Who you ARE

Chapter V Duress Alarm Devices and Their Role in Crisis Management

Resources: Books, Publications, Web Sites, and Conferences

CHAPTER I—THE BIG PICTURE: SECURITY CONCEPTS AND OPERATIONAL ISSUES

Most schools in the United States are safe institutions, with disciplinary issues creating most disruptions. However, because of the 1998 campus slayings involving students, firearms, and multiple victims, schools and school programs are working harder to reach out to students, to teach them to be good citizens, to identify potentially dangerous personalities, and to develop appropriate intervention strategies. There are many excellent programs around the country that address the issues of bullying, anger, hate, abuse, drugs, alcohol, gangs, lack of role models, vandalism, and so forth. It is of great importance to the United States that these programs be pursued expeditiously. Unfortunately, these programs cannot be successful overnight (indeed, many must be initiated early in a child's life in order to be most effective) and do not yet exist in all schools. Meanwhile, security incidents are occurring in schools that must be dealt with now—perpetrators must be caught and consequences must be administered. School administrators would like to discourage security infractions by means of any deterrent available to them. One such approach sought more often today involves security technologies.

Security technologies are not the answer to all school security problems. However, many security products (e.g., cameras, sensors, and so forth) can be excellent tools if applied appropriately. They can provide school administrators or security officials with information that would not otherwise be available, free up manpower for more appropriate work, or be used to perform mundane tasks. Sometimes they can save a school money (compared to the long-term cost of personnel or the cost impact of not preventing a particular incident). Too often, though, these technologies are not applied appropriately in schools, are expected to do more than they are capable of, or are not well maintained after initial installation. In these cases, technologies are certainly not cost effective.

Why Security Technologies?

To reduce problems of crime or violence in schools: (1) the opportunities for security infractions should be eliminated or made more difficult to accomplish, (2) the likelihood of being caught must be greatly increased, and (3) consequences must be established and enforced. Item 3 is a social and political issue and needs to be addressed head on by school boards and communities across the country. This guide addresses only items 1 and 2. Simply providing more adults, especially parents, in schools will reduce the opportunities for security infractions and increase the likelihood of perpetrators being caught. However, adding dedicated professional security staff to perform very routine security functions has many limitations:

- Locating qualified people may be difficult.
- Humans do not do mundane tasks well.
- Manpower costs are always increasing.
- Turnover of security personnel can be detrimental to a security program.
- As in other security environments, more repetitious tasks become boring.

Hence, the possible role of security technologies expands. Through technology, a school can introduce ways to collect information or enforce procedures and rules that it would not be able to afford or rely on security personnel to do.

Why Security Technologies Have Not Been Embraced by Schools in the Past

Anyone working in the security field is aware that there are thousands of security products on the market. Some of them are excellent, but many claim to be "the very best of its kind." And, unfortunately, there are a significant number of customers in the country who have been less than pleased with the ultimate cost, maintenance requirements, and effectiveness of security technologies they have purchased. Schools have been no exception to this and have a few inherent problems of their own:

- Schools do not usually have the funding for aggressive and complete security programs.
- Schools generally lack the ability to procure effective security technology products and services at the lowest bid.
- Many school security programs cannot afford to hire well-trained security personnel.
- School administrators and their staff rarely have training or experience in security technologies.
- Schools have no infrastructures in place for maintaining or upgrading security devices—when something breaks, it is often difficult to have it repaired or replaced.
- Issues of privacy and potential civil rights lawsuits may prohibit or complicate the use of some technologies.

The issues come down to applying security technologies in schools that are effective, affordable, and politically acceptable but still useful within these difficult constraints.

Effectiveness Versus Affordability Versus Acceptability   Effectiveness, affordability, and acceptability are difficult trade-offs and, occasionally, a seemingly ineffective solution to a security problem is chosen because of a lack of funding or pressure from the community to do something. Although many effective security measures are too expensive for schools, cost alone is not often the ultimate driver. Most major changes to security policies, including the introduction of technologies, are often brought on not by foresight but as a response to some undesirable incident.

This is not to say that a good argument should be made for applying every physical security approach in every school. "Appropriate" preparation is, by far, the greater "art" in security system design, and it includes an evolving plan, beginning with defining a particular school's risks.

A Systematic Approach to Identifying the Security Risks at a School

Note: The following discussion considers all security risks to schools—violence, drugs, theft, and vandalism—not just those that may be addressed by the technologies covered in this volume. Depending on the acceptance and demand for this guide, future additional volumes will address the remaining technologies in greater detail.

In the past, schools have rarely understood the need or had the time or resources to consider their security plans from a systems perspective—looking at the big picture of what they are trying to achieve in order to arrive at the optimal security strategy. A school's security staff must understand what it is trying to protect (people and/or high-value assets), who it is trying to protect against (the threats), and the general environment and constraints that it must work within—the characterization of the facility. This understanding will allow a school to define its greatest and/or most likely risks so that its security strategy consciously addresses those risks. This strategy will likely include some combination of technologies, personnel, and procedures that do the best possible job of solving the school's problems within its financial, logistical, and political constraints.

Why is this careful identification of risk important? Because few facilities, especially schools, can afford a security program that protects against all possible incidents. No two schools are alike and, therefore, there is no single approach to security that will work ideally for all schools. From year to year, even, a school's security strategy will need revision because the world around it and the people inside it will always be changing.

Defining a school's assets.   For this school year, what is most at risk? The protection of the students and staff is always at the top of this list, but the measures taken to protect them will usually be driven by the defined threats. Are the instruments in the band hall very attractive targets for theft or vandalism? Is the new computer lab full of the best and most easily resold computers? Though desirable, a school cannot possibly afford to protect everything to the same level of confidence.

Defining a school's threats.   For this school year, who or what is your school threatened by? Gang rivalries? Fights behind the gym? Drugs hidden in lockers? Guns brought to school? Outsiders on campus? Drinking at lunchtime? Vehicle break-ins? Graffiti in the bathrooms? Accidents in the parking lot? How sophisticated (knowledgeable of their task of malevolence) or motivated (willing to risk being caught or injured) do the perpetrators seem to be? Measures taken to protect against these threats are driven by the characterization of the facility and its surroundings as mentioned earlier.

Characterizing a School's Environment

Any security strategy must incorporate the constraints of the facility so that all strengths, weaknesses, and idiosyncrasies are realized and provided for. How risks are approached will largely be driven by facility constraints. If theft and vandalism are primary risks for your school, answers to questions regarding the physical plant will determine the optimal security measures. Is the school new or old? Are the windows particularly vulnerable? Does everyone who ever worked at the school still have keys? What is the nighttime lighting like? Does the interior intrusion sensor system work well, or do the local police ignore the alarms due to a high false-alarm rate? Are visitors forced or merely requested to go through the front office before accessing the rest of the school?

If outsiders on campus are a primary concern, it will be necessary to recognize the facility's ability to control unauthorized access. How many entry points are there into the buildings? Are gangs present in the area? Are the school grounds open and accessible to anyone, or do fences or buildings restrict access? Is there easy access to the school roof? Where are hiding places within the building or on the premises? Is the student population small enough so that most of the staff would recognize most of the students and parents?

If issues of violence are a major concern, a thorough understanding of employees, student profiles, and neighborhood characteristics will be necessary. What is the crime rate in the neighborhood? Is the school administration well liked by the students? Are teachers allowed access to the school at night? Are students allowed off campus at lunch time? How much spending money do students generally have? Are popular hangouts for young people close by and, for business establishments, does management collaborate with the school? Are expelled or suspended students sent home or to an alternative school? How many incidents of violence have occurred at the school over the past 4 years? What is the general reputation of the school, and how does it appear to an outsider? Are your most vocal parents prosecurity or proprivacy? Do your student like and respect your security personnel well enough to pass them pieces of information regarding security concerns? Once the school's threats, assets, and environmental constraints are understood, the security needs can be prioritized such that the school's security goals are understood by all those involved.

Identifying security needs and then securing the funding to pay for them are usually unrelated at most schools. Schools have to have a "Plan B," for program design which may be the perfect "Plan A"—but spread out over several years of implementation. If the desirable strategies (e.g., fencing, sensors, locker searches, speed bumps) are too costly or unpalatable to the community, a school may then need to modify the facility constraints (e.g., back entrances locked from the outside, no open campus for students, no teacher access after 10 p.m., all computer equipment bolted down, no lockers for students, and so forth).

Most school districts or school boards will be more supportive of security measures and the requested funding if they are well educated about the most likely risks faced each year and the options available. A security staff should not have the wide-open charter to "keep everything and everybody safe." A school board should be briefed as often as once a month as to what the current security goals are and what strategies are recommended, realizing that these will and must continue to evolve. If a school board member is clearly aware of a school's most important concerns and what is required to achieve them, then he or she is less likely to be swayed by an irate parent into making a decision that will handicap reasonable security efforts.

Designing the School Security System

After identifying the risks or concerns at a noneducational facility, a methodical approach to the security plan would then examine possible solutions to each area of vulnerability from the perspective of:

$$\text{Detection} \longrightarrow \text{Delay} \longrightarrow \text{Response}$$

For any problem, it is necessary first to detect that an incident or problem is occurring. For example, when someone is breaking into a building, it is necessary that this act be detected and that information be supplied to the authorities as soon as possible. Next, this adversary must be delayed as long as possible so that the response force may arrive. A simple example of delay would be firmly bolting computer components onto large heavy desks, so that a thief is forced to use more time removing the bolts. Finally, someone, such as the police, must respond to the incident to catch the thief redhanded.

For a school environment, it is probably more appropriate to expand this model:

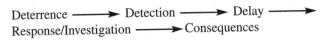

The most appealing step in any school security system should be to convince the perpetrator that he or she should not do whatever it is he or she is considering, whether the action is perceived as too difficult, not worthwhile, or the chances of being caught are quite high. Clearly, most security measures employed in facilities are intended for the precise purpose of deterrence, whether it be to discourage a thief, a drug dealer, or an errant employee. (Note: Deterrence is not generally considered part of the security strategy for most high-risk government facilities; this is due in part to the fact that quite a bit of deterrence comes "free" with other security measures, and it would be difficult to attribute a lack of security problems to any particular deterrence effort.)

Unlike other facilities, where a perpetrator would be handed over to the authorities, and the consequences determined by law, a school often has the authority and/or opportunity to establish the consequences for incidents that occur on their campus. It is imperative, however, that schools do not assume authority that they do not have. Issues governed by law must be reported to the appropriate authority.

To illustrate the application of this model, consider the problem of nighttime break-ins and theft in a school building. A model for the security strategy to address this might be:

Deterrence   Close off the parking lot or driveways to vehicle traffic at night. Post signs that video cameras are in use on the campus (but only if you actually do have cameras). Use fencing strategically, but where fencing would be unacceptable, consider a barrier of thorny pyracantha bushes. Allow a law enforcement officer to live on campus.

Detection   Install an intrusion detection system in all school hallways, administrative offices, and rooms with high-value assets. Use motion sensors, magnetic switches on doors, heat sensors, and/or glass-break sensors as appropriate. Send alarm signals to the police, the officer on campus, and the school principal.

Delay   Bolt computers and TVs to desks and walls so that removing them is difficult and time-consuming.

Response/Investigation   Police and/or campus security arrives on the scene, makes arrests.

Consequences   Enforce consequences when possible and the school has the authority to do so. (This becomes an additional deterrent for the future, especially if nonsensitive pieces of information regarding the incident are released to staff, students, and the community.)

Schools do not normally have the opportunity for real-time detection and real-time response to security incidents; after-the-fact investigation is normally the best a school can hope for.

Although this model may not be appropriate for all aspects of security at a school, it can serve as a methodology for consideration. Its use can prevent some less-thought-out strategies. A true example of this is a large urban high school that was planning to purchase $100,000 worth of exterior cameras to combat nighttime vandalism being inflicted on the exterior of the building. This plan was halted abruptly when the school was asked who would be available to watch the monitors from the 40-plus cameras (detection) and who would be able to respond quickly enough to these sporadic and relatively small incidents (response). A better and cheaper alternate plan was devised that included using antigraffiti sealer on all brick surfaces, some strategically located wrought iron fencing that could not easily be climbed, and the replacement of a few particularly vulnerable windows with glass block.

A Spectrum of Physical Security Approaches

It will be assumed that consequences for undesirable actions have been put into place at a school; otherwise, there is little or no deterrence to be gained from any physical security measures designed to detect, delay, and respond to an incident. A wide array of security measures involving people, campus modifications, and/or technologies can be considered for most concerns, keeping in mind the unique characteristics of each school. A recurring message from school administrators is that the majority of their problems are brought onto campus by outsiders or expelled/suspended students so measures to keep outsiders off campus will generally be of global benefit. (Although this is not the case in all incidents, school administrators quite often find it more palatable to parents if security measures are justified based on the exterior threat rather than the suspicion of their children.) The following is a partial list of possible security measures to address various security issues:

(Most of the following suggested security measures are in use in one or more U.S. schools, but a few may not yet have been attempted. In any case, there is no comprehensive body of knowledge regarding their effectiveness. More research is needed to get a national picture on particular technologies. Also keep in mind that a school should always contact its legal counsel before participating in any new security program that involves searching or testing of people or property.)

Outsiders on campus

- Posted signs regarding penalties for trespassing.
- Enclosed campus (fencing).
- Guard at main entry gate to campus.
- Greeters in strategic locations.
- Student IDs or badges.
- Vehicle parking stickers.
- Uniforms or dress codes.
- Exterior doors locked from the outside.
- A challenge procedure for anyone out of class.
- Cameras in remote locations.
- School laid out so all visitors must pass through front office.
- Temporary "fading" badges issued to all visitors.

Fights on campus

- Cameras.
- Duress alarms.
- Whistles.
- Vandalism
- Graffiti-resistant sealers.
- Glass-break sensors.
- Aesthetically pleasing wall murals (these usually are not hit by graffiti).
- Law enforcement officers living on campus.
- 8-foot fencing.
- Well-lit campus at night.

Theft

- Interior intrusion detection sensors.
- Property marking (including microdots) to deter theft.

- Bars on windows.
- Reinforced doors.
- Elimination of access points up to rooftops.
- Cameras.
- Doors with hinge pins on secure side.
- Bolting down computers and TVs.
- Locating high-value assets in interior rooms.
- Key control.
- Biometric entry into rooms with high-value assets.
- Law enforcement officer living on campus.

Drugs

- Drug detection swipes.
- Hair analysis kits for drug use detection (intended for parental application).
- Drug dogs.
- Removal of lockers.
- Random searches.
- Vapor detection of drugs.

Alcohol

- No open campus at lunch.
- Breathalyzer test equipment.
- No access to vehicles.
- No lockers.
- Clear or open mesh backpacks.
- Saliva test kits.

Weapons

- Walk-through metal detectors.
- Handheld metal detectors.
- Vapor detection of gunpowder.
- Crimestopper hot line with rewards for information.
- Gunpowder detection swipes.
- Random locker, backpack, and vehicle searches.
- X-ray inspection of book bags and purses.

Malicious acts

- Setback of all school buildings from vehicle areas.
- Inaccessibility of air intake and water source.
- All adults on campus required to have a badge.
- Vehicle barriers near main entries and student gathering areas.

Parking lot problems

- Cameras.
- Parking decals.
- Fencing.
- Card ID systems for parking lot entry.
- Parking lots sectioned off for different student schedules.
- Sensors in parking areas that should have no access during school day.
- Roving guards.
- Bike patrol.

False fire alarms

- Sophisticated alarm systems that allow assessment of alarms (and cancellation if false) before they become audible.
- Boxes installed over alarm pulls that alarm locally (screamer boxes).

Bomb threats

- Caller ID on phone system.
- Crimestopper program with big rewards for information.
- Recording all phone calls, with a message regarding this at the beginning of each incoming call.
- All incoming calls routed through a district office.
- Phone company support.
- No pay phones on campus.
- Policy to extend the school year when plagued with bomb threats and subsequent evacuations.

Bus problems

- Video cameras and recorders within enclosures on buses.
- IDs required to get on school buses.
- Security aides on buses.

- Smaller buses.
- Duress alarm system or radios for bus drivers.

Teacher safety

- Duress alarms.
- Roving patrols.
- Classroom doors left open during class.
- Cameras in black boxes in classrooms.
- Controlled access to classroom areas.

Legal Issues

Within each section of this manual, some legal issues have been noted regarding the use of various technologies. A reasonable approach to using any new security device would include checking with your legal organization, talking to schools in the area that have already implemented the measure, and inviting local law enforcement to come in to discuss the device's possible use. Although every possible ramification cannot be foreseen, it does help to be aware of issues that might be raised and to be aware of current thinking about ways to address each of these.

Evaluating a School's Security System Design

The staff assigned to handle security concerns should plan to meet on a regular basis for collaboration on new problems, needed changes to existing approaches, and the exchange of information and intelligence. New problems and proposed solutions may sometimes be presented (where appropriate) to school employees, the student council, the parent advisory group, the local police, or other schools in the area. Although including more people may lengthen the decisionmaking process, making representatives of these groups a part of the security upgrade team for issues that would involve them will ensure buy-in. A side benefit will be that word will spread throughout the community that the school is taking active security measures, which will act as a deterrent.

New School Design

Many school buildings in the United States have been constructed to achieve an inviting and open-to-the-community feeling, with multiple buildings, big windows, multiple entrances and exits, and many opportunities for privacy. Needless to say, these layouts are not conducive to many current requirements to address security needs. To combat broken windows and nighttime thefts, the country also went through a brief period of designing schools with almost no windows; the cave-like results these designs produced were soon found to be objectionable to many people.

Incorporating the principles of Crime Prevention Through Environmental Design (CPTED) in the design or remodeling of a school can contribute greatly to the control and security of the campus. There are several good sources of CPTED literature available through the Web; CPTED as applied specifically to schools will be covered in a subsequent volume.

If a district has the luxury of looking forward to a new school in the future, it is imperative that trained security personnel, who are familiar with the area and the community, and who will be responsible for day-to-day security operations in the new facility, are involved in every step of the new design. This is critical to ensuring that the design of the new school minimizes vulnerabilities. There are architectural firms specializing in schools that incorporate good security principles; a security-conscious design can actually help compensate in the long term for tight security budgets, fewer security personnel, and less sophisticated security gadgets. The following are some suggestions to keep in mind for a new facility; the funding, location, geography, streets, and neighborhood will usually drive which ideas are feasible for each new school. Although this list includes only a few basic security technologies (such as cameras, sensors, and so forth), the facility design should not preclude their straightforward installation in the future.

- Limit the number of buildings—one building is best—to limit outsiders on the campus.
- Minimize the entrances to the school building—having one or two main entrances/exits will support efforts to keep outsiders off campus. Allow enough room at the main entry in the event that a screening area (i.e., for weapon or drug detection) needs to be incorporated later on. Alarm other exits for emergency use only.
- Minimize the line of sight from secluded off-campus sites onto student gathering areas, the main entry doors, playgrounds, patios, and so forth (This suggestion must be tempered against the benefits gained from the natural, desirable surveillance by neighbors, passers-by, officers on patrol, and so forth.)
- Allow for a security person to be posted at a single entrance onto campus to challenge each vehicle for identification of all occupants. Buses and school employees should have a separate (and controlled) entrance.
- Provide a dropoff/pickup lane for buses only.
- Minimize the number of driveways or parking lots that students will have to walk across to get to the school building.
- Build single-stall bathrooms to mitigate bathroom confrontations and problems.
- Enclose the campus. (This is more a measure to keep outsiders out rather than to keep insiders in.) Beside defining property boundaries, a robust fence forces a perpetrator to consciously trespass, rather than allowing casual entry.
- Make certain that the school building and classroom areas can be closed and locked off from the gym and other facilities used during off hours.
- Minimize secluded hiding places for unauthorized persons, both inside and outside buildings.
- Do not eliminate windows, but use them strategically. Consider incorporating clerestories or secure skylights that allow light in but that are less vulnerable than typical windows.
- Maximize the line of sight within buildings.

- Large wide spaces, like hallways or commons, should have sufficient vertical dimension so space does not feel restrictive to students.

- Consider installing student lockers in classrooms or other areas easy to monitor so that there is no single locker area that becomes a bottleneck, and there is always the deterrence of an adult nearby.

- Do not cut corners on communications, especially those required for security. Make certain that your facility has built in the necessary receivers and transmitters throughout the structure to allow for dependable two-way radio and cellular phone use. (Sometimes radio frequency communication is not possible deep within a large, structurally dense facility.)

- Where possible, have buildings and other student gathering areas set back from the streets, driveways, or parking areas by at least 50 feet.

- Install a basic security alarm system throughout all hallways, administrative offices, and rooms containing high-value property, such as computers, VCRs, shop equipment, laboratory supplies, and musical instruments.

- Allow a law enforcement officer to live on campus. (In some school districts, an officer is allowed to move his or her own trailer to a strategic location on campus and receive free utilities in exchange for prenegotiated and formally contracted responsibilities.) The deterrent effect of a police vehicle parked on campus all night and weekend can be great. Such an arrangement can also provide both detection and response in situations where damage is being inflicted upon the facility, but no alarm system would normally detect it.

- Provide a separate parking area for work-study students or those who will be leaving during the school day. (This allows the main student parking lot to be closed off during the school day.)

- Make certain that exterior lighting is sufficient for safety. Lights mounted on the exterior of buildings often are inadequate for adjoining driveways or parking lots.

- Do not underestimate the value of trees and landscaping on a school campus. An attractive, well-maintained school is generally less attractive to thieves.

The Role of Order Maintenance

One additional consideration that cannot be overlooked is the perception of a lack of order on a school campus. If a school is perceived as unsafe (i.e., it appears that no adult authority prevails on a campus), then "undesirables" will come in, and the school will actually become unsafe. This is an embodiment of the broken window theory: One broken window left unrepaired will encourage additional windows to be broken. Seemingly small incidents or issues such as litter on a school campus can provide the groundwork for (or even just the reputation of) a problem school. Issues of vandalism and theft can be almost as harmful to a school as actual violence because they can create a fertile environment for loss of control and community confidence.

Issues contributing to a school's overall order maintenance must therefore be taken seriously, not unlike any other public facility. Reducing theft, deterring vandalism and graffiti, keeping outsiders off campus, keeping the facility in good repair, improving poor lighting, maintaining attractive landscaping, and getting rid of trash are all important to school security.

Technologies such as cameras, sensors, microdots (for identifying ownership), and antigraffiti sealers can contribute significantly in many (but not all) situations and are possible approaches to further support a school's order maintenance.

Too often school districts undervalue the ultimate importance of reliable and conscientious maintenance, janitorial, and groundskeeping staff. Their ultimate contribution to the order maintenance of a school can be enormous. Additionally, the janitorial staff needs to be selected with almost the same care as the teaching staff because they have great access to and knowledge of a school facility. Contracting out this work without complete background checks of all workers can lead to many problems in the long run.

CHAPTER II—VIDEO SURVEILLANCE

A. Video Cameras

1. Why Video Cameras?   The peace of mind of both students and faculty at a school can often be quickly enhanced by the installation of video cameras as part of a closed circuit television (CCTV) system. This change of attitude may result in even further-reaching effects on a campus than would be expected by the use of cameras alone. As mentioned in the introductory chapter of this guide, a sense of safety and authority will directly influence people's opinions and impressions, which will ultimately contribute to the overall order maintenance of a facility and how that facility is treated by occupants and outsiders.

To the school's security personnel who must handle day-to-day security issues, the best thing about cameras is the deterrence factor they introduce to outsiders who do not belong on campus and to students and employees who do. Information regarding security measures, such as cameras at the local school, will generally spread through a community. This type of reputation can make outsiders reconsider an unwelcome visit to the historically easy mark of the neighborhood—the school. It can be assumed that most kids are not going to step way out of bounds if they believe they will likely be caught, which is often possible through the appropriate application of cameras. In a school security system, the ideal goal should be to convince kids not to even attempt to do something that is unacceptable.

Addressing an incident after it occurs is good, but not as good as if it had never happened. Once a perpetrator is caught, there is a chain of events involving confrontation, denial, parental involvement, consequences, and perhaps even the involvement of law enforcement and the legal system. School administrators will be forced to spend a great deal of time on the matter, and all participants will find the process distasteful.

Another strength of cameras is the strong evidence they can preserve on tape. Even if law enforcement is not brought in regarding an incident, the recorded tape can be invaluable to a school administration. Many schools report that when students are brought into the school office after an incident and shown a tape of themselves in an illegal or unacceptable act—even if the tape might not have been of sufficient resolution and detail to use for prosecution purposes in a court of law—the student will usually admit to the incident.

The ultimate usability of a video recording is dependent on many variables. It is possible for a camera system to produce tapes on which individuals are unidentifiable or their actions are indiscernible. Be certain that a camera system provides the kind of information you need before you pay for it. These requirements should be clearly spelled out in the purchase agreement, along with a specified time period during which the school can adequately test it.

Video recordings are also beneficial for use with parents. Although nearly all parents want to believe their children are innocent of wrongdoing, some parents will deny their child's guilt despite the credible testimony of others to the contrary. However, as many school administrators and teachers have discovered, parents quickly accept their child's role in an incident when shown a videotape of the incident. Most parents want to do the right thing, but hard evidence is often required for some to concede over a matter involving their own child.

From a cost standpoint, the use of CCTV in public areas on school grounds can free up manpower. If cameras are covering a large patio area where students congregate during breaks, adults who normally would be assigned to oversee that area can instead be made available to monitor other areas of concern.

Finally, the solid documentation that a video recording provides can be invaluable in situations involving liability claims. Although it is possible that this may occasionally work against a school, most schools welcome this concrete evidence so that testimony regarding an incident does not consist solely of hearsay.

2. Why Not Video Cameras?

- CCTV systems are expensive. Installation can also be expensive, as well as logistically difficult.
- Choosing the correct camera equipment requires some technical knowledge.
- A single camera can effectively view a smaller area than would be intuitively expected; hence many applications can require more cameras, equipment, and expense than was originally expected.
- Cameras can be stolen or vandalized.
- Ongoing maintenance and operational support are required.
- Some applications or areas do not warrant camera use.
- Some communities or individuals will challenge the legality of using cameras.
- Insiders with full knowledge of the installed video system's capabilities can possibly circumvent the system to their advantage.
- If it becomes well known where cameras are being used at a school, students may simply move their misbehaviors to a different part of campus.

3. Good Applications Versus Poor Applications   An effective use of cameras in schools is viewing the recorded tape after an incident has occurred. Examples of reasonable goals for a school video system are capturing scenes indicating who started a fight in the hallway, who is smoking marijuana in the parking lot, who stole all the blank computer disks out of the computer laboratory, or if a particular person did indeed try to run down someone with his or her truck in the school driveway. Less reasonable goals, or at least more difficult or manpower intensive, are trying to use camera scenes to stop a student fight in its early stages, prevent someone from bringing weapons into the facility, or catch a thief before he makes his escape.

A visible camera may not help if a school's goal is to identify a nighttime thief in the band hall or computer lab if the thief simply covered his or her face or disguised himself or herself. However, it may still add substantially to deterrence; a would-be thief may never be sure if there will be some type of immediate response to the video recording or exactly where all the cameras are located. Depending upon each situation, video cameras can support security initiatives in the following applications:

- Parking lots and driveways.
- Cafeterias.
- Patio and entry areas.
- Hallways.
- Gymnasiums.
- Main administrative offices.
- Band halls.
- School stores.
- Computer rooms.
- Science laboratories.
- Supply closets.

Schools may want to consider classroom installation of the cameras and recorder enclosures that are currently so popular for use on school buses. For buses, a camera is placed in the black box only when requested by a bus driver, thereby reducing the number of camera systems that must be purchased. Usually, the deterrence factor derived from students never knowing when a camera is actually present can discourage much of the misbehavior. (This is not to be confused with the use of a dummy camera, where a potential victim is under the illusion that he or she is being monitored and, therefore, help will be forthcoming in the event of an attack; this can create extensive liability concerns for a facility.)

In an application with a camera looking in an easterly or westerly direction, extreme glare may occur during sunrise or sunset. If this type of placement cannot be avoided, the camera should be mounted as high as possible and then angled downward to view below the horizon. If sunrise and/or sunset are not critical time periods for a particular application, then it may be acceptable simply to have an unusable picture during these times.

Similarly, vehicle headlights and other sources of glaring light, particularly during night operations, should be considered. A system that is designed with the potential problem sources recognized can be compensated for. After initial installation is complete, it is much more difficult to compensate for these problems. Oftentimes, funding is no longer available to make needed adjustments.

Viewing a scene such as a dark doorway that contains a significant shadow can be quite difficult. Newer cameras with better electronics help compensate for these types of applications, but they are more expensive.

Seasonal problems should be anticipated and addressed before purchasing an exterior camera system. Conditions to be aware of are blowing snow, built-up ice on a camera housing, dust storms, trees that block the scene in summer, temperature extremes, or north sides of buildings with shadows that may affect scene assessment during winter months.

4. To Monitor or Not to Monitor   Each year, a great number of camera systems are bought in the United States with the objective of assigning a security person to constantly monitor the scenes from the video cameras in real time. The objective of such installations is that some sort of response may then be dispatched immediately and an undesirable incident prevented or stopped, basically using the live person watching the monitor as a detector. This is quite often an unrealistic approach to security, particularly in school applications.

Experiments were run at Sandia National Laboratories 20 years ago for the U.S. Department of Energy to test the effectiveness of an individual whose task was to sit in front of a video monitor(s) for several hours a day and watch for particular events. These studies demonstrated that such a task, even when assigned to a person who is dedicated and well intentioned, will not support an effective security system. After only 20 minutes of watching and evaluating monitor screens, the attention of most individuals has degenerated to well below acceptable levels. Monitoring video screens is both boring and mesmerizing. There are no intellectually engaging stimuli, such as when watching a television program. This is particularly true if a staff member is asked to watch multiple monitors, with scenes of teenagers milling about in various hallways, in an attempt to watch for security incidents.

A practical security application of real-time viewing of a video monitor might be the intent to actively allow or disallow individuals to enter a particular locked door. In this case, the security person at or near the video monitors receives an alarm or other announcement that a person desires entry into that facility or area. The security person would then focus his or her attention directly on the screen and make a decision (according to procedures) as to whether to release the remote lock on a door to allow the person access.

Most schools have a security staff, whether it be an assistant principal assigned security as one of his or her duties, a few security aides equipped with two-way radios, or an impressive number of sworn police officers. Few schools, however, find themselves with surplus security-staff time. Because of the ineffectiveness of people monitoring video scenes in real time, it would seem to be a very poor use of school security staff. One possible exception is when a certain incident is expected at a school during a finite time period. For example, if cars in a parking lot are frequently broken into during the noon hour, security staff may want to actively monitor their cameras' outputs during this period so that they may immediately assess an incident in progress and apprehend the suspect. This would be particularly appropriate if the suspect is not known and not a member of the school community.

The use of cameras and a real-time display unit without the benefit of a recorder is not recommended. It is true that a video camera and monitor alone are much cheaper than a complete video system with recording and multiplexing capabilities. However, the hard evidence made available in the form of a video recording can more than make up for the cost of a recording system. Ease of prosecution and the likely prevention of future incidents by this individual are additional benefits.

CHAPTER III—METAL DETECTION

A. Walk-Through Metal Detectors for Personnel

1. Do Metal Detectors Really Work?—The Basics   Metal detectors work very well—they are considered a mature technology and can accurately detect the presence of most types of firearms and knives. However, metal detectors work very poorly if the user is not aware of their limitations before beginning a weapon detection program and is not prepared for the amount of trained and motivated manpower required to operate these devices successfully.

A metal detection device in school security applications is used primarily to locate undesirable objects that are hidden on a person's body. When a questionable item or material is detected by the device, the detector produces an alarm signal; this signal can be audible, visible (lights), or both. Unfortunately, a metal detector alone cannot distinguish between a gun and a large metal belt buckle. This shortcoming is what makes weapon detection programs impractical for many schools; trained employees are needed to make these determinations.

Metal detectors are usually not effective when used on purses, book bags, briefcases, or suitcases. There is usually a large number of different objects or materials located in or as part of the composition of these carried items that would cause an alarm.

If you ask the average person what a metal detector does and what property to which it is most sensitive, the answer to the first question would probably be that it is a device that detects only metal. The answer to the second question likely would be that a metal detector is more likely to detect metal objects with heavier mass. Both answers are incorrect.

A metal detector actually detects any conductive material—anything that will conduct an electrical current. The typical pulsed-field portal metal detectors generate electromagnetic pulses that produce very small electrical currents in conductive metal objects within the portal archway which, in turn, generate their own magnetic field. The receiver portion of a portal metal detector can detect this rapidly decaying magnetic field during the time between the transmitted pulses. This type of weapon detection device is "active" in that it generates a magnetic field that actively looks for suspicious materials or objects. A magnetometer, a passive device, was much more in use 20 years ago in the detection of weapons. The magnetometer depends on the Earth's magnetic field—it looks for a distortion caused by the presence of ferromagnetic (attracted to a magnet) material.

Counter to intuition, the mass of a particular object is not significant in metal detection. The size, shape, electrical conductivity and magnetic properties are the important properties.

For example, when a long thin wire is taken through a portal (walk-through) metal detector, and the wire is in any geometry except one in which the two ends (or any two points on the wire) are touching, it will rarely be detected. However, shape this same wire into a closed circle and the metal detector will most likely go off, even though the mass of the wire has not changed.

Delving even deeper into metal detector sensitivity, consider the orientation of an object. Take the same closed-loop wire described in the previous paragraph. Lay this loop on its side so that it is parallel to the ground. In this configuration, the portal metal detector is less likely to see it, but, if the wire loop is upright and parallel to the side panels of the metal detector, the detector will be much more likely to go off in this orientation.

Some people fear the use of a metal detector on themselves because of the possible side effects of being subjected to the magnetic field. This fear is unfounded; metal detectors emit an extremely weak magnetic field, weak enough to be of no concern even to heart patients with pacemaker-type devices. Indeed, the use of an electric hair dryer subjects the user to a much stronger field than would be received by a metal detection device.

Another widely held belief about metal detectors is that they are a straightforward technology, where the equipment does all the work. This is not true at all. The average first-time consumer will undoubtedly expect a metal detector to be much smarter and more helpful than it can possibly be. A metal detector is only as good as the operator overseeing its use.

In many facilities, the misconception exists that someone known by the operator, such as a fellow employee or a security person, should be allowed to circumvent the system. It must be clearly established that in order to ensure the integrity of any routine metal detection program, everyone must be subjected to the program requirements, including students, parents, teachers, custodial and maintenance staff, security personnel (except for sworn police officers who are required to carry a weapon), school administrators, and visitors. To require less would be counterproductive and prejudicial. Signage can be of great help: a sign at the school entrance explaining the importance of the detectors in maintaining a safe and comfortable learning environment provides policy notification. If a more aggressive approach is needed for a particular community, entry signs could spell out a particular school or district policy that requires the screening of all who enter the school, with access denied to those who refuse.

CHAPTER IV—ENTRY-CONTROL TECHNOLOGIES

Many school administrators contend that the majority of the security problems and incidents at their schools are the result of an unauthorized person being on campus (albeit the vast majority of these unauthorized persons are in some way related to the school or to students at the school). These trespassers can include a school's own suspended or expelled students, students from rival schools, irate parents seeking revenge against a student or employee, gang members, or even drug dealers. It is logical, then, that if a school were able to carefully control exactly who was able to enter the campus or school buildings, security incidents would drop significantly. This is easier said than done.

Schools can often prevent or discourage the casual intruder. Some of the less technical, though often quite effective, approaches to deterring unauthorized entry are:

- Posted signs warning that unauthorized trespassers are subject to arrest.
- Signs that inform visitors that all vehicles brought onto campus are subject to search by the school.
- A guard who is checking identifications at the main entrance gate to the campus.

- Vehicle parking stickers so that any vehicle found parked on campus without a sticker, other than in the monitored visitor lot, is subject to being ticketed and towed.

- Uniforms for students, which make outsiders very identifiable.

- A school policy of no hats; no droopy pants; no shirts with alcohol, drug, violence,, or gang affiliation messages; or no exposed tattoos, which again can help make outsiders identifiable.

- Greeters at all open entrances to school (these can be parent volunteers).

- Minimal numbers of entrances to the campus and to the school. Superfluous exterior doors should be locked to prevent entry from the outside and labeled inside: "For emergency exit only—alarm will sound."

- A policy that anyone walking around campus during class time will be challenged for a pass and/or student ID and is subject to being searched or even scanned by a metal detector to be checked for weapons and/or drugs.

- The main student parking lot (which does not include parking for work-study students) closed off and locked during the day. Make entry to school during the school day possible only through the front office.

- Fencing around campus that will discourage the casual intruder and better define school property.

- A policy that, when a student is expelled or suspended, his or her student ID is confiscated and (for a larger school) his or her picture is made available to the security staff.

A. Limiting Entry/Exit Points

Most U.S. school buildings in use today were originally designed to foster learning, mimicking universities to some extent. Often, their layouts provided many secluded niches to allow students privacy in which to study; separate buildings to house the various disciplines; multiple entrances and exits in buildings to maximize fire safety and emphasize freedom; and spread-out campuses to prevent congestion and to be open to the community. Fences became, perhaps for appearance but more likely to cut expenses. Some schools even have public streets running through the campus. These designs were very appropriate and greatly enjoyed 30 to 40 years ago. Entry control in these facilities has been limited in the past to the coincidence of an adult noticing an outsider on campus and challenging that outsider.

For current security needs, controlling the access of students, employees, and visitors has become paramount. Without major remodeling for some schools, the manpower required to accomplish access control could be enormous, both for entry into buildings and onto the campus itself. (One fairly new high school in Colorado consists of 1 large building but has more than 100 exterior doors.) Technologies such as card swipes or keypads can greatly reduce this manpower requirement, but not without significant expense.

To best control a school building and/or campus, the number of entryways into the building or onto the campus must be severely limited. Just as with any high-security facility, restricting normal entrance to only one or two locations can greatly reduce the number of security personnel or security devices that must be supported. But limiting entry points can be very difficult for some schools, due to building layout, required emergency egress, property boundaries, the surrounding neighborhood, and adjacent streets.

Some urban schools have no campus per se; their buildings sit directly on streets on one or more sides. This can somewhat reduce the control problem but has some inherent problems of its own.

For those schools with campuses, fencing is usually important to control entry onto the school grounds. It is important that schools and communities recognize that enclosing a campus with fencing is more to keep outsiders out than to keep insiders in, although its presence does tend to reduce truancy during the school day. Controlling campus entry requires fencing or other physical barriers.

Fencing does not have to be unattractive. Razor tape or barbed wire is rarely appropriate for a school setting but may sometimes be necessary due to vandalism or theft at a school. If adequate funding is available, wrought iron fencing can enhance the appearance of some campuses, while providing a very difficult barrier to climb over. Less expensive but still providing an excellent barrier is an 8-foot chain link fence with small mesh (1-inch to $1\frac{1}{2}$-inch). Unlike a typical 6-foot chain link fence, it is difficult to pull up on an 8-foot-high fence and a smaller mesh will not allow toeholds. This more desirable 8-foot fencing material is usually about twice the cost per running foot as the cost of standard 6-foot fencing material, but it is probably worth the extra cost, depending on the particular school's risks.

A robust fence defines property boundaries and forces a perpetrator to consciously trespass rather than allowing idle wandering onto a campus that has no fencing. The goal of fencing is to deter the casual or unmotivated trespasser. No fence can keep out someone determined to enter the campus who comes prepared or who is very motivated (i.e., brings a ladder or wire clippers, smashes through the fence with a vehicle, and so forth). Fencing may be less important for a school that is located in a somewhat remote location. If the majority of students, faculty, and visitors must necessarily get to a particular school on buses or in cars, then the act of restricting vehicle entry to one or two driveways and posting a guard at these locations to validate all vehicle occupants may be adequate without the enclosure of fencing. For campuses on where entry into the building(s) is controlled/restricted and students do not congregate outside during the day, again, fencing may be less useful.

CHAPTER V—DURESS ALARM DEVICES AND THEIR ROLE IN CRISIS MANAGEMENT

It would be very unusual for a school never experience a crisis situation. A crisis can be any incident whereby the health or well-being of one or more students or one or more employees is in imminent danger, or part or all of the school facility will potentially be destroyed or made unavailable.

A list of crises could include:

- A threatening or drunk student or employee.
- A trespasser on campus.

- A fight.
- The breakout of a contagious disease.
- An irate and threatening parent on campus.
- Sudden unavailability of a teacher or a bus driver.
- A weapon known to be on campus.
- Massive vandalism.
- A utility outage (no water, electricity, heating, cooling, or telephone service).
- Bad weather (weather too bad to allow students to return home via normal methods or at normal times).
- A vehicular accident with injuries, either in or near the school parking lot or during a school-sponsored event.
- An extremely ill student or employee.
- A gas main leak or toxic spill on or near campus.
- A bomb threat.
- A gang confrontation on or near school property.
- A suicide.
- A hostage situation.
- A shooting, stabbing, murder, or rape.
- A bomb detonation inside the school facility or adjacent to school facilities (a car bomb).
- A local or National emergency that sends community residents to seek temporary shelter at the school.

For a school, a crisis that requires immediate response can be as harmless (but inconvenient) as the lack of a key to open the gym for an evening sporting event. Unfortunately, recent tragedies in the United States have demonstrated the need for schools to be prepared to respond to emergencies as serious as shootings or bombs.

How a school responds to this wide range of incidents is in itself an entire discipline—that of crisis management and planning. Every school needs a well-thought-out, annually updated crisis plan, with regular training for all those who might be involved. Not all schools have a plan, and many plans in existence were issued by the school district such that, by virtue of their generic nature, they may be inadequate for a true emergency. This plan needs to make assignments of who is in charge during different types of emergencies; who is the alternate in charge; who is called first, by whom, from where, and using what; whether students are relocated and how; how students are provided food, water, or shelter in the interim; what type of statement is made to the press and by whom; and who is in charge when emergency teams (fire, police, and so forth) arrive on the scene. These are only a few of the specifications called for. In the best of all possible situations, a predetermined team of school employees will immediately muster upon occurrence of a serious situation. Team members would know who[m] to look to for decisions and then proceed automatically in their roles for the particular plan chosen to be implemented.

For the sake of this discussion, it will be assumed that a school has a current crisis plan in place. The issue that will be of concern here is how an employee (or student) can notify security, school personnel, and/or local emergency services that a crisis is occurring or is imminent. Types of communication that may be viable are yelling/screaming, sending someone else for help, using the public address (PA) system, using a telephone, or calling on a two-way radio. (Two-way radios will be a selected technology topic in a subsequent manual.)

Now consider that the person who needs to summon help is in a situation in which these options are not viable. This situation may be constrained by the need for extreme urgency or discretion (because of an intimidating situation) or because of the vulnerable location of the person summoning help. The provision that allows a person to summon help under one or more of these constraints is defined as a "duress alarm."

Modern duress alarms are generally electronic devices that vary widely in capabilities and price. There are three general overlapping categories of duress alarms that can send one or more levels of distress signals to a particular location:

- A panic-button alarm—a push button mounted in a fixed location.
- An identification alarm—a portable device that identifies the owner of the device.
- An identification/location alarm—a portable device that identifies, locates, and tracks the person who activated the duress alarm.

(One additional category could possibly be the cellular telephone. While this approach is neither as discrete nor as automatic as the other three categories of alarm devices, a cellular telephone is highly recommended equipment for every principal and the primary security person. Land lines for telephone service are occasionally unavailable, whether due to inclement weather, accidents, or through malicious actions.)

The panic button is by far the most common type of duress alarm presently found in schools. The simplest application would be a strategically located button that, when initiated, would engage a dedicated phone line. A prerecorded message specifying the school, its location, and the urgency is sent to several locations, such as the police department, the district security office, and so forth. Such a system could be pulled together for a few hundred dollars by the local handyman, plus the ongoing cost of the phone line.

Commercially available duress panic button systems provide a push button mounted on classroom walls or under teachers' desks. In a duress situation, a teacher or other employee depresses the panic button, which transmits a signal, via wiring, to a location where a visible and/or audio alarm would be activated at a console. This console would provide information that would identify the classroom where the panic button was activated, but not who activated it. A more advanced system may incorporate the PA system, which allows the teacher and the administrative personnel to hold a two-way conversation by using the existing room PA speakers and installed internal wiring. The cost of this system for an average school would be approximately $10,000.

There are several weaknesses to a panic-button system. In a classroom situation, it is possible that the panic button would not be readily available in a duress situation. It may be across the room from the teacher's desk or even accidentally blocked by furniture or posters. Also, this configuration lends itself to nuisance alarms triggered by mischievous students. This problem can be offset by hiding the push button or requiring a teacher to enter a PIN on a keypad before use. (The latter is not recommended for schools because of the potential liability of a student attempting, unsuccessfully, to summon help in a threatening situation.) Such a system does not actually identify the person using it, only the owner of the device, but does locate the alarm to a particular classroom or wherever the push button is physically mounted. A panic-button system is cost effective when installed during the school's initial construction, rather than as a retrofit, and can be a simple and effective system for many types of emergencies.

A second type of system incorporates a pager-like device that has a panic button built in and is either worn by school personnel or may be installed within a foot switch located under a desk. When the panic button is pushed, a wireless alarm signal is sent to the closest installed wireless sensing unit (a type of repeater) which would then send the signal on to the alarm console. The personnel at the console would receive a coded number and this number would correspond to a teacher. This system does not usually give specific locations other than to the general preprogrammed zone of the repeater. Increasing the number of zones requires more wireless sensing units to be installed, which increases the cost and complexity of the system. A major limiting factor for this system is that the pager-like device must have a clear line of sight to the nearest sensing unit for an accurate transmission. In other words, walls, glass, roofs, floors, and so forth will degenerate the transmitted signal, which decreases the precision of identifying an individual under duress.

This type of system may also incorporate a two-way radio built into the pager that would allow communication between the console operator and person under duress, but this larger pager is more awkward to wear. Also, if a school has an existing PA system, a duress system could utilize the existing PA system wiring to send the signal from the sensing unit to the alarm console. This hybrid system would use both wireless and preexisting wires to reduce the hardware and installation costs. An estimated cost for this type of system would be about $50,000.

A third system, a smarter version of the previous system, can identify, locate, and track the person who activated the duress alarm of his or her pager. Again, school personnel would push the panic button in a duress situation, and this action would send a wireless alarm signal to a more sophisticated wireless sensing unit. The sensing unit would forward the signal to the alarm console. An extensive wireless infrastructure identifies, locates, and tracks the pager device (and hence the person under duress) within school property. The electronics and software of such a system produces a positioning symbol on a console panel or map-like display. (Telephone calls to several vendors during the summer of 1998 revealed that these systems generally cost approximately $100,000 for a 40-acre school area.)

Advanced and promising technologies. The Global Positioning Satellite (GPS) technology that is currently identifying, locating, and tracking everything from military soldiers to car rental vehicles has not been shown to be as successful when used inside buildings or around large or tall buildings. GPS requires an unobstructed signal from the ground transmitter unit to an Earth-orbiting satellite. Some advanced duress systems use a hybrid design that tracks outside personnel with GPS technology and RF or infrared systems for tracking personnel inside facilities. The cellular phone system infrastructure is improving greatly in capabilities and coverage, which in the future may be a great asset to duress alarm signals. Advances in low Earth-orbiting satellite technology that transmits data may also prove to be beneficial in making duress alarm systems more intelligent in the future.

Duress alarm system technologies are improving at a very fast pace but will likely have to come down substantially in cost before they will be affordable to most schools. Before going out on bid for the purchase of such a system, it is recommended that school administrators communicate with current users or request to participate in a demonstration of the proposed system.

11

A Guide to Effective School-Based Prevention Programs: Early Childhood Education and Environmentally Focused Programs

Sharon Mihalic and Tonya Aultman-Bettridge

Over the past several years, a large amount of information has been collected on the causes of violence and prevention programs that can modify risk and protective factors that contribute to violence. Much attention has been focused nationally on selecting and implementing quality programs.

One of the first challenges in school-based prevention efforts is how to choose a program from the multitude of those available. In the midst of sophisticated program marketing, multiple lists of best practices and programs are made available to school districts. Some programs may have the potential to be harmful to youth, and competitive resources may be wasted on such programs that could be used to implement more effective programs. It is imperative to disseminate research findings on the causes of violence and programs that have been found to be effective or ineffective in preventing or reducing violence.

Effective programs should be grounded in sound theory of the causes of youth violence. Research has determined that risk and protective factors can be found in the multiple contexts in which youth are embedded, including the school context. Within the school context, multiple factors lead to a higher risk of violence and behavioral problems. These risk factors for violence are discussed in this chapter, as are the school-based programs that address these causal factors.

Chapter 11's explicit goal is to identify those programs that focus on early childhood education and contribute to a safe and orderly school environment. Having a multitude of prevention programs is a benefit only if there is some meaningful way to determine what program(s) might be best for a particular problem, location, or group. This chapter's attempt to accomplish that goal is achieved admirably.

INTRODUCTION

As violence has climbed to the top of the national agenda, the pressure on schools to assume the primary role in prevention has grown. Although the family has the predominant role in socializing youth in mainstream values and providing positive support through the transition from childhood to adolescence and into adulthood, today schools are assuming a larger share of that role. Schools provide a prime setting to promote the acquisition of developmental competencies necessary for life success and to prevent socioemotional, behavioral, and academic difficulties (Felner et al., 2001). With increased curriculum demands, many school personnel argue that their primary role is in educating youth in academics; however, a consensus is growing that a safe and orderly school that provides a positive developmental context can help to achieve that objective. Additionally, schools provide an efficient way of reaching large numbers of children, represent a stable institution that can sustain a program over time, and provide accessibility to outcome data such as school disciplinary records (Farrell, Meyer, Kung, & Sullivan, 2001).

Several factors are useful in explaining the interest and surge in school-based prevention activities. First is the rising rate of violence throughout the late 1980s and early 1990s. Second is the emergence of a new type of violence—multiple shootings of students by peers at school. Third, public perception has made violence a top national priority. Fourth, as perceptions of the magnitude of violence and school safety lose touch with the reality of the situation, youth feel unsafe at school, and parents fear that schools are no longer a safe haven for the children. Each of these factors is briefly elaborated upon.

Violence Trends.   Findings that are reported annually by local law enforcement agencies across the country to the FBI's Uniform Crime Reporting program show that after years of relative stability, a rising trend in youth violence and homicide through the late 1980s and early 1990s appeared, heightening public awareness of the problem. Between 1988 and 1994, there was a 64% increase in the violent crime arrest rate. Violent Crime Index offenses include murder, forcible rape, robbery, and aggravated assault. There was a subsequent decline of 36% between the 1994 peak and 1999, with the 1999 arrest rate the lowest in the decade (Snyder, 2000). In 1999, while murder, forcible rape, and robbery were at or below their lowest points in the 1980s, aggravated assault was 69% higher than the 1983 low point. Homicide arrests more than doubled between 1987 and its peak in 1993, then declined 68% from 1993 to 1999, when it reached its lowest level since the 1960s (Snyder, 2000). The increase in juvenile homicides through 1993 is tied to the increased use of firearms. The subsequent decline is also related to a decline in the use of firearms. While in 1994, 82% of juvenile homicides were committed with firearms (Snyder & Sickmund, 2000), in 1999, 52% of all juvenile murder victims were killed with a firearm (Snyder, 2000).

While official arrest data have shown a dramatic increase in violence from the mid-1980s to the 1993–1994 peaks followed by declines, self-reports by youth indicate no such decline. After rising by about 50%, the incident rate of serious assault and robbery have remained essentially the same from 1993 through 1998 (U.S. Department of Health and Human Services, 2001).

School Shootings.   Although rare, shootings of students by classmates have elevated concerns about school safety. While these incidents are shocking and tragic, we must not build our perception of the problem and policy around them. In fact, children are safer on school grounds than any other place, with school homicides representing less than 1% of all youth homicides. According to the National School Safety Center (2001), there has been a decreasing trend in school-associated violent deaths between the school years 1992–1993 ($n=56$) and 2000–2001 ($n=23$). With 52 million American schoolchildren, this means that there was a 1 in 2 million chance of being killed in a school. Despite this decline in school-associated violent deaths and the decline in serious school violence, Americans are becoming more fearful for their children's safety in school.

Public Perception.   The perception of risk is often greater than the reality, despite all the indicators that violence and crime are declining. In 1982, only 3% of adults polled nationally considered crime and violence the most important problem facing this country. In 1994, more than half identified it as a major problem (Maguire & Pastore, 1996). This change in attitude coincides with the rising arrest rates through the late 1980s and early 1990s. The perception that schools were safe also took a downturn during the 1990s, perhaps a result of the increased presence of gangs and certainly linked with the increase in multiple school shootings. For instance, a 1999 Gallup poll found that 43% of parents feared for their children's safety while at school (Gallup Organization, 1999), a 49% increase over 1998. Additionally, teenagers in 1998 reported violence to be the largest problem in their school (Maguire & Pastore, 1998). A phone poll of 1,004 adults for the *Wall Street Journal* and NBC News revealed that 71% of adults believed that a school shooting could occur in their community (Brooks, Schiraldi, & Ziedenberg, 2001). Despite the perception that violence is a major problem in the community and in schools, between 1995 and 1999 students reported feeling safer at school and while traveling to and from school (Kaufman et al., 2000).

School Safety.   In light of recent highly publicized tragic acts of school violence, such as Columbine in 1999, it is important to gain an accurate assessment of the extent of violence on school grounds. Contrary to public perception, schools are among the safest places for children to be, and school crime appears to be on the decline. A joint study by the Bureau of Justice Statistics and the National Center for Education Statistics (Kaufman et al., 2000) shows that in 1998, students were about twice as likely to be a victim of serious violent crime away from school as at school. Between 1995 and 1999, school victimization decreased from 10% to 8%. Younger students (ages 12–14) were more likely than older students (ages 15–18) to be victims of crime at school.

In 1996–1997, only 10% of all public schools reported at least one serious violent crime (murder, rape, suicide, assault with weapon, or robbery) to the police, 47% reported a less serious or nonviolent crime (e.g., assault without a weapon, theft/larceny, and vandalism), and 43% did not report any crimes.

The Centers for Disease Control and Prevention (2001) conducts the Youth Risk Behavior Survey (YRBS) biennially to assess the prevalence of health-risk behaviors among high school students. The YRBS, using data from 1993–1999, shows a decline in weapon carrying in the last 30 days from 12% to 7%, and in carrying a gun from 8% to 5%. The percentages for gun carrying in two other national surveys are even lower. The Monitoring the Future (MTF) study asks a single item question about carrying a gun to school in the last 30 days. In 1998, 3.1% of grade 8, 3.6% of grade 10, and 2.1% of grade 12 students carried a gun. In the National Longitudinal Study of Adolescent Health, a more conservative estimate is gleaned from two questions inquiring about how often students had carried a weapon to school in the last 30 days, followed by what type of weapon. A student was counted as a gun carrier if he or she reported carrying a handgun, rifle, or shotgun. In 1995, 1.4% of eighth-grade students, 1.2% of tenth-grade students, and 1.1% of twelfth-grade students had carried a gun to school in the preceding 30 days (Kingery & Coggeshall, 2001).

In contrast to these improvements in risk behaviors, rates of some types of school crime have not changed or changed little (Kaufman et al., 2000). Between 1993 and 1997, students in grades 9–12 who reported being threatened or injured with a weapon in the past 12 months on school grounds remained relatively constant, at about 7% or 8% (this is also shown in the YRBS). Also, being in a physical fight on school property in the past 12 months remained constant, at about 15% (the YRBS showed a slight decline in fighting at school from 1993 to 1999, from 16% to 14%), while the prevalence of fighting anywhere decreased between 1993 and 1997, from 42% to 37%.

Thus, many indicators suggest that youth are relatively safe from being victimized by serious violence. The National Study of Delinquency Prevention in Schools (Gottfredson, Gottfredson, & Czeh, 2000), which includes student reports from 37% of the 847 secondary schools asked to participate, suggests that it is minor forms of problem behavior that are more common in school and that interfere with educational objectives. For instance, 27% of teachers report that student misbehavior keeps them from teaching a fair amount or a great deal. Although thefts have declined between 1992 and 1998, this form of victimization is more common at school than away from school (Kaufman et al., 2000).

A major emphasis has also been placed on bullying in schools. In 1999, about 5% of students ages 12–18 reported they had been bullied at school in the last six months. Bullying is more common in lower grades than in higher grades, with about 10% of students in grades 6 and 7 being bullied, compared with about 5% in grades 8 and 9, and 2% in grades 10–12 (Kaufman et al., 2000).

These factors have brought the problem of violence to the forefront of the national agenda. Effective strategies for reducing and eliminating the problem are being sought. Although numerous violence-prevention programs have been developed, few have been systematically evaluated. Efforts to enhance school safety have relied more commonly on revised disciplinary codes, locker searches, conflict-resolution programs, establishment of dress codes, multicultural sensitivity training, designation of schools as "gun-free" and "drug-free" zones, and suspensions for weapons violations (Sheley, 2000). Most of the interventions that are introduced into schools are not linked to the knowledge of the success or failure of the intervention. This often results in schools initiating and then terminating various interventions until they encounter one that seems to work for them. Resources are wasted on ineffectual programs that could be used to implement more effective programs. Elliott and Tolan (1999) note that "doing something is not always better than doing nothing" because some interventions have been shown to be harmful to adolescents. However, today we have a wealth of information about the patterns of youth involvement in violence, identifiable risk factors and their role in the developmental trajectory toward violence and antisocial behavior, and effective interventions that are built upon theoretical foundations that address the risk factors that play a crucial role in the development of antisocial behavior. More information and assistance is available to help schools and communities assess their own body of risk factors and select programs that address those risks and the populations they want to target.

The demand for effective programs has never been greater. This has moved several federal and state agencies and a few nonprofit organizations to identify and disseminate "best practices" and/or "best programs." Because each organization creating these lists defines the criteria for effectiveness differently (some have more or less rigorous criteria for program inclusion), and because the universe of programs reviewed or outcomes sought may vary, there are many differences from list to list. Just as having too little information often results in a school or agency continuing with current practices, an overload of information with no way to sort out the details effectively may also result in a failure to adopt research-based practices and programs. This chapter is intended to provide information on a wide range of effective school-based programs.

Criteria for Program Selection

The list of programs selected for this chapter include, but are not limited to, school-based programs adopted in the Blueprints series (the first author of this chapter directs the Blueprints Project and has been involved in the identification of Blueprints programs since the inception of the project). The criteria for a Blueprints Model program include:

1. *Evidence of deterrent effect with a strong research design.* This is the most important of the selection criteria. Blueprints accepts evidence of deterrent effects for violence (including childhood aggression and conduct disorder), drug use, and/or delinquency. Designs must involve either random assignment to treatment and control conditions or a control group that is matched as closely as possible to the experimental group on relevant characteristics (e.g., gender, race, age, socioeconomic status, income). The research design must be of such high quality to rule out alternative explanations for effects found. This means that particular attention is given to several key aspects such as sample size, selection bias, equivalency of conditions, differential attrition (loss of study participants over time such that the treatment and control groups look different on key characteristics), analyses, and measurements.

2. *Sustained effect.* Blueprints requires a sustained effect at least one year beyond treatment with no subsequent evidence that this effect is lost. Many programs lose their effect once treatment ends. This criterion helps ensure that effects are maintained through the high-risk years of adolescence.

3. *Multiple site replication.* Blueprints requires at least one replication with demonstrated effects. This helps to ensure that a program can be implemented

successfully in a new setting with different providers and populations. It helps to establish that program effectiveness is not due to a particular person or specific characteristics at a site.

Promising Blueprints programs must meet the first criterion. The Model and Promising programs for this chapter come directly from the Blueprints list. These programs have undergone a peer review in which a distinguished advisory board have come to a consensus that the programs meet Blueprints criteria. Because the criteria for Blueprints selection is so rigorous and the outcomes confined to violence, delinquency, or substance abuse, a third list of favorable programs have been identified for this chapter that includes a broader range of outcomes relevant for school safety and success, such as school disciplinary problems, suspensions, truancy, dropout, and academic achievement. These programs may also have slightly weaker research designs than the standard held for Blueprints. The authors of this chapter, however, agree that there is *reasonable* scientific evidence that behavioral effects are due to the intervention and not a result of weak methodological rigor. These programs all have experimental or matched control group designs. Each program write-up includes an overview of the intervention, the target population, and a brief description of the evaluation.

Categorizing the Programs

Programs are classified into 10 categories. Most of these categories were identified in a major study of delinquency prevention in schools, a project undertaken to determine the levels of problem behavior in U.S. schools and the activities and programs undertaken by schools to promote a safe and orderly environment (Gottfredson, Gottfredson, & Czeh, 2000). The 10 categories include:

Early Childhood Education Programs
Environmentally Focused Programs
Interventions to Establish Norms or Expectations for Behavior
Reorganization of Grades or Classes
School and Discipline Management Interventions
Classroom or Instructional Management
Individually Focused Programs
Social Skills, Behavioral, and Cognitive-Behavioral Programs
Other Instructional Programs
Counseling, Social Work, and Other Therapeutic Interventions
Mentoring, Tutoring, and Work Study
Recreation, Community Service, Enrichment, and Leisure Activities

In the original study that identified these categories, as well as in the Maryland Report describing "What Works and What Doesn't Work" in the field of prevention and treatment (Gottfredson, 1997), some practices proved more effective than others:

1. Strategies that focus on changing the environment were somewhat more effective than those focusing only on changing individuals' attitudes, behaviors, or beliefs.

2. The most effective strategies (across the outcomes of crime, substance use, dropout/truancy, and antisocial behavior/aggression) were school and discipline management interventions; interventions to establish norms and expectations for behavior; and instructional programs that teach social competency skills using cognitive-behavioral methods.

3. The least effective strategies (across all four outcomes) were instructional programs that do not use cognitive-behavioral methods; counseling, social work, and other therapeutic interventions; and recreation and leisure programs.

For this study, a total of 382 programs were examined, 199 of which were school based (i.e., the intervention occurred in the school or was delivered by school staff or under the school system auspices). Among the school-based programs, 116 involved an experimental or matched control group design. After elimination of some programs because of methodological weaknesses or outcomes not pertinent to our criteria, 59 studies are reported in this chapter and the next. Each program is ranked into one of three groups: exemplary, promising, and favorable.

EARLY CHILDHOOD EDUCATION PROGRAMS

A small percentage of teenagers typically account for the majority of crimes. Many of these youth are life course persistent offenders (Loeber & Farrington, 1998; Moffit, 1993) who have an early onset of aggressive and behavioral problems, often associated with inattention-hyperactivity, neurocognitive risk, difficult temperament, and poor parenting (Moffitt & Caspi, 2001). The Cambridge study of 411 working-class boys in London indicated that boys rated by their teachers and peers as "most troublesome" at ages 8 to 10 represented 22% of the entire sample, but 70% of future chronic offenders (i.e., had repeatedly committed offenses by the age of 19 and continued for at least five years or more) (Farrington, 1987). The Dunedin Multidisciplinary Health and Development Study in New Zealand showed that 10% of boys and 1% of girls were on a life course persistent path (Moffitt & Caspi, 2001).

Early initiators have often experienced neuropsychological impairments, such as poor reading, language, and problem-solving skills; inattentiveness and impulsivity; and memory difficulties. These problems compromise healthy development and increase the risk for significant impediments to later wellness, such as violence, delinquency, school dropout, and depression (Cowen & Durlak, 2000; Kazdin, 1985) and drug abuse (Brook, Whiteman, Gordon, & Cohen, 1986; Dishion, Patterson, Stoolmiller, & Skinner, 1991). Although the majority of young children with behavioral problems will not become life course persistent offenders (Derzon, 2001; Yeager & Lewis, 2000), conduct disorder and other forms of antisocial behavior become resistant to change over time. The prognosis for those early starters who continue exhibiting problems into adolescence is poor unless early intervention, designed to improve the child's behavioral adjustment at home and at school, is offered (Kazdin, 1987). Intervention performed during early childhood, focused on preventing health and developmental problems, can prevent later delinquency by interrupting the negative socialization processes that begin during childhood and continue through adolescence (Herrenkohl et al., 2001).

Factors within the family that place children at risk include harsh or ineffective parenting, poor parental monitoring, poor attachment, lack of warmth and nurturance; and for the child, lack of social and intellectual competence, impulsiveness, and lack of self-control (Webster-Stratton et al., 2001). Emmy Werner (1989, 1990; Werner & Smith, 1992) followed a cohort of children born in 1955 on the island of Kauai for 30 years, and found that despite children having four or more debilitating risk factors by age two (such as parental psychopathology, extreme poverty, perinatal birth disorders, low parental educational level), certain children were able to overcome the adversity in their lives. These resiliency, or protective, factors can be classified according to three major domains (see Garmezy 1985; Greenberg, Domitrovich, & Bumbarger, 1999; Masten & Garmezy, 1985):

- Individual characteristics (i.e., dispositional attributes of the individual that may have a strong genetic base) such as easy temperament, positive orientation, intelligence, self-esteem, autonomy, and sociability
- Family characteristics, such as secure attachments, lack of family conflict, cohesive and warm family interactions to provide emotional support and affection
- External (environmental) support systems at school, work, or church that encourage and reinforce a child's coping efforts, reward the individual's competencies and determination, and provide him or her with a sense of meaning and an internal locus of control

While some children are born with innate characteristics that help them to overcome early childhood adversity, others will need supportive families and strong external support systems to overcome the risks in their lives. Intervening early with high-risk preschool-age children and their parents, through early childhood development and education programs, helps to foster resiliency in the child.

Early interventions that focus on promoting parent knowledge, attitudes, or behavior related to effective child rearing; children's health and development; preventing child abuse and neglect; and enhancing maternal life course can have an important impact on the subsequent development of antisocial behavior by interrupting the developmental trajectory toward delinquency and related behavioral disorders. Many early childhood education (ECE) programs work with the parents to provide them with support and skills designed to alter the parent–child interaction. Parent training helps to overcome the problems generally associated with poor family management practices by instructing parents in providing consistent and supportive forms of discipline (Patterson, 1986). These programs provide skills training to the parents to encourage the development of a solid attachment with the child to promote the emotional and social development of the child and help build the child's capacity for impulse regulation and empathy (Olds, Hill, Mihalic, & O'Brien, 1998). Building a solid foundation between the parent and child at the earliest ages encourages the growth and development of children with a strong sense of self-esteem, self-control, and emotional, social, and cognitive skills that will help protect them against a multitude of health risks, such as violence and drug use. In addition to rooting a strong parent–child attachment is the need to promote early age-appropriate child competencies and preparedness for school.

Most of the early childhood programs that have been successful contain similar elements. For instance, they are intensive, multicomponent programs that address the various systems and influences that affect a child's development. Most also include home visits to provide parenting skills and support, as well as an early educational component that focuses on the child's development (Wasserman, Miller, & Cothern, 2000). Home visitation and ECE programs have been most beneficial to high-risk populations, such as poor families and unmarried women. Although intervention may begin earlier, most ECE programs target children at about age 2 through school entry. Some of the most powerful and effective interventions seek to attain multiple goals (Gomby, Larson, Lewit, & Behrman, 1993) by combining preschool or daycare with home visits. Programs with a home visit component typically include weekly to monthly home visits to provide parents with information about parenting and/or child development, emotional and social support, counseling, and referrals to outside agencies. Parents are also taught to support and maintain the social, emotional, and cognitive gains that children achieve in the daycare or preschool setting.

The primary goal of ECE programs is school readiness—preparing at-risk children for entering school by improving cognitive development and constructing a role for the child that places him or her on a trajectory for success. These programs focus directly on the child by seeking to improve cognitive development through language, reading, improving health and nutrition, and cognitively stimulating play. The early cognitive gains achieved often result in later school readiness and academic achievement, thus strengthening bonds to school (Schweinhart & Weikart, 1980). The outcomes of the ECE programs have primarily focused on the cognitive development and academic success of the child, with less emphasis on antisocial behavior. However, several programs described here have demonstrated in long-term follow-ups that they can reduce behavior problems at the time when children are at risk for violent offending.

Exemplary Programs   None.

Promising Programs   *High/Scope Perry Preschool* provides high-quality early childhood education to children ages 3 and 4 from low socioeconomic families and seeks to combat the relationship between childhood poverty and school failure by fostering social, emotional, and intellectual competence. The two-year intervention operates 2.5 hours per day, five days per week, for seven months per year, and includes weekly home visitations by teachers. Based on the theory that early success, or failure, in school may set children on a life course trajectory of success or failure, High/Scope helps children start out in school with a role conducive to success (Schweinhart & Weikart, 1980). This goal is achieved by providing children with cognitive stimulation that may be lacking in the home environment, which leads to greater cognitive ability when children enter school. In addition, the program teaches children to be active and independent learners, helps parents to support the child's education, and provides teachers with effective training methods and support (Parks, 2000). The success achieved by this program stems from the increased school readiness, which results in positive reinforcement from teachers and students, enhanced academic performance, and stronger commitment to school (Parks, 2000; Schweinhart & Weikart, 1980).

The evaluation, based on the random assignment of 123 African-American youth in five subsequent years (1962–1966) to preschool and no preschool groups, demonstrated greater school success (academic achievement and commitment); socioeconomic success (increased employment, economic independence, satisfaction with work) at age 19; social responsibility, including reductions in antisocial behavior and misconduct during elementary school through age 15; and fewer fights, criminal justice contacts, and arrests (31% of program participants had been arrested for a crime, compared to 51% of controls) through age 19 (Berrueta-Clement et al., 1984; Schweinhart & Weikart, 1980; Weikart, Bond, & McNeil, 1978). At age 27, the experimental group had half as many arrests as the control group, as well as higher earnings. More of the women in the experimental group had graduated from high school, attended college or vocational training, were married, and had fewer children out of wedlock (Schweinhart, Barnes, & Weikart, 1993).

The program provides a savings to the public of nearly seven times the initial investment per child, with a return of $7.16 per dollar spent (Barnett, 1993; Parks, 2000) incurred through savings in welfare assistance, special education and criminal justice costs, savings to crime victims, and increased tax revenue from higher earnings. An independent cost analysis, provided by the RAND Corporation (Karoly et al., 1998), eliminates the victim costs, the least reliable savings category, and still found a return of more than twice the initial investment.

Three other programs, the *Yale Child Welfare Project,* the *Syracuse Family Development Program,* and the *Houston Child Development Center,* also target low-income families and are designed to provide family support and early education. These programs offer a broad range of support for both mothers and children. Through home visits, mothers receive individualized training and support on child development issues, appropriate interactions with children, nutrition, health and safety, immediate family crises, achieving long-term goals, and accessing community resources. Each program also provides some form of high-quality daycare/education for the children. Two programs begin during pregnancy and continue until the infants are 30 months old (Yale) or through the child's fifth year (Syracuse). The Houston Program targets children two months to three years.

The Houston Program, through random assignment of 102 Mexican-American mother–child pairs, demonstrated increases in IQ and cognitive ability at 24 months for program children; less destructive, overactive, and negative attention-seeking behavior at ages 4–7; and lower teacher ratings of impulsive, obstinate, disruptive, hostile, and fighting behaviors at ages 8–11 (Johnson & Breckenridge, 1982; Johnson & Walker, 1987). The Yale (Seitz, Rosenbaum, & Apfel, 1985) and Syracuse Programs (Lally, Mangione, Honig, & Wittner, 1988), using quasi-experimental designs with matched control groups, primarily targeting African-American women, demonstrated long-term effects 10 years after the intervention on social adjustment, school attendance, and achievement. The Syracuse Program also reduced juvenile delinquency. Specifically, at age 15, 6% of program participants had a juvenile record, compared to 22% of controls, and those with criminal records had fewer and less serious offenses. Additionally, the Yale Program demonstrated dramatic effects on program mothers by increasing educational achievement, reducing family size, and creating more economically independent families.

Favorable Programs   *Abecedarian* is a preschool program that operates year-round for low-income children from infancy through age 5 (Campbell & Ramey, 1995). The infant curriculum strives to enhance cognitive, language, perceptual-motor, and social development skills. In the later preschool years, the emphasis is on language development and preliteracy skills. Primary medical care is also received on site. During the preschool portion of the program, efforts are made to involve parents by providing voluntary programs and supportive social services. During the school-age treatment, a Home School Resource Teacher individualizes sets of supplemental educational activities addressing specific learning needs that serve as the focal point for biweekly home visits in which parents are taught to use the learning activities with their children.

The evaluation of this program involved 109 families who were randomized into a preschool group and a control group, with a second randomization occurring prior to kindergarten entry. Comparisons were made not only between treatment and no treatment, but also between students who received the treatment in preschool and those who received it during elementary school. The experimental design resulted in four groups: (1) preschool treatment followed by early elementary treatment (infancy to 8 years), (2) preschool treatment only (infancy to 5 years), (3) early elementary school treatment only (5–8 years), and (4) untreated controls. Attrition from birth to the treatment endpoint, based on the number of subjects with 8-year IQ data, was 18.9%. The sample was 98% African-American. Although there were no IQ differences in the first 3 months of the program, by 18 months and thereafter through age 8 years, experimental group children displayed a significant advantage in IQ test scores relative to the control group. The age 12 follow-up (Campbell & Ramey, 1994), conducted 4 years after the treatment endpoint, and after 7 years in public school, showed that positive effects of preschool treatment on children's intellectual test performance and on academic tests of reading and mathematics had been maintained into early adolescence. Results also suggest that the longer the duration of treatment, the larger the effect. The most effective treatment condition, relative to the control group, was combined preschool and early elementary treatment, followed by preschool only, and lastly followed by early elementary treatment (Campbell, Burchinal, Skinner, & Gardner, 2000).

Project Care was developed after the success of the Abecedarian educational daycare curriculum, supplementing that program with a strong family support component, based upon the assumption that without family involvement, intervention is likely to be unsuccessful or disappear once the intervention is discontinued. The family education component involves a home-based intervention designed to help the parent foster the cognitive and social development of the child. Visits occur weekly during the first three years, and during later years the visits are weekly to every six weeks, depending upon parental preference. The evaluation involved random assignment of 65 families at the time of the child's birth to one of three conditions: (1) Child Development Center plus family education, (2) family education alone, or (3) a control group. All the families had infants who were at elevated risk for delayed development due to the disadvantaged educational or social circumstances of the parents. Results showed that cognitive performance was higher for the children in the educational daycare plus family support group (tests performed from 6 months through 54 months of age). No cognitive intervention effects were obtained for the family education alone group.

Chicago Child–Parent Center and Expansion Program (CPC) provides a half-day preschool, half-day or all-day kindergarten, and all-day service in primary grades. The CPC targets economically and educationally disadvantaged children and focuses on three major areas: providing children and parents with comprehensive services (e.g., free breakfasts and lunches, health screening; coordinated adult supervision through CPC head teachers, teacher's aides, parent-resource teachers, and school-community representative; and funding for instructional supplies and in-service child development teacher training); increasing parental involvement in school, especially during preschool and kindergarten in which half-day involvement each week is required; and utilizing a child-centered, basic skills focus on reading and mathematics. Children may participate in the program from one to six years, from preschool to the third grade.

The quasi-experimental design included 1,262 youth (956 CPC students who participated in the 20 Chicago CPCs during preschool and kindergarten and 306 comparison students from six randomly selected schools participating in a locally funded, all-day kindergarten program for low-income families) and assessed the impact of the program on delinquency at ages 13–16. Although the results were mixed, the most consistent finding was that participation in the primary grade component of the CPC program after participation in preschool/kindergarten was significantly associated with a lower rate of school-reported delinquency at ages 13–14, but duration of program participation was only marginally significant at ages 15–16. There were no differences on students' self-reports of delinquency or arrests (Reynolds, Chang, & Temple, 1998). These mixed findings elicit caution.

Al Pals is a 47-lesson, resiliency-based classroom prevention program that targets 3- and 4-year-old children in Head Start and preschool. The curriculum is designed to teach young children the skills necessary for appropriate expression of feelings, problem-solving and coping skills, managing self-control, and engaging in positive interactions and relationships with peers and adults. In 37 classrooms randomly assigned to treatment or control conditions, the program classrooms showed improvement on social skills and resilience-related behaviors. Additionally, while problem behaviors, including aggression, increased for controls, they remained stable for the intervention group (Lynch, 1998).

First Step to Success targets at-risk kindergarteners who show clear signs of antisocial behavior. The program includes three modules. First, a screening component determines program eligibility. Second, the classroom component enables children to earn privileges for themselves and other classmates based upon good behavior. Third, the home-based component consists of six lessons that enable parents to build child competencies and skills in areas that affect school adjustment and performance. Home visits are made weekly for approximately three months. A randomized, experimental, wait-list control group design was used to evaluate intervention effects. It included two cohorts of 24 and 22 students who were exposed to the program in subsequent years. At postintervention, program children had better ratings than control children on teacher-rated aggression. The effects were maintained through the second grade for cohort one and the first grade for cohort two (Walker et al., 1998).

ENVIRONMENTALLY FOCUSED PROGRAMS

Changing School Systems

Many individual-level risk factors for crime and violence may be brought into the school environment by individual students, for example, abuse and neglect, behavioral disorders, impulsiveness, and risk-taking temperaments. Moreover, when there is a concentration of children with these characteristics, there is an emergent contextual effect at school, in which physical aggression, bullying, and disrespect for teachers, other students, and authority figures become normative. Further, the way the school is structured and the training and competence of the staff can also function to undermine a successful course of youth development, facilitating the creation and maintenance of delinquent or antisocial peer groups, low expectations for academic success, intimidation of teachers, and low value on education. The overall climate, structure, and environment of a school can thus contribute to students' behavioral problems or, at the least, impede any successful resolution of them. School ecology programs recognize these problems and seek to identify and change conditions in the school that might negatively impact students. Such factors may include school norms and behavioral expectations, administrative policies, tracking strategies, school structure and size, and teacher attitudes and practices.

The goals of school ecology programs is to reduce the conditions of risk in the environment to prevent the onset of adaptive difficulties and to enhance the school context to help ensure that *all* youth acquire competencies and strengths to ensure their success (Felner et al., 2001). To create and maintain systemic changes in school climate and structure, as well as to generalize effects across settings, programs must involve teachers, administrators, parents, students, and interested community members as partners in implementation. School-based strategies can be roughly grouped into four categories: Interventions to Establish Norms or Expectations for Behavior, Reorganization of Grades or Classes, School Discipline and Management Interventions, and Classroom Instructional Management.

Interventions to Establish Norms or Expectations for Behavior

Research on school discipline problems indicates that the ways in which norms and expectations for behavior are established can have a strong impact on levels of school crime and violence. In schools in which behavioral norms are clearly stated and well known by students and also are consistently and fairly enforced, levels of student and teacher victimization are reduced (Gottfredson, 1997). In many cases, programs aim to change all of the normative environments experienced by students, including the family and the community. These interventions operate under the assumption that risk factors in multiple domains (which is to say, those in society, in the family, in the individual, and in the peer group, as well as in the school) must be addressed in order to affect substantial changes in youth behavior.

Exemplary Programs   *Bullying Prevention Program* focuses on restructuring the social environment of primary and secondary schools in order to provide fewer opportunities for bullying behavior to occur and also to reduce the positive social "rewards" (such as peer approval and support) gained through bullying behavior. Overall, the program aims to create a school normative environment characterized by positive interest and involvement by adults and establish firm limits to unacceptable behavior, in which norm and rule violations consistently result in sanctions and adults act as authority figures and positive role models for youth. While the Bullying Prevention Program actively involves students, adults in the school are the driving force in changing the normative environment. To facilitate such a sweeping change, the program seeks to ensure that adults are aware of bullying problems and are actively involved in their prevention, conveying the message that "bullying is not accepted in our class/school and we will see to it that it comes to an end" (Olweus, Limber, & Mihalic, 1999).

Interventions in the Bullying Prevention Program occur at the school, classroom, and individual student level. The program begins with the creation of a coordinating committee and a schoolwide survey to assess the extent and nature of the bullying problem at the participating school. Following the survey, a school conference day is held to review questionnaire results. The coordinating committee then begins planning for implementation of the program, including the creation of a system to improve the monitoring of students during recess and lunchtimes (based on "hot spots" identified by the survey) and to plan for parent and staff meetings to discuss implementation progress. The classroom-level intervention involves the creation of class rules regarding bullying behavior and regular class meetings to discuss issues and/or rule infractions. In addition, meetings with parents of children of a given classroom may occur to discuss elements of the program. The program is also implemented at the individual student level with bullies, their parents, and victims in order to ensure that any ongoing behavior is stopped and that victims receive needed support.

Research on the Bullying Prevention Program utilized a quasi-experimental design with time-lagged contrasts between age-equivalent groups (successive cohorts of children for particular grade levels) involving 2,400 students in grades 4 to 7 in 42 schools (28 elementary and 14 junior high) in Bergen, Norway, who were followed over 2.5 years. This evaluation documented decreases of (typically) 50% or more in reported frequency with which students reported being bullied by others. In addition, substantial reductions in student involvement in vandalism, fighting, thefts, and truancy were also demonstrated by the project. Students reported better order and discipline at school, improved social relationships, and increases in positive attitudes toward school (Olweus, Limber, & Mihalic, 1999). A program replication with 6,388 students in grades 4 through 6 in 39 schools in three matched pairs of rural South Carolina districts revealed a decrease in the frequency with which children bullied other children (by approximately 25%), while students in control schools reported a corresponding increase. Additionally, self-reported antisocial behavior increased in the control group, while there was either no increase or a slower rate of increase with regard to general delinquency, vandalism, school misbehavior, and punishment for school-related misbehaviors among the treated children (Olweus, Limber, & Mihalic, 1999).

Midwestern Prevention Project (MPP) includes school normative environment change as one of many components of a comprehensive, three- to five-year community-based prevention program that targets "gateway" drug use of tobacco, alcohol, and marijuana—those substances that traditionally precede the use of other illicit substances. The program involves schools, parents, and community organizations; uses mass media to communicate messages regarding the dangers of gateway drug use; and seeks changes in health policies and community practices to reduce youth access to targeted substances. Lasting a period of five years, the program introduces each segment (school, parent, community organization, and health policy) on a specific timeline, beginning with the school intervention in year one and ending with targeted health policy change in the final years of the project.

The school-based segment of MPP is the central component of the program and is the first to be introduced. The program begins in either sixth or seventh grade, depending on the school district and which grade represents the transition to middle or junior high school. It consists of 10 to 13 classroom sessions, delivered by teachers trained in the curriculum, and may be facilitated by peer leaders. Peer leaders are nominated by the class and trained by teachers in the program components. Classroom sessions focus on increasing drug-resistance skills and also aim to change the social climate of the school to encourage non-drug-use norms. Five booster sessions are offered in year two to reinforce concepts learned previously, and follow-up peer counseling and support are made available through the high school years.

School activities are followed by a parent component designed to develop norms within the family and the neighborhood that discourage drug use. Parent education and organization efforts continue throughout the middle/junior high school years. School climate change is facilitated by a group comprised of the school principal, teachers, parents, and peer leaders. This group works to change the school climate by institutionalizing the school-based curriculum, helping to monitor drug use on the school grounds and in the community, and planning and implementing the parent training program. Parent intervention is followed by the community component, in which community leaders plan and implement drug abuse prevention services within the neighborhood, plan community activities that complement the school and family programs, and develop strategies to change health policies (such as local ordinances restricting cigarette smoking in public venues). This final goal is achieved via subcommittees of local government and community leaders and is largely aimed at reducing supply and demand of gateway substances. A mass media campaign using television, radio, and print is delivered throughout the life of the project to convey to the larger community messages that are central to the student and parent skills training components of the program.

MPP was first evaluated in Kansas City (Pentz, Mihalic, & Grotpeter, 1997) using a quasi-experimental design in which schools ($n=50$) and communities were assigned to program conditions on the basis of scheduling flexibility and demographic matching where possible. Three sampling plans were used to collect data, including the random assignment of eight schools to treatment or control groups, for a total of 1,607 students who were tracked over a three-year period. Although follow-up interviews were conducted with 84% of the original panel participants, 69% had complete data. The evaluations have shown net reductions of up to 40% in daily smoking and marijuana use, along with smaller reductions in alcohol use. These results were maintained by youth in participating communities through high school graduation. Reductions in use of other illicit substances (amphetamines, LSD, and inhalants) have been shown in participating youth into early adulthood (age 23). The program has also demonstrated reductions in parent alcohol and marijuana use, and increased positive parent–child communications regarding drug use and abuse prevention. In addition, communities participating in MPP have reported that it has successfully facilitated the development of community services for drug abuse prevention.

Promising Programs   *Project Northland* is a three-year comprehensive, community-based program designed to prevent alcohol use in middle school students. Each year of the program has a specific theme. In the first year, the intervention targets sixth graders with a goal of improving parent–child communication. Children, with the assistance of their parents, complete homework assignments focusing on adolescent alcohol use.

A communitywide task force is also established in the project's first year to address issues of community norms and youth access to alcohol. The second year, focusing on seventh-grade students, involves a teacher-led classroom curriculum that emphasizes resistance skills. Parent involvement is encouraged, and youth are given opportunities to participate in structured, alcohol-free activities. In the final year, eighth-grade students are encouraged to become community activists against teen alcohol use, thereby generalizing the lessons learned in the first two years of the project to the larger community.

Evaluation of the program involved 24 Minnesota school districts (4 smaller districts were combined with nearby districts to ensure adequate sample size in each unit, for a total of 20 combined districts) that were blocked by size and then randomly assigned to treatment and control groups. By the end of the eighth grade, the program demonstrated lower scores on a "tendency to use alcohol" scale, less use of alcohol in both the past week and past month, and lower frequency of the combination of alcohol and cigarette use for program youth. In addition, students who were nonusers of alcohol at the beginning of the intervention demonstrated significantly lower onset rates for alcohol, and cigarette and marijuana use were significantly lower in the intervention districts (Perry et al., 1996).

Favorable Programs   *Peacebuilders* aims to change the school environment at the elementary school level to reinforce positive behaviors and emphasize rewards and praise for prosocial behavior. The intervention focuses on training school staff and teachers to be Peacebuilder "coaches," to use a common language of "community norms," to model prosocial behavior, and to provide a variety of rewards to students for good behavior. Through parent education, marketing to families, and mass media tie-ins, children are taught to praise people, avoid put-downs, seek out wise people as advisers and friends, notice and correct hurts caused, and right wrongs (Embry et al., 1996).

Evaluation of the program was conducted with four schools receiving treatment and four matched control schools, with each school randomly assigned to either the treatment or control group. One control school dropped out of the program midyear. Results indicated increases in prosocial behavior, such as compromising and coping with anger, and with lower self- and teacher-reports of aggressive behavior in schools participating in the program (Flannery et al., 1998). Another study found that nurse visits (overall visits and visits for injuries due to fighting) decreased in schools participating in the Peacebuilders program when compared to control schools (Krug et al., 1997).

Mass Media Smoking Prevention Program targets youth in grades 5 through 10 by combining a classroom curriculum designed to prevent/reduce youth smoking with a media campaign aimed at changing norms and attitudes about youth smoking. The curriculum includes lessons on decision-making skills to resist peer and media pressure to smoke, social support for nonsmoking, and information about health effects of smoking (Flynn et al., 1992). For the evaluation, four standard metropolitan statistical areas were selected, based on being an independent media market, having a population of 50,000 to 400,000, and having matched demographic characteristics, including education, income, and ethnicity. Two communities received the mass media intervention and school program, while the two matched communities received only the school program. The program demonstrated significantly less smoking in groups receiving both the school curriculum and the mass media program, compared with youth receiving only the school curriculum. The school and media group also reported less intention to smoke and norms and attitudes favoring nonsmoking than the school only groups. These results persisted through five years of the program (Flynn et al., 1994). A follow-up study (Flynn et al., 1995) found that those in the school and media group reported less smoking at grades 10 through 12, than did those in the school only group. The results demonstrate that mass media campaigns can boost the effects of a school-based prevention program.

Safe Dates aims to improve student interpersonal relationships and reduce dating violence through student education, changing stereotypes, and providing student support. Safe Dates is designed to prevent dating violence through both school- and community-based activities. The school program consists of a 10-week curriculum, theater production, and poster contest. In addition, community support services, such as a crisis line and support groups, are made available in the community for adolescents already involved in abusive dating relationships. The purposes of these activities are to change norms regarding dating violence, prevent gender stereotyping, and inform youth about services available to them. The evaluation included 1,700 eighth and ninth graders in 14 rural public schools matched on school size and stratified by grade. One member of each matched pair was randomly assigned to a treatment or control condition. The program has shown reductions in abuse for those participating in treatment services and less psychological abuse and sexual violence perpetration for those participating in the school-based prevention program (Foshee et al., 1998).

Reorganization of Grades or Classes

Many schoolwide interventions focus on the school climate, or environment, by making changes to the substantive structure of the school itself. These efforts are designed to buffer the negative effects of large schools or class sizes on students (particularly at-risk adolescents), as well as to help avoid or overcome problems some students encounter when transitioning into new and large urban junior or high school settings, especially in districts involving multiple feeder schools. In some cases, restructuring is aimed at making the school environment more relevant for some students, including offering work-study training and community service in addition to traditional academic subjects.

Exemplary Programs   None.

Promising Programs   *School Transitional Environment Program (STEP)* aims to ease the transition of high-risk youth entering larger, more complex school settings (Felner & Adan, 1988). STEP involves a reorganization of the social system to eliminate the flux and complexity that students confront when entering a new school. Incoming ninth-grade students are assigned to teams of 60 to 100 students, who are then assigned to homerooms in which all students are STEP participants. Homeroom teachers serve as guidance counselors and assist students in making a successful transition. They also maintain contact with parents regarding students' progress. All students participating in the project are assigned to the same core courses, which are located physically close together in order to facilitate stable peer groups and create a smaller "school within a school" physical environment.

An initial study of STEP was conducted in a large urban high school with a total enrollment of approximately 1,700 students. Students were randomly selected for participation in STEP from approximately 450 entering freshmen who were showing generally satisfactory school adjustment and not in need of any special mental health programming. The 65 participating STEP students were matched by sex, age, and ethnic background with 120 control students who met the same criteria. A total of 59 experimental and 113 control group students completed all assessments. By the end of the ninth grade, students participating in the program demonstrated better attendance, school performance, and more stable levels of self-confidence than controls. STEP students also perceived the school environment as more stable, understandable, well organized, involving, and supportive than did control students (Felner, Ginter, & Primavera, 1982). A long-term follow-up (Felner & Adan, 1988) of this initial sample through the high school years (in which 90% of school records were obtained) showed that STEP students had higher grades and fewer absences than control subjects in the ninth and tenth grades, although this gap closed in the last two years of high school. The dropout rate of STEP students was half that of the control group (21% vs. 43%).

Student Training Through Urban Strategies (STATUS) combines school climate change with classroom restructuring in order to establish stronger ties between youth and their communities. The program targets high-risk youth in middle/junior high and high school. The school climate segment of the intervention consists of four components. A student leadership class allows students to participate in school policy making and problem solving. Staff development and training prepare school staff to support and facilitate student involvement. Action committees within the community are organized to provide resources and guidance to students. Finally, parent meetings increase awareness of school processes and activities and allow parents to participate in school decision making. The "options" class (law-related education), which uses instructional methods emphasizing active student involvement, focuses on social institutions, including the school, human behavior, family, social contracts and social order, and the criminal justice system. In high school, the curriculum adds job market and life-planning skills (Gottfredson, 1990).

The evaluation of the program included aproximately 120 students, self-referred or referred by school staff, in grades seven and nine, in each of two schools that were randomly assigned to treatment or control conditions. Shifting of students occurred after randomization because of scheduling difficulties resulting in nonequivalent groups. However, differences were statistically controlled. Results showed less delinquency for participating students, less drug involvement for middle school students, less negative peer influence, and better school performance and attitudes (Gottfredson, 1990).

Favorable Programs   None.

School and Discipline Management Interventions

Like programs designed to change behavioral norms or restructure the school environment, programs featuring school and discipline management interventions involve a comprehensive, schoolwide change effort, with school climate as a primary focus. Unlike other types of strategies, however, these interventions involve a more targeted focus on behavior management and school discipline practices. In addition, in contrast to many restructuring programs, they typically target *all* students within a particular school setting, rather than individual high-risk students. Many of these programs also strive to establish closer relationships between schools and communities by including parents, local leaders, and members of the community in the initiative.

Exemplary Programs   None.

Promising Programs   *Promoting Action Through Holistic Education (PATHE)* targets middle and high schools that serve students at risk of school failure and subsequent delinquency. The program generally involves all students in the school and provides additional treatment for low-achieving and disruptive students. This comprehensive intervention uses a number of strategies to affect schoolwide change. School improvement programs are designed and implemented through a partnership of staff, students, parents, and community members. Specific academic weaknesses and discipline problems within the school are identified and targeted for change through staff training and the creation of clear and fair rules. A variety of strategies, including "school pride" campaigns, extracurricular activities to foster greater student engagement in the school, and peer counseling services, are all used to promote a positive school climate. In addition, the school provides job-seeking skills programs and career exploration programs to promote career development within the entire student body.

In addition to these services and interventions designed to benefit the entire student body, PATHE also provides additional services for at-risk students. These include mentoring, tutoring, and counseling programs aimed at improving self-concept, academic success, and bonding to prosocial norms (Gottfredson, 1990).

A nonequivalent comparison group design involving all teachers and students in five middle schools (four program and one comparison) and four high schools (three program and one comparison) in low-income, predominantly African-American, urban, and rural areas was utilized to evaluate the program. Schools were the unit of analysis. To test the program among the high-risk sample, a pool of students developed through teacher referrals and examination of academic and behavioral referrals from each school were randomly assigned to treatment or control conditions. The evaluation demonstrated decreases in levels of serious delinquency, drug involvement, suspensions, and school disciplinary actions in the schools participating in the program. The results also indicated decreased school alienation, increases in attachment to school, and improvements in school climate and discipline management. Additionally, higher risk youth targeted by the program had higher graduation rates, higher standardized test scores, and increases in school attendance, but no changes in delinquency, and self-reported drug involvement was higher for the treatment group. This suggests that the mentoring, tutoring, and counseling components for the high-risk sample were not enough to change problem behaviors (Gottfredson, 1990).

Favorable Programs   *Child Development Project* is a comprehensive, ecological approach designed to influence all aspects of the school. The goal is to foster healthy youth development; inspire social, ethical, and intellectual growth; and create a meaningful, challenging, and motivating school curriculum. The program targets elementary schools (K–8) in various geographic and socioeconomic areas. The program components are a cooperative learning environment, a values-rich reading and language arts program, a teaching (rather than punitive) approach to student discipline, school community-building activities, and activities to foster greater parental involvement.

The evaluation involved urban, suburban, and rural schools in six school districts (two experimental and two control schools in each district) across the country. Program schools were chosen based on the likelihood of successful implementation and then matched to control schools by socioeconomic status, ethnicity, and academic achievement. Comparisons showed that the schools were comparable at baseline. Final year two data were collected from 5,303 (80%) students. The results studywide (the 12 program schools vs. the 12 comparison schools) showed no differences in delinquency outcomes but did show a significant difference in alcohol use and a marginally significant difference in the composite of three substance use items (alcohol, marijuana, and tobacco). Effects were strongest for the five high-implementation schools, in contrast to their matched controls, with the differences in alcohol use, marijuana use, and the three-item composite all statistically significant. Marginally significant declines were found at the high-implementation program schools for running away from home, taking a vehicle without the owner's permission, and being involved in gang fights, while these behaviors increased at the control schools. Other positive outcomes were observed at the high-implementation schools including liking school, intrinsic academic motivation, task orientation toward learning, commitment to democratic values, acceptance of outgroups, conflict-resolution skills, intrinsic motivation for prosocial behavior, and concern for others (Battistich, Schaps, Watson, & Soloman, 1996).

In a follow-up study, students participating in the original project in six treatment (three were high-implementation schools) and six control schools were assessed during middle school (grades 6 to 8). Results showed significant improvements in positive group activities, higher educational aspirations, and fewer acts of misconduct at school for students participating in the program during elementary school (Battistich et al., in press). The findings overall suggest that this program must be implemented with high fidelity to the original model to achieve successful outcomes.

Comer School Development Program includes comprehensive school, community, and parent interventions aimed at improving the overall school environment for inner-city youth in elementary grades. The Comer project focuses on building diverse teams to oversee governance and management of the school (made up of administrators, parents, and staff) and student mental health and other services (made up of the principal, psychologist, social worker, counselor, and/or nurse) (Haynes, 1996). Additionally, a parent team works to motivate parents to become more involved in school activities and to improve communication between the school and parents.

Three evaluations of the project have been completed, two using matched treatment and control schools. Twenty-three middle schools were included in an evaluation of the Comer program in Prince George's County. In Chicago, the intended design was based on a pilot year of work in four program schools followed by a multi-year randomized experiment with 10 matched school pairs, with one school within each pair assigned to Comer and one to the control group. All were elementary schools with grades K–8. Five of the 24 schools dropped out of the study at different times. In a third evaluation project in Bent Harbor, Michigan (Haynes, Comer, & Hamilton-Lee, 1988), 7 participating elementary schools were compared to the school district as a whole. These evaluations of the Comer program, while showing many mixed results (at Prince George's County, there were no effects on student outcomes, and results were mixed in Chicago), did indicate some improvements in mental health (lack of anger), decreases in negative social behaviors (less acting out), and improvements in self-concept and school climate. Although implementation fidelity was lax in many of these schools and may have weakened program results, the mixed findings over three evaluations elicit caution.

Other school programs targeting schoolwide discipline and management issues utilize zero tolerance policies, student problem solving, and student training in prosocial behaviors. The *CAPSLE* project (Creating a Peaceful School Learning Environment) combines zero tolerance policies and a structured discipline plan with student training and support services with an aim to reduce levels of bullying within the school. An evaluation of the project, involving one treatment elementary school matched with one control school, indicates some decline in disciplinary problems, improved academic achievement, and decreases in hostility and withdrawal for students in schools participating in the program, as well as a marginally significant reduction in the prevalence of bullying (Tremlow et al., 1999). The *Preventing School Vandalism and Disruptive Behavior* program showed reductions in vandalism costs through teacher training in analyzing school and classroom environment, positive reinforcement, and behavioral modification (Mayer, Butterworth, Nafpaktitis, & Sulzer-Azaroff, 1983). Students from classrooms receiving treatment also showed a significantly greater decrease in off-task behavior (e.g., hitting, yelling, throwing objects, talking without permission, not doing assigned work). This evaluation involved 18 elementary and junior high schools, which were randomly assigned to either the treatment or the control group. However, not all schools in the treatment group completed the program. The *School Safety Program*, evaluated in two matched high schools and implemented in 13 eleventh-grade government and history classrooms with more than 250 students, produced some reductions in student fear, conflict, and school suspensions through police participation in schoolwide problem-solving efforts of students. Participants are trained in a four-stage problem-solving model in order to address issues around school behavior (Kenney & Watson, 1996).

Classroom or Instructional Management

Prevention and intervention strategies focusing on classroom management generally combine teacher training in effective instructional and disciplinary practices with student training or curricula. Ultimately, the goal of such strategies is to equip teachers with the necessary skills to positively manage student behavior. Generally, these approaches involve the entire school population, rather than high-risk students (Thornton et al., 2000). However, the interventions are often designed to be implemented in more "at-risk" schools, such as those located in large urban areas, or that have histories of student behavior and learning problems.

Exemplary Programs   None.

Promising Programs   *Seattle Social Development Project* is a long-term intervention for grades 1 through 6 that combines parent and teacher training to intervene early in a child's development to foster prosocial bonds, strengthen school attachment and commitment, and decrease youth delinquency. The program is based on social control and social learning theories. Teachers receive training in proactive classroom management as well as interactive teaching and cooperative learning. These strategies focus on establishing clear rules and rewards for positive behavior. Teachers are encouraged to frequently assess each child to ensure that he or she is learning, and to remediate where necessary. Additionally, students are encouraged to work in small, diverse groups in order to promote healthy relationships with peers. At the first-grade level, teachers provide instruction in communication, decision making, and negotiation and conflict-resolution skills. The sixth-grade curriculum includes refusal-skills training (Hawkins et al., 1992).

Throughout the program, parents can participate in training sessions and child development sessions that are age-specific. For children in first and second grades, parents receive training in child monitoring and discipline techniques. The second- and third-grade parents are offered sessions geared toward parent–child communication, school engagement, and support for their child's academic progress. In fifth and sixth grades, sessions focus on family communications regarding drugs and encouraging a child's refusal skills (Hawkins et al., 1992).

The evaluation of the project included two elementary schools assigned to be full control or full experimental sites. In the remaining six schools, entering first-grade students and teachers were randomly assigned to intervention or control classrooms. During grades 1 through 4, newly entering students were randomly assigned to classrooms. When the initial students entered the fifth grade, the panel was expanded to include all fifth-grade students in 18 Seattle elementary schools. At the end of the second grade (Hawkins, Von Cleve, & Catalano, 1991), participating students exhibited lower levels of aggression and antisocial behaviors (white males) and lower levels of self-destructive behavior (white females). Older students (those entering fifth grade) were less likely to begin using alcohol and engaging in delinquent behavior than controls, and experienced increases in school attachment and improved family relationships (Hawkins et al., 1992). At age 18, students who had participated in the project from grades 1 through 6, compared to students who had received the program in grades 5 and 6 only and those in control groups, had reduced involvement in violent delinquency and sexual activity, reductions in alcohol use including drinking and driving behavior, improved attachment and commitment to school, and improved school achievement compared to controls (Hawkins et al., 1999).

Favorable Programs   *Success for All* reorganizes instruction to teach all students to read at or near grade level by grade 3. The program utilizes reading instruction, tutoring, coordination of services, and parent involvement (Slaven et al., 1994). The evaluation of Success for All included 15 elementary schools in seven school districts located across the country. Program schools were matched with control schools (based on socioeconomic status, ethnicity of students, and student achievement), and individual students were matched based on vocabulary test scores. Success for All participants performed better than students in control schools in reading improvements and reductions in grade repeating.

Two programs, *Consistency Management and Cooperative Discipline (CMCD)* and *Proactive Classroom Management Techniques,* provide teacher training in effective classroom management and discipline practices, as well as in instructional techniques. The CMCD program, implemented in grades 2 through 5, includes a strong student involvement program and teacher training, whereby students increasingly gain responsibility for various aspects of classroom management. The program focuses on teaching caring for students, cooperation between students and teachers, student ownership and responsibility, and parent and community involvement. A study of program effectiveness included five urban elementary schools participating in the program, matched as closely as possible to five control schools. Students participating in the program demonstrated increases in academic performance, compared with students in control schools (Freiberg, 1996). Proactive Classroom Management seeks to change teacher practices and increase student involvement in classroom activities. The program was evaluated with 513 treatment students and 653 control students from seventh-grade classrooms in five middle schools, randomly assigned to treatment or control classrooms. Students participating in the program demonstrated more positive attitudes and attachment to school, higher expectations for education, and lower rates of suspension and expulsion from school than students not participating. In contrast with these positive findings, there were no significant differences in achievement, self-reported delinquency, or drug use (Hawkins, Doueck, & Lishner., 1988).

DISCUSSION

In light of an increasing demand by funders for accountability and the growing perception that children are not safe at school, efforts to identify effective violence and drug-prevention programs are intensifying. Although numerous programs are being implemented in schools, relatively few of these have met even minimal criteria for effectiveness. Evaluations that cannot rule out alternative explanations for the effects found weaken our confidence in the results. Randomized designs provide the "gold standard" for evaluation. This chapter has provided descriptions of various school-based early childhood and environmental programs that have been proven effective through high-quality evaluations.

The programs meeting our criteria suggest that intervening early in the developmental life course is important to interrupt negative socialization processes that may place a child on a life course persistent path that may involve antisocial behavior, school dropout, and poor adult socialization. Several programs were shown to immediately impact cognitive performance and academic improvement. These early successes, in all likelihood, set these children on a positive developmental path in which readiness for school is enhanced, helping them to more successfully navigate that early transition. Success for many children participating in these programs continues into adolescence and is demonstrated by reductions in behavior problems such as fighting, delinquency, arrests, school attendance, and disruptive and hostile acts up to 10 years beyond program completion. The longest follow-up, at age 27, shows that children who attended the Perry Preschool were also more successful than the control children in navigating the transition into adulthood with fewer arrests, higher school completion and post-secondary enrollment (females) and higher earnings.

While early childhood education programs may emphasize individual-level risk factors, these programs specifically target environmental factors by focusing on children living in economically poor and high-risk neighborhoods. The school environment may also play a significant role in contributing to the violence and delinquency of students. Comprehensive, schoolwide programs that create environments that support teachers, staff, and students; emphasize organization and open lines of communication; create and reinforce academic and disciplinary policies that promote prosocial norms; and instruct teachers in techniques of effective classroom management have been effective in reducing school-related problem behaviors, delinquency, and drug use. Schoolwide improvement efforts also promote a positive school climate and help to improve academic performance.

REFERENCES

Barnett, W. S. (1993). Benefit-cost analysis of preschool education: Findings from a 25-year follow-up. *American Journal of Orthopsychiatry, 63,* 25–50.

Battistich, Victor, Schaps, Eric, Watson, Marilyn, & Soloman, Daniel (1996). Prevention effects of the Child Development Project: Early findings from an on-going multi-site demonstration trial. *Journal of Adolescent Research, 11,* 12–35.

Battistich, Victor, Schaps, Eric, Watson, Marilyn, Solomon, Daniel, & Lewis, Catherine (in press). Effects of the Child Development Project on students' drug use and other problem behaviors, *Journal of Primary Prevention.*

Berrueta-Clement, J. R., Schweinhart, L. J., Barnett, W. S., Epstein, A. S., & Weikart, D. P. (1984). *Changed lives: The effects of the Perry Preschool Program on youths through age 19* (Monographs of the High/Scope Educational Research Foundation, No. 8). Ypsilanti, MI: High/Scope Press.

Brook, J. S., Whiteman, M., Gordon, A. S., & Cohen, P. (1986). Dynamics of childhood and adolescent personality traits and adolescent drug use. *Developmental Psychology, 22,* 403–414.

Brooks, Kim, Schiraldi, Vincent, & Ziedenberg, Jason (2001). *School house hype: Two years later. Executive summary.* Justice Policy Institute/Children's Law Center. [Online]. Available: *http://www.cjcj.org/schoolhousehype/shh2exec.html.*

Campbell, Frances A., Burchinal, Margaret, Skinner, Martie L., & Gardner, David M. (2000). Persistent effects of early childhood education on high risk children and their mothers. *Applied Development Science, 4,* 2–14.

Campbell, Frances A., & Ramey, Craig T. (1995). Cognitive and school outcomes for high-risk African-American students at middle adolescence: Positive effects of early intervention. *American Educational Research Journal, 32,* 743–772.

Campbell, Frances A., & Ramey, Craig T. (1994). Effects of early intervention on intellectual and academic achievement: A follow-up study of children from low-income families. *Child Development, 65,* 684–698.

Centers for Disease Control and Prevention (2001). *Fact sheet: Youth risk behavior trends from CDCs 1991, 1993, 1995, 1997, and 1999 Youth Risk Behavior Surveys.* Silver Spring, MD: Centers for Disease Control and Prevention, National Center for Chronic Disease Prevention and Health Promotion.

Cowen, Emory L., & Durlak, Joseph (2000). Social policy and prevention in mental health. *Development and Psychopathology, 12,* 815–834.

Derzon, James H. (2001). Antisocial behavior and the prediction of violence. *Psychology in the Schools, 38,* 93–106.

Dishion, T. J., Patterson, G. R., Stoolmiller, M., & Skinner, M. L. (1991). Family, school, and behavioral antecedents to early adolescent involvement with antisocial peers. *Developmental Psychology, 27,* 172–180.

Elliott, D. S., & Tolan, P. H. (1999). Youth violence, prevention, intervention, and social policy. In D. J. Flannery & C. R. Huff (Eds.), *Youth violence: Prevention, intervention, and social policy* (pp. 3–46). Washington, DC: American Psychiatric Press.

Embry, D. D., Flannery, D. J., Vazsonyi, A. T., Powell, K. E., & Altha, H. (1996). Peacebuilders: A theoretically driven, school-based model for early violence prevention. *American Journal of Preventative Medicine, 12,* 91–100.

Farrell, Albert, Meyer, Aleta, Kung, Eva, & Sullivan, Terri (2001). Development and evaluation of school-based violence prevention programs. *Journal of Clinical Child Psychology, 30,* 207–220.

Farrington, D. P. (1987). Early precursors of frequent offending. In J. Q. Wilson & G. C. Loury (Eds.), From children to citizens: Families, school, and delinquency prevention (pp. 27–50). New York: Springer-Verlag.

Felner, Robert, & Adan, Angela (1988). The School Transitional Environment Project: An ecological intervention and evaluation. In R. H. Price, E. L. Cowen, R. P. Lorion, & J. Ramos-McKay (Eds.), *14 ounces of prevention: A casebook for practitioners.* Washington DC: American Psychological Association.

Felner, Robert, Favazza, Antoinette, Shim, Minsuk, Brand, Stephen, Gu, Kenneth, & Noonan, Nancy (2001). Whole school improvement and restructuring as prevention and promotion: Lessons from STEP and the Project on High Performance Learning Communities. *Journal of School Psychology, 39,* 177–202.

Felner, R. D., Ginter, M., & Primavera, J. (1982). Primary prevention during school transitions: Social support and environmental structure. *American Journal of Community Psychology, 10,* 277–290.

Flannery, D. J., Vazsonyi, A. T., Powell, K. E., & Altha, H, Versterdal, W., & Embry, D. D. (1998). Longitudinal evidence of effective violence prevention: A randomized controlled trial of Peacebuilders Elementary School Intervention. Draft Copy.

Flynn, Brian S., Worden, John K., Secker-Walker, Roger H., Badger, Gary J., & Geller, Berta M. (1995). Cigarette smoking prevention effects of mass media and school interventions targeted to gender and age groups. *Journal of Health Education, 26,* S45–S51.

Flynn, Brian S., Worden, John K., Secker-Walker, Roger H., Badger, Gary J., Geller, Berta M., & Costanza, Michael C. (1992). Prevention of cigarette smoking through mass media intervention and school programs. *American Journal of Public Health, 82,* 827–834.

Flynn, Brian S., Worden, John K., Secker-Walker, Roger H., Pirie, Phyllis L., Badger, Gary J., Carpenter, Joseph H., & Geller, Berta M. (1994). Mass media and school interventions for cigarette smoking prevention: Effects 2 years after completion. *American Journal of Public Health, 84,* 1148–1150.

Foshee, V. A., Bauman, K. E., Arriaga, X. B., Helms, R. W., Koch, G. G., & Linder, G. F. (1998). An evaluation of Safe Dates, an adolescent dating violence prevention program. *American Journal of Public Health, 88,* 45–50.

Freiberg, H. J. (1996). From tourists to citizens in the classroom. *Educational Leaders, 51,* 32–37.

Gallup Organization (1999). Gallup poll topics: A–Z. Children and violence. [Online]. Available: *http://www.gallup.com.*

Garmezy, N. (1985). Stress-resistant children: The search for protective factors. In J. E. Stevenson (Ed.), *Recent research in developmental psychopathology* (pp. 213–233). Oxford: Pergamon Press.

Gomby, Deanna, Larson, Carol, Lewit, Eugene, & Behrman, Richard (1993). Home visiting. Analyis and recommendations. In Richard E. Behrman (Ed.), *The future of children: Home visiting: Vol. 3.* Los Altos, CA: David and Lucile Packard Foundation.

Gottfredson, Denise (1997). School-based crime prevention. In L. W. Sherman, D. C. Gottfredson, D. MacKenzie, J. Eck, P. Reuter, & S. Bushway (Eds.), *Preventing crime: What works, what doesn't, what's promising: A report to the United States Congress.* Washington, DC: U.S. Department of Justice, Office of Justice Programs.

Gottfredson, Denise (1990). Changing school structures to benefit high-risk youths. *Understanding troubled and troubling youth: Multidisciplinary perspectives.* Newbury Park, CA: Sage.

Gottfredson, Gary, Gottfredson, Denise, & Czeh, Ellen (2000). Summary: National study of delinquency prevention in schools. Ellicott City, MD: Gottfredson Associates, Inc.

Greenberg, Mark, Domitrovich, Celene, & Bumbarger, Brian (1999). *Preventing mental disorders in school-age children: A review of the effectiveness of prevention programs.* Prevention Research

Center for the Promotion of Human Development, Pennsylvania State University. Submitted to Center for Mental Health Services, Substance Abuse and Mental Health Services Administration, U.S. Department of Health and Human Services; July 1999. Available at: *http://www.psu.edu/dept/prevention/cmhs.html.*

Hawkins, J. D., Catalano, R. F., Kosterman, R., Abbott, R., & Hill, K. G. (1999). Preventing adolescent health-risk behaviors by strengthening protection during childhood. *Archives Pediatric Adolescent Medicine, 153,* 226–234.

Hawkins, J. D., Catalano, R. F., Morrison, D., O'Donnell, J., Abbot, R., & Day, E. (1992). The Seattle Social Development Project: Effects of the first four years on protective factors and problem behaviors. In J. McCord & R. E. Trembly (Eds.), *Preventing antisocial behavior: Interventions from birth through adolescence.* New York: Guilford Press.

Hawkins, J. D., Doueck, H. J., & Lishner, D. M. (1988). Changing teacher practices in mainstream classrooms to improve bonding and behavior of low achievers. *American Educational Research Journal, 25,* 31–50.

Hawkins, J. D., Von Cleve, E., & Catalano, R. F. (1991). Reducing early childhood aggression: Results of a primary prevention program. *Journal American Academy Child Adolescent Psychiatry, 30,* 208–217.

Haynes, Norris (1996). Creating safe and caring school communities: Comer School Development Program schools. *Journal of Negro Education, 65,* 308–314.

Haynes, Norris, Comer, James, & Hamilton-Lee, Muriel (1988). The School Development Program: A model for school improvement. *Journal of Negro Education, 57,* 11–21.

Herrenkohl, Todd, Huang, Bu, Kosterman, Rick, Hawkins, J. David, Catalano, Richard, & Smith, Brian (2001). A comparison of social development processes leading to violent behavior in late adolescence for childhood initiators and adolescent initiators of violence. *Journal of Research in Crime and Delinquency, 38,* 45–63.

Johnson, Dale L., & Breckenridge, James N. (1982). The Houston Parent-Child Development Center and the primary prevention of behavior problems in young children. *American Journal of Community Psychology, 10,* 305–316.

Johnson, Dale L., & Walker, Todd (1987). Primary prevention of behavior problems in Mexican-American children. *American Journal of Community Psychology, 15,* 375–385.

Karoly, L. A., Everingham, S. S., Hoube, J., Kilburn, R., Rydell, C. P., Sanders, M., & Greenwood, P. W. (1998). Investing in our children: What we know and don't know about the costs and benefits of early childhood interventions. MR-898. Santa Monica, CA: RAND Corporation.

Kaufman, P., Chen, X., Choy, S. P., Ruddy, S. A., Miller, A. K., Fleury, J. K., Chandler, K. A., Rand, M. R., Klaus, P., & Planty, M. G. (2000). *Indicators of school crime and safety, 2000.* Washington DC: U.S. Departments of Education and Justice. NCES 2001-017/NCJ-184176.

Kazdin, Alan E. (1987). Treatment of antisocial behavior in children: Current status and future directions. *Psychological Bulletin, 102,* 187–203.

Kazdin, Alan E. (1985). *Treatment of antisocial behavior in children and adolescents.* Homewood, IL: Dorsey Press.

Kenney, D. J., & Watson, T. S. (1996). Reducing fear in the schools: Managing conflict through student problem solving. *Education and Urban Society, 28,* 436–455.

Kingery, Paul, & Coggeshall, Mark (2001). Surveillance of school violence, injury, and disciplinary actions. *Psychology in the Schools, 38,* 117–126.

Krug, E. G., Brener, N. D., Dahlberg, L. L., Ryan, G. W., & Powell, K. E. (1997). The impact of an elementary school-based violence prevention program on visits to the school nurse. *American Journal of Preventative Medicine, 13,* 459–463.

Lally, J. Ronald, Mangione, Peter L., Honig, Alice S., & Wittner, Donna S. (1988). More pride, less delinquency: Findings from the ten-year follow-up study of the Syracuse University Family Development Research Program. *Zero to Three,* April 13–18.

Loeber, R., & Farrington, D. (1998). *Serious and violent juvenile offenders: Risk factors and successful interventions.* Thousand Oaks, CA: Sage.

Lynch, Kathleen (1998). Results of Michigan replication study 1996–97: Child outcomes - Al's Pals: Kids Making Healthy Choices. Richmond, VA: Virginia Institute for Developmental Disabilities, Virginia Commonwealth University.

Maguire, K., & Pastore, A. (Eds.) (1998). Sourcebook of criminal justice statistics 1997 (p. 102). Washington, DC: U.S. Department of Justice, Bureau of Justice Statistics, U.S. Government Printing Office.

Maguire, K., & Pastore, A. (Eds.) (1996). Sourcebook of criminal justice statistics 1995. Washington, DC: U.S. Department of Justice, Bureau of Justice Statistics, U.S. Government Printing Office.

Masten, A. S., & Garmezy, N. (1985). Risk, vulnerability, and protective factors in developmental psychopathology. In B. B. Lahey & A. E. Kazdin (Eds.), *Advances in clinical child psychology*: *Vol. 8* (pp. 1–52). New York: Plenum Press.

Mayer, G. Roy, Butterworth, T., Nafpaktitis, M., & Sulzer-Azaroff, B. (1983). Preventing school vandalism and improving discipline: A three-year study. *Journal of Applied Behavior Analysis, 16,* 355–369.

Moffitt, Terrie (1993). Adolescence-limited and life-course-persistent antisocial behavior: A developmental taxonomy. *Psychological Review, 100,* 674–701.

Moffitt, Terrie, & Caspi, Avshalom (2001). Adulthood predictors differentiate life-course persistent and adolescence-limited antisocial pathways among males and females. *Development and Psychopathology, 13,* 355–375.

National School Safety Center (2001). School associated violent deaths. In-house Report of the National School Safety Center, Westlake Village, CA.

Olds, David, Hill, Peggy, Mihalic, Sharon, & O'Brien, Ruth (1998). *Prenatal and Infancy Home Visitation by Nurses.* In D. S. Elliott (Series Ed.), *Blueprints for Violence Prevention* (Vol. 7). Boulder, CO: Center for the Study and Prevention of Violence, Institute of Behavioral Science, University of Colorado.

Olweus, D., Limber, S., & Mihalic, S. F. (1999). *Bullying Prevention Program.* In D. S. Elliott (Series Ed.), *Blueprints for Violence Prevention* (Vol. 9). Boulder, CO: Center for the Study and Prevention of Violence, Institute of Behavioral Science, University of Colorado.

Parks, Greg (2000). *The High/Scope Perry Preschool Project.* Washington, DC: OJJDP Juvenile Justice Bulletin, U.S. Department of Justice, Office of Justice Programs.

Patterson, Gerald (1986). Performance models for antisocial boys. *American Psychologist, 41,* 432–444.

Pentz, Mary Ann, Mihalic, Sharon, & Grotpeter, Jennifer (1997). *The Midwestern Prevention Project.* In D. S. Elliott (Series Ed.), *Blueprints for Violence Prevention* (Vol. 1). Boulder, CO: Center for the Study and Prevention of Violence, Institute of Behavioral Science, University of Colorado.

Perry, Cheryl, Williams, Carolyn, Veblen-Mortenson, Sara, Toomey, Traci, Komro, Kelli, Anstine, Pamela, McGovern, Paul, Finnegan, John, Forster, Jean, Wagenaar, Alexander, & Wolfson, Mark (1996). Project Northland: Outcomes of a communitywide alcohol use prevention program during early adolescence. *American Journal of Public Health, 86,* 956–965.

Reynolds, Arthur J., Chang, Heesuk, & Temple, Judy A. (1998). Early childhood intervention and juvenile delinquency: An exploratory analysis of the Chicago Child-Parent Centers. *Evaluation Review, 22,* 341–372.

Schweinhart, L. J., Barnes, H. V., & Weikart, D. P. (1993). *Significant benefits.* Ypsilanti, MI: High/Scope Press.

Schweinhart, L. J., & Weikart, D. P. (1980). *Young children grow up: The effects of the Perry Preschool Program on youths through age 15.* Ypsilanti, MI: High/Scope Press.

Seitz, Victoria, Rosenbaum, Laurie K., & Apfel, Nancy H. (1985). Effects of family support intervention: A ten-year follow-up. *Child Development, 56,* 376–391.

Sheley, Joseph (2000). Controlling violence: What schools are doing. In S. Kellam, R. Prinz, & J. Sheley (Eds.), *Preventing school violence: Plenary papers of the 1999 conference on criminal justice research and evaluation: Enhancing policy and practice through research: Vol. 2.* Washington DC, U.S. Department of Justice, Office of Justice Programs.

Slaven, R. E., Madden, N. A., Dolan, L. J., Wasik, B. A., Ross, S. M., & Smith, L. J. (1994). Whenever and wherever we choose: The replication of Success for All. *Phi Delta Kappa,* April, 639–647.

Snyder, Howard (2000). *Juvenile arrests 1999.* OJJDP Juvenile Justice Bulletin. Washington DC: U.S. Department of Justice, Office of Justice Programs, Office of Juvenile Justice and Delinquency Prevention.

Snyder, H. N., & Sickmund, M. (2000). *Challenging the myths* (1999 National Report Series). Washington, DC: U.S. Department of Justice, Office of Justice Programs, Office of Juvenile Justice and Delinquency Prevention.

Thornton, Timothy N., Craft, Carole A., Dahlberg, Linda L., Lynch, Barbara S., & Baer, Katie (2000). Best practices of youth violence prevention: A sourcebook for community action. Atlanta, GA: Centers for Disease Control and Prevention.

Tremlow, S. W., Fonagy, P., Sacco, F., Fies, M., Evans, R., & Ewbank, R. (1999). Creating a Peaceful School Learning Environment: A controlled study of an elementary school intervention to reduce violence. Agawam, MA: Tremlow and Sacco Group.

U.S. Department of Health and Human Services (2001). *Youth violence: A report of the Surgeon General.* Rockville, MD: U.S. Department of Health and Human Services, Centers for Disease Control and Prevention, National Center for Injury Prevention and Control; Substance Abuse and Mental Health Services Administration, Center for Mental Health Services; and National Institutes of Health, National Institute of Mental Health.

Walker, Hill, Kavanagh, Kate, Stiller, Bruce, Golly, Annemieke, Severson, Herbert, & Feil, Edward (1998). First step to success: An early intervention approach for preventing school antisocial behavior. *Journal of Emotional and Behavioral Disorders, 6,* 66–76.

Wasserman, Gail, Miller, Laurie, & Cothern, Lynn (2000). *Prevention of serious and violent juvenile offending.* OJJDP Juvenile Justice Bulletin. Washington DC, U.S. Department of Justice Programs, Office of Justice Programs, Office of Juvenile Justice and Delinquency Prevention.

Webster-Stratton, Carolyn, Mihalic, Sharon, Fagan, Abigail, Arnold, David, Taylor, Ted, & Tingley, Charles (2001). *The Incredible Years: Parent, Teacher and Child Training Series.* In D. S. Elliott (Series Ed.), *Blueprints for Violence Prevention* (Vol. 11). Boulder, CO: Center for the Study and Prevention of Violence, Institute of Behavioral Science, University of Colorado.

Weikart, D. P., Bond, J. T., & McNeil, J. T. (1978). *The Ypsilanti Perry Preschool Project: Preschool years and longitudinal results through fourth grade.* (Monographs of the High/Scope Educational Research Foundation, No. 3). Ypsilanti, MI: High/Scope Press.

Werner, Emmy E. (1990). Protective factors and individual resilience. In Meisels & Shonkoff (Eds.), *Handbook of early childhood intervention.* New York: Cambridge University Press.

Werner, Emmy E. (1989). Vulnerability and resiliency: A longitudinal perspective. In M. Brambring, F. Losel, & H. Skowronek (Eds.), *Children at risk: Assessment, longitudinal research, and intervention.* Berlin: Walter de Gruyter.

Werner, Emmy E., & Smith, Ruth S. (1992). Protective factors and adult adaptation. *Overcoming the odds: High risk children from birth to adulthood.* Ithaca: Cornell University Press.

Yeager, Catherine A., & Lewis, Dorothy O. (2000). Mental illness, neuropsychologic deficits, child abuse, and violence. *Juvenile Violence, 9,* 793–798.

12

A Guide to Effective School-Based Prevention Programs: Individually Focused Programs

Sharon Mihalic and Tonya Aultman-Bettridge

Authors Mihalic and Aultman-Bettridge now continue discussing the selection and implementation of quality school-crime reduction and/or prevention programs. Whereas Chapter 11 focused on programs directed toward the environment and early childhood programs, this chapter is directed specifically toward the individual.

The groundbreaking work these authors accomplish relates to their assessment of school-based programs. They examine a substantial number of programs and systematically evaluate how well each program accomplishes its goals. What works and what does not? This is the key question. There are a multitude of programs available for schools—which one(s) provide a high-quality probability for success?

INDIVIDUALLY FOCUSED PROGRAMS

The most common form of intervention focuses on individuals with an aim to promote social competencies and/or ameliorate deficits within troubled adolescents. As opposed to a focus on unhealthy environments (as exemplified in the school environmental programs described in Chapter 11), individually focused interventions mostly consider the environment irrelevant and instead seek to change a person's thoughts, beliefs, attitudes, or behaviors. Many multicomponent programs consider both theories of change and incorporate environmental and individually focused strategies into the intervention, with great success (Lipsey, 1992). The individually focused programs are grouped into five categories: Social Skills, Behavioral, and Cognitive-Behavioral Programs; Other Instructional Programs;

Counseling, Social Work, and Other Therapeutic Interventions; Mentoring, Tutoring, and WorkStudy; and Recreation, Community Service, Enrichment, and Leisure Activities.

Social Skills, Behavioral, and Cognitive-Behavioral Programs

Teaching youth self-control and social skills enables them to interact competently with others and resolve problems without force or violence. These skills are typically taught through programs utilizing behavioral or cognitive-behavioral techniques.

Behavioral programs focus on rewarding desired behavior and providing mild forms of punishment for undesired behavior. These interventions rely on external reinforcers (e.g., contingency contracting, token economies) to shape behavior.

Cognitive skills programs, on the other hand, focus on thinking skills and the ways in which individuals process social information (Fraser, 1996). The cognitive approach seeks to improve a child's ability to think through a problem situation, identify consequences to a certain action, and evaluate and generate optional solutions to problems, with repeated emphasis on the links between thought and action. Cognitive approaches typically combine some behavioral strategies (cognitive-behavioral), especially when targeting antisocial or delinquent youth to promote prosocial behavior. The assumption is that by changing internal factors (i.e., cognition), as opposed to purely external factors (i.e., reinforcement contingencies), the behavior will be learned and generalized to everyday situations (Tolan & Guerra, 1994).

Cognitive-behavioral programs are similar to the social skills-building programs that utilize behavioral and cognitive techniques; however, the former are typically delivered to small groups of at-risk adolescents or youth already displaying behavioral problems, rather than to a general population of students. These programs work more intensely with these youth to change behavior by utilizing behavioral techniques of punishments and rewards or by altering deficiencies in thinking skills. This strategy is based upon the premise that delinquent youth, who generally score lower on cognitive tests than their nondelinquent peers (Henggeler, 1989), are deficient in a number of thinking and social problem-solving skills necessary for social adaptation. For instance, many delinquents act impulsively, giving little thought to their actions and generating fewer alternative solutions to interpersonal problems; believe that what happens to them depends on fate, chance, or luck, and fail to see the consequences of their own actions; focus on ends or goals rather than the intermediate steps to obtain them; exhibit a rigid or concrete thinking style making it difficult for them to understand the reasons for rules or laws; lack thinking skills required for solving problems and interacting with others; and misinterpret the actions and intentions of others (Kazdin, 2000; Ross & Ross, 1989; Spivack, Platt, & Shure, 1976). The development of cognitive skills helps youth to adapt successfully to their environment and reduces the likelihood that they will adopt a criminal lifestyle.

Social and cognitive skills are learned skills greatly influenced by environmental factors (Ross & Ross, 1989). For example, extreme poverty may impede the successful adoption of cognitive skills, as economically deprived neighborhoods tend to be more disorganized and provide less social control over residents, in that there may be fewer adults or peers to model effective problem-solving strategies. Inadequate or coercive parental supervision and discipline, abuse, or neglect may also have a retarding effect on the development of cognitive skills in general, and social perspective taking and empathetic understanding in particular. Children who are disciplined in a controlling, erratic, or excessively punitive manner may perceive that they have little control over their own environment; fail to learn adequate problem-solving skills; believe that what happens to them is not dependent upon their behavior; and are especially likely to act aggressively, due to their inability to solve problems and satisfy needs in a more socially acceptable way. Parents with a history of criminal behavior, substance use, or depression, may model cognitive deficits, such as lack of self-management or ineffectual problem solving, ultimately resulting in cognitive deficits in the child.

Many effective programs utilize social and cognitive skills training approaches, and these types of interventions have been shown to reduce crime, substance use, school dropout and truancy, and other antisocial behavior and conduct problems (Gottfredson, Wilson, & Najaka, in press). Social skills programs have typically been offered to general and at-risk populations (Davis & Tolan, 1993). They have also been effectively delivered at various developmental stages, including preschool, elementary, junior high, and senior high school (Gottfredson, Wilson, & Najaka, in press). Cognitive programs, however, have been more beneficial for those older than 10 or 11, due to their more advanced stage of cognitive development (Kazdin, 2000). These programs are typically multifaceted and include elements of modeling, behavioral rehearsal (practiced role-playing), feedback, social reinforcement, and mild punishment (loss of points or tokens) (Kazdin, 1987; Sarason & Sarason, 1981). Although cognitive development strategies have been offered as primary prevention programs, as well as in treatment and correctional settings, they do not work as well for conduct-disordered children who have co-morbid diagnoses, academic delays and dysfunction, and lower reading achievement, and who come from families with high levels of impairment (Kazdin, 2000).

Other approaches in this general area seek to reduce children's misconduct by modifying parents' behavior, with the overall goal of altering the pattern of interchanges so that prosocial, rather than coercive, behavior is reinforced and supported within the family (Kazdin, 2000; Ross & Ross, 1989). Parents are taught to establish a consistent set of rules and provide reinforcements for prosocial behaviors as well as mild forms of punishment to suppress negative behaviors. Parents are also taught social skills such as communication, contracting, and problem solving. Children thus develop better cognitive strategies and social skills by observing their own parents deal with problem-solving issues.

Goals of Social Skills Training Programs (Davis & Tolan, 1993)

- Verbal skills
- Support utilization
- Perspective taking
- Other-enhancement
- Assertion
- Communication
- Peer pressure resistance strategies

Goals of Cognitive Skills Training Programs (Ross & Ross, 1989)

- Learn thinking and problem-solving skills
- Learn general strategies for recognizing problems, analyzing them, and conceiving and considering alternative, noncriminal solutions
- Learn to calculate the consequences of behavior and stop and think before acting
- Broaden social perspective (go beyond egocentrism)
- Understand the perspective of other people
- Develop interpersonal problem-solving skills and coping behaviors

---

Exemplary Programs *Incredible Years: Parent, Teacher, and Child Training Series* is a comprehensive set of curriculums designed to promote social competence and prevent, reduce, and treat conduct problems in young children, ages 2 to 8. In all three training programs, trained facilitators use videotape scenes to encourage group discussion, problem solving, and sharing of ideas. The BASIC parent series is "core" and a necessary component of the program delivery. The other parent training components and teacher and child components are recommended. The parent training intervention (comprised of three series: BASIC, ADVANCED, and Supporting Your Child's Education—SCHOOL) is focused on strengthening parenting competencies (monitoring, positive discipline, confidence) and fostering parents' involvement in children's school experiences in order to promote children's academic and social competence. The teacher training intervention is focused on strengthening teacher classroom management strategies to promote children's prosocial behavior and school readiness and reduce classroom aggression and non-cooperation with peers and teachers. The child training intervention, known as Dina Dinosaur Social Skills and Problem-Solving Curriculum, teaches children (ages 4 to 8) social skills, empathy training, anger management, and conflict-management skills. The child training program, which can be used in a clinic or school setting, targets children with conduct problems and should be offered to groups of five to six children in two-hour sessions held once a week for 18 to 20 weeks. It is organized to dovetail with the parent and teacher training programs. In the school setting, aggressive children can be pulled out of the classroom to receive the small group training taught by school counselors.

Overall, two randomized trials of the child training series indicate that combining the child and teacher training with parent training significantly improves the long-term outcome for children with conduct problems and results in a more positive classroom atmosphere with less aggressive peer problems. Results of one study, in which children received the Dina Dinosaur Curriculum and their parents received the BASIC and ADVANCED training series, indicated that combining these components was effective in improving children's problem-solving skills and parenting behaviors (Webster-Stratton & Hammond, 1997). Another study, which included a combination of parent, teacher, and child training, demonstrated effectiveness in strengthening children's academic and social skills at school, improving children's interactions with peers, and reducing children's behavior problems at home and school (Webster-Stratton et al., 2001). Currently, the effectiveness of the classroom-based version of the Dinosaur Curriculum for all children is being evaluated. Additionally, six randomized trials of the parent series indicate increases in positive parent affect, effective limit setting, reductions in parental depression and increases in parental self-confidence, increases in positive family communication and problem solving, reduced conduct problems in children's interactions with parents and increases in their positive affect and compliance to parental commands, and increases in school bonding and involvement.

Promoting Alternative Thinking Strategies (PATHS) is a comprehensive program for promoting social and emotional competencies, including the expression, understanding, and regulation of emotions. The curriculum is designed to be used by educators and counselors throughout the year with entire classrooms of children from kindergarten through fifth grade. PATHS has been researched with children in regular education classrooms, as well as with a variety of special needs students (deaf, hearing impaired, learning disabled, emotionally disturbed, mildly mentally delayed, and gifted). The curriculum provides teachers with systematic, developmentally based lessons, materials, and instructions for teaching their students emotional literacy, self-control, social competence, positive peer relations, and interpersonal problem-solving skills. Focusing on these protective factors provides tools that enable youth to achieve academically and helps enhance classroom atmosphere and the learning process. A key objective of promoting these developmental skills is to prevent or reduce behavioral and emotional problems. PATHS lessons include instruction in identifying and labeling feelings, expressing feelings, assessing the intensity of feelings, managing feelings, understanding the difference between feelings and behaviors, delaying gratification, controlling impulses, reducing stress, self-talk, reading and interpreting social cues, understanding the perspectives of others, using steps for problem solving and decision making, having a positive attitude toward life, self-awareness, nonverbal communication skills, and verbal communication skills.

Studies have compared classrooms receiving the intervention to matched controls using populations of normally adjusted students, behaviorally at-risk students, and deaf students. Program effects include teacher-, child sociometric-, and child self-report ratings of behavior change on such constructs as hyperactivity, peer aggression, and conduct problems (Greenberg, Kusche, & Mihalic, 1998).

Life Skills Training (LST) is a three-year intervention designed to prevent or reduce gateway drug use (tobacco, alcohol, and marijuana) by teaching social resistance skills which helps students identify pressures to use drugs and provides students with the skills needed to resist drug offers (Dusenbury & Falco, 1995). LST is primarily implemented in school classrooms by schoolteachers, although it has also been successfully taught by health professionals and peer leaders. LST targets all middle/junior high school students (initial intervention in grade 6 or 7, depending on the school structure, with booster sessions in the two subsequent years). The curriculum includes 15 sessions in year one, 10 sessions in year two, and 5 sessions in year three, which last an average of 45 minutes and can be delivered once a week or as an intensive three-week minicourse. The three basic components of the program teach youth (1) personal self-management skills (e.g., decision making and problem solving, self-control skills for coping with anxiety, and self-improvement skills); (2) social skills (e.g., communication and general social skills); and (3) information and skills designed to have an impact on youth's knowledge and attitudes concerning drug use, normative expectations concerning drugs, and skills for resisting drug use influences from the media and peers. Teachers use techniques such as instruction, demonstration, feedback, reinforcement, and practice.

Using outcomes averaged across more than a dozen studies, LST has been found to reduce alcohol, tobacco, and marijuana use by 50% to 75%, compared to controls. Reductions in smoking, inhalants, narcotics, and hallucinogens have been demonstrated through the 12th grade (Botvin, Mihalic, & Grotpeter, 1998).

Promising Programs *Interpersonal Cognitive Problem Solving Program (ICPS)* trains children in generating a variety of solutions to interpersonal problems, considering the consequences of these solutions, and recognizing thoughts, feelings, and motives that generate problem situations. By teaching children *to* think, rather than *what* to think, the program changes thinking styles and, as a result, enhances children's social adjustment, promotes prosocial behavior, and decreases impulsivity and inhibition. The program was originally designed for use in nursery school and kindergarten, but it has also been successfully implemented with children in grades 5 and 6. Throughout the intervention, instructors use pictures, role-playing, puppets, and group interaction to help develop students' thinking skills, and children's own lives and problems are used as examples when teachers demonstrate problem-solving techniques. Small groups of 6 to 10 children receive training for approximately three months. The intervention begins with 10 to 12 lessons teaching students basic skills and problem-solving language. The next 20 lessons focus on identifying one's own feelings and becoming sensitive to others' emotions. Students learn to recognize people's feelings in problem situations and realize that they can influence others' responses. The last 15 lessons utilize role-playing games and dialogue to promote problem-solving skills. Students generate solutions to hypothetical problem situations and consider the possible consequences of their decisions.

A two-year study of ICPS that included 219 African-American students attending 20 federally funded day care centers (10 intervention and 10 control) revealed significant benefits for intervention students. There were 131 students remaining in year two, and students were further divided to either receive or not receive a second year of the program. Immediately following and one year after the program ended, ICPS children, compared to control students, demonstrated less impulsive (scale that included measures of dominance-aggression) and less inhibited classroom behavior and better problem-solving skills (Shure & Spivack, 1980; 1982). There were additional analyses to determine whether students trained for two years did better in generating alternative solutions and in behavior than those with only one year of training. The results showed that students receiving two years scored the highest at generating alternative solutions, followed by students trained for one year, and then controls. However, the second year of training made no difference in terms of behavioral ratings. One year of exposure to the program was sufficient to produce adequate behavioral adjustment.

A replication with fifth- and sixth-grade students found that ICPS ($n = 222$) children, compared to an alternative treatment group ($n = 97$) that received training in critical thinking, demonstrated more positive, prosocial behaviors, healthier relationships with peers, and better problem-solving skills at the end of grade 5 (Shure & Healy, 1993). At the end of grade 6, all ICPS students achieved greater gains in ICPS skills than control groups, and the group receiving two years of training was superior in all positive behaviors as measured by teachers, peers, and independent observers.

Preventive Treatment Program is designed to prevent antisocial behavior of boys who display early problem behavior. This two-year program combines parent training with social skills training for youth to decrease delinquency, substance use, and gang involvement. The intervention has been successfully implemented for white, Canadian-born males, ages 7 to 9, from low socioeconomic families, who were assessed as having high levels of disruptive behavior in kindergarten. Parents attend an average of 17 sessions that focus on monitoring their children's behavior, giving positive reinforcement for prosocial behavior, using punishment effectively, and managing family crises. The boys receive 19 sessions aimed at improving prosocial skills and self-control. The training is implemented in small groups containing both disruptive and nondisruptive boys, and it utilizes coaching, peer modeling, self-instruction, reinforcement contingency, and role-playing to build skills.

The evaluation included boys who were rated as highly disruptive by their teachers at the end of kindergarten. Although 1,161 boys were evaluated from 53 schools, eligibility criteria reduced this sample to 904. All boys with a disruptive score above the 70th percentile were considered at risk ($n = 319$); of these, 249 boys met the selection criteria and were randomly assigned (prior to elimination because of failure to meet the selection criteria) to one of three groups: a treatment group (46 families after selection screening and consent to participate in the study), a no-treatment contact group (84 families), and a no-treatment, no-contact control group (42 families). This evaluation demonstrated both short- and long-term gains for youth receiving the intervention. At age 12, three years after the intervention, treated boys were less likely to report the following offenses: trespassing, taking objects worth less than $10, taking objects worth more than $10, and stealing bicycles. Treated boys were rated by teachers as fighting less than untreated boys. Also, 29% of the treated boys were rated as well adjusted in school, compared to 19% of the untreated boys; 22% of the treated boys, compared to 44% of the untreated boys, displayed less serious difficulties in school; and 23% of the treated boys, compared to 43% of the untreated boys, were held back in school or placed in special education classes. At age 15, those receiving the intervention were less likely than untreated boys to report gang involvement; having been drunk or taken drugs in the past 12 months; committing delinquent acts (stealing, vandalism, drug use); and having friends arrested by the police (Tremblay, Masse, Pagani, & Vitaro, 1996; Tremblay et al., 1992; Tremblay et al., 1991).

Good Behavior Game (GBG) is a behavior modification program involving students and teachers that aims to decrease early aggressive and shy behaviors to prevent later criminality. The GBG is universal and can be applied to general populations of early elementary school children, although the most significant results have been found for children demonstrating early high-risk behavior. The GBG improves teachers' ability to define tasks, set rules, and discipline students, and allows students to work in teams in which each individual is responsible to the rest of the group. Before the game begins, teachers clearly specify those disruptive behaviors (e.g., verbal and physical disruptions, noncompliance, etc.) that, if displayed, will result in a team's receiving a checkmark on the board. By the end of the game, teams that have not exceeded the maximum number of marks are rewarded, while teams that exceed this standard receive no rewards. Eventually, the teacher begins the game with no warning and at different periods during the day so that students are always monitoring their behavior and conforming to expectations. The evaluation of this program at first assessment included 1,084 first-grade children from 19 schools in five urban areas of Baltimore. Three or four more similar schools were matched within each of the urban areas and assigned to one of two treatments (GBG or an alternative treatment called Mastery Learning, which targets reading skills) or control conditions. Classrooms within each school were randomly assigned either to the intervention or to serve as an internal control class (receiving no intervention). Entering first-grade children were then randomly assigned to classrooms. At the end of first grade, GBG students, compared to a control group, had less aggressive and shy behaviors according to teachers and fewer peer nominations of aggressive behavior. Additionally, the alternative treatment, Mastery Learning, produced a significant short-term impact on reading achievement for both males and females. While there was no long-term follow-up of the Mastery Learning group, at the end of sixth grade, GBG students, compared to a control group, demonstrated decreases in levels of aggression for males who were rated highest for aggression in first grade (Kellam, Rebok, Ialongo, & Mayer, 1994).

Fast Track is a comprehensive and long-term prevention program that aims to prevent chronic and severe conduct problems for high-risk children. It is based on the view that antisocial behavior stems from the interaction of multiple influences, and it includes the school, the home, and the individual in its intervention. Fast Track's main goals are to increase communication and bonds between these three domains; enhance children's social, cognitive, and problem-solving skills; improve peer relationships; and ultimately decrease disruptive behavior in the home and school. The primary intervention is designed for all youth in a school setting. It specifically targets children identified in kindergarten for disruptive behavior and poor peer relations. The program spans grades 1 through 6, but is most intense during the key periods of entry to school (first grade) and transition from grade school to middle school. It is multidimensional, including the following components:

1. Parent training occurs in first grade and emphasizes fostering children's academic performance, communicating with the school, controlling anger, and using effective discipline.
2. Home visitations occur biweekly to reinforce parenting skills, promote parents' feelings of efficacy and empowerment, and foster parents' problem-solving skills.
3. Social skills training enhances children's social-cognitive and problem-solving skills, peer relations, anger control, and friendship maintenance.
4. Academic tutoring is offered three times per week to improve children's reading skills.
5. Classroom intervention utilizes the PATHS curriculum, a program designed to be used in grades 1 through 5 to help children develop emotional awareness skills, self-control, and problem-solving skills.

The evaluation of the program included 6,715 first graders from selected elementary schools in four different areas of the country. Approximately 12 schools from high-risk neighborhoods in each of the following sites were selected: Durham, North Carolina; Nashville, Tennessee; Seattle, Washington; and central Pennsylvania. Most of the sites were characterized by their ethnic diversity and low to middle socioeconomic standing. All of the neighborhoods met the high-risk criteria because they exhibited higher levels of delinquency and juvenile arrests. All participating schools were placed into matched sets whereby they were grouped with other schools with similar characteristics (i.e., racial makeup, size, poverty level, and achievement level). Schools from common sets were then randomly assigned to treatment and control groups. Results have been published for only a first-grade sample in which three different cohorts were examined. Consent was obtained to study 7,560 students; however, 845 students were "high risk." High-risk children were classified as "high-risk intervention" or "high-risk control" and were not considered in the first analysis of classroom effects, bringing the total n down to 6,715. Analyses of classroom effects showed that intervention classes displayed lower levels of aggression than control classes, improved classroom atmosphere, decreases in hyperactive-disruptive behavior, and fewer conduct problems (Conduct Problems Prevention Group, 1999a). The high-risk sample demonstrated improved emotional recognition, emotional coping, and social problem solving; decreases in aggressive retaliation; and some improvement in aggressive-disruptive behaviors on 4 of 12 measures (Conduct Problems Prevention Group, 1999b).

Linking the Interests of Families and Teachers (LIFT) is a population-based intervention for the prevention of conduct problems such as antisocial behavior, involvement with delinquent peers, and drug/alcohol use. The program is designed for elementary school-aged children and their families living in at-risk neighborhoods characterized by high rates of juvenile delinquency. LIFT targets the school, peers, and family through the following program components: (1) A classroom component contains 20 one-hour sessions taught over 10 weeks using a lecture and role-play format that focuses on a specific social or problem-solving skill, unstructured free play, skills review, and daily awards. (2) A modification of the Good Behavior Game serves as the playground component. Each class is divided into small groups for playground play. Children can earn rewards by exhibiting positive problem-solving skills and suppressing negative behaviors while on the playground. (3) Parents are taught how to create a home environment that is conducive to the ongoing practice of good discipline and supervision through a series of six meetings at their child's school. Each meeting provides a review of the results from home practice exercises, a lecture, discussion and role-plays of issues for the current week, and a presentation of home practice exercises for the following week.

The evaluation involved 12 schools that were randomly assigned to LIFT or the control condition, with first- and fifth-grade classrooms also randomly chosen for participation. Measurements were collected during the fall and spring of each year for three years. Evaluation of posttest results (Reid, Eddy, Fetrow, & Stoolmiller, 1999) showed that LIFT children significantly decreased acts of physical aggression on the playground, compared to the control group, and these effects were most dramatic for children who were rated most aggressive at pretest. Teacher ratings indicated a significant increase in positive social skills and classroom behavior in children receiving the LIFT program. Additionally, LIFT mothers who displayed the highest preintervention levels of aversive behaviors showed the largest reductions, compared to control mothers. After three years, fifth-grade children in the control group were 2.2 times more likely to initiate affiliation with misbehaving peers and 1.8 times more likely to initiate patterned alcohol use than LIFT children. In the first-grade sample, intervention children were less likely to show an increase in inattentive, impulsive, and hyperactive behaviors, as perceived by teachers (Eddy, Reid, & Fetrow, 2000).

Preventive Intervention is a behavioral intervention that helps prevent juvenile delinquency, substance use, and school failure for high-risk adolescents. The two-year intervention begins when participants are in seventh grade and includes monitoring student actions, rewarding appropriate behavior, and increasing communication between teachers, students, and parents. Program staff checks school records for participants' daily attendance, tardiness, and official disciplinary actions, and staff members contact parents by letter, phone, and occasional home visits to inform them of their children's progress. Teachers submit weekly reports assessing students' punctuality, preparedness, and behavior in the classroom, and students are rewarded for good evaluations. Each week, three to five students meet with a staff member to discuss their recent behaviors, learn the relationship between actions and their consequences, and role-play prosocial alternatives to problem behaviors.

The program evaluation included two sets of 40 students from two schools who demonstrated at least two of the following characteristics: low academic motivation, family problems, or frequent or serious school discipline referrals. These students were matched into 20 pairs and randomly assigned to treatment or control conditions. At the end of the intervention, program students showed higher grades and better attendance when compared to control students (Bry & George, 1980). Results from a one-year follow-up showed that intervention students, compared to control students, had less self-reported delinquency; drug abuse (including hallucinogens, stimulants, glue, tranquilizers, and barbiturates); school-based problems (suspension, absenteeism, tardiness, academic failure); and unemployment (20% and 45%, respectively). A five-year follow-up found that intervention students had fewer county court records than control students (Bry, 1982).

Preparing for the Drug Free Years (PDFY) is a family competency training program for parents of children in grades 4 through 8 (ages 8 to 14) that promotes healthy, protective parent–child interactions and reduces children's risk for early substance use initiation and other common adolescent problems. PDFY is a weekly five-session, two-hour multimedia program that strengthens parents' child-rearing techniques, parent–child bonding, and children's peer resistance skills. Children are required to attend one session, which focuses on building skills to resist peer pressure to engage in inappropriate behavior. The other four sessions involve only parents and include instruction in the following areas: (1) identifying risk factors for adolescent substance use and creating strategies to enhance the family's protective processes; (2) developing effective parenting skills, including creating clear guidelines regarding substance use, monitoring compliance with these guidelines, and providing effective and appropriate consequences when necessary; (3) managing anger and family conflict; and (4) providing opportunities for positive child involvement in family activities.

The program has been successfully implemented with families of middle school children in nine schools who resided in rural, economically stressed neighborhoods in the Midwest who were selected to receive the program and then were randomly assigned to the intervention or a wait-list control. Compared to the control condition, the PDFY intervention was more effective in promoting proactive communication from parent to child and in improving the quality of the parent–child relationship (Kosterman et al., 1997). A longitudinal study included 33 rural low-income schools in 19 midwestern counties that were blocked on the proportion of students that resided in lower-income households and on school size, and then schools within each block were randomly assigned to one of two treatment conditions or to a minimal contact control condition. PDFY children compared to controls demonstrated significantly less alcohol initiation and positive trends in reducing tobacco and marijuana use (Spoth, Redmond, & Shin, 1999).

Strengthening Families 10–14 (formerly Iowa Strengthening Families) is a universal, family-based intervention that enhances parents' general child management skills, parent–child affective relationships, and family communication. The long-range goal for the program is to delay the onset of adolescent substance use and behavior problems by improving family practices. During the seven two-hour sessions each week, parents and children learn individual skills, then are brought together to improve family communication and practices. During the parent training sessions, held in groups with an average of eight families, parents are taught to clarify expectations of children's behavior, especially regarding substance use; utilize appropriate and consistent discipline techniques; manage strong emotions concerning their children; and use effective communication. In the child sessions, adolescents learn similar skills, as well as peer resistance and refusal techniques; personal and social interaction skills; and stress and emotion management. In the combined parent and children classes, families practice conflict resolution and communication skills, and engage in activities designed to increase family cohesiveness.

The program was evaluated with all sixth-grade students and their families in 33 rural midwestern schools in which most of the program families were white and middle class and most parents had obtained at least a high school education. A randomized block design was used in which schools were blocked on the proportion of students who resided in low-income households and on school size. The schools were randomly assigned to one of two treatment groups or a minimal contact control condition. At posttest, program parents showed improved child management practices, including monitoring, discipline, and standard setting; increased parent–child communication; more child involvement in family activities and decisions; and strengthened family affective quality (Spoth, Redmond, & Shin, 1998). One- and two-year follow-ups revealed that participating adolescents had lower rates of alcohol initiation at both years and 30% to 60% relative reductions in alcohol use, using without parents' permission, and being drunk (Spoth, Redmond, & Lepper, 1999). The four-year follow-up (at the end of grade 10) indicated lower proportions of youth reporting lifetime use of alcohol, tobacco, and marijuana (Spoth, Redmond, & Shin, 1999).

Favorable Programs   *Open Circle* is a K–5 curriculum that teaches children communication, self-control, and social problem-solving skills to enhance academic and social competency. Teachers and principal lead a whole school initiative program in which there is work on schoolwide projects. Parents are also encouraged to be involved. There is a five-session parent program, and newsletters are sent out through the year to keep parents informed about aspects of the curriculum and to help reinforce the program elements at home. In four matched urban and suburban schools with eight fourth-grade classrooms, teachers rated program students significantly higher on Social Skills, Self-Control, Assertion, and Cooperation, and significantly lower on Problem Behavior, Externalizing, Internalizing, and Hyperactivity. There were no differences on academic competence (Hennessey & Seigle, unpublished).

Positive Action is a K–6 curriculum that consists of over 140 fifteen- to twenty-minute lessons per year delivered in school classrooms on a near daily basis, covering self-concept, positive actions for body and mind, self-management, getting along with others, being honest with yourself and others, and improving yourself. The school climate component of the program reinforces the classroom curriculum through coordinating the efforts of the entire school in practicing positive actions to promote improved behavior. Using a posttest matching design, school-level academic achievement and disciplinary data were examined. The program improved achievement by 16% in one school district and 52% in another, and reduced disciplinary referrals by 78% in one district and 85% in the other, compared to controls (Flay, 2001).

Improving Social Awareness-Social Problem Solving Program teaches elementary school-aged children social problem-solving skills in order to cope with the stresses and pressures associated with entering adolescence and the adjustment to a middle school environment. Therefore, the program is particularly relevant for fifth-grade students. The program consists of weekly sessions and provides instruction in self-control and improving social awareness, an instructional phase that provides an eight-step framework for making decisions, and an application phase that focuses on structured opportunities to apply the skills students are learning to real-life problems and decisions. Lessons are taught through presentations, videotaped vignettes, role-playing, discussion, and storytelling.

The evaluation included 158 fifth-grade children from four elementary schools who averaged approximately one year above grade level on standardized academic tests. There were three quasi-experimental conditions: no training, full training (instructional and application), and partial training (instructional phase only). All fifth-grade teachers were involved in carrying out the program under a delayed control design, with the instructional phase begun in two schools, and the other two schools being used as a delayed comparison group. Two schools received the partial intervention and two schools received the full intervention. No significant differences were found among the four schools. The no-training control group consisted of children entering middle school during the prior year. When comparing all three conditions, the overall pattern of differences indicated that full training was superior to partial training, and both conditions were associated with a significant reduction in children's self-reported level of difficulty with commonly occurring stressors in middle school, when compared to controls. Social problem solving was also shown to be a mediator of improved response to difficulty with stressors regarding peers and coping (Elias et al., 1986).

A second study included two years of intervention in grades 4 and 5. Follow-up data indicated that intervention children showed higher levels of positive prosocial behavior and lower levels of antisocial, self-destructive, and socially disordered behavior four to six years later, compared to control students. Academic achievement was also higher five years after the program, but not after six years (possibly because a remedial procedure had been instituted in that year to raise academic scores of all students) (Elias et al., 1991).

Earlscourt Social Skills Group Program provides instruction to small groups of five to seven children between the ages of 6 and 12 identified as moderately aggressive or non-compliant. Eight basic skills are taught: problem solving, knowing your feelings, listening, following instructions, joining in, using self-control, responding to teasing, and keeping out of fights. Each skill is taught in three sessions: one in which the need for the skill is discussed, and two sessions that provide opportunities for skill acquisition through role-play and rehearsal and reinforcement activities. In one study (Pepler, King, & Gyrd, 1991), 40 referred children were randomly assigned to treatment or a wait-list control group that received the intervention in the spring. Teacher ratings showed that children in the social skills group had improved their externalizing behaviors and had fewer behavioral problems than the wait-list control group, and these gains were maintained three months after treatment ended. Parent ratings also showed improvement in externalizing behaviors from Time 1 to Time 3, and in internalizing behaviors at Time 2 and through Time 3. Interestingly, there was no effect on the social problem-solving ability of children, an expected mediator of program effects. A second study (Pepler et al., 1995) of 74 children with similar problems, randomly assigned to treatment or a wait-list control group, showed more mixed findings with reductions in externalizing behaviors as reported by teachers not blind to condition, but not by parents and peers. The mixed findings and small sample sizes in these two studies elicit caution.

Anger Coping Program is a cognitive-behavioral problem-solving skills intervention for anger management that was delivered to boys in grades 4 to 6 identified by classroom teachers as being aggressive and disruptive. The program includes 12 to 18 sessions and focuses on inhibiting impulsive behavior, identifying social cues, generating prosocial responses to different social circumstances, evaluating responses, and enacting problem-solving strategies. The intervention also applies behavioral techniques to reward compliance with group rules. The evaluation included 76 boys from 8 elementary schools who were not randomly assigned to conditions, but the differences among the conditions were statistically controlled in analyses. At the four- to six-month follow-up, boys in the anger-coping treatments displayed significant reductions in classroom observations of disruptive and aggressive off-task behaviors and parent reports of aggression, but no changes in teachers' and peers' perceptions of the treated boys. A follow-up study, $2\frac{1}{2}$ to $3\frac{1}{2}$ years after treatment ended (when boys were 15 years of age), showed that the treated boys displayed higher self-esteem and lower levels of substance use (measured by a substance use summary) than controls. The intervention had no long-term effects on general behavioral deviance (Lochman, 1992). The mixed findings elicit caution.

Peer Coping Skills (PCS) teaches elementary children to cope with peer-related social challenges and to become part of a prosocial support network to reduce youth reliance on antisocial, aggressive behaviors. Children are taught, as speakers, to describe their feelings, thoughts, and behaviors in a genuine manner and, as listeners, to understand another's point of view. Sessions, approximately 50 minutes, occur weekly throughout the school year, outside the classroom, and typically include a mixed, but small group (approximately eight) of aggressive and competent-nonaggressive classmates. The competent peers serve as role models and as sources of new friends and sources of social support for prosocial conduct. A total of 25 first- through third-grade classes in six elementary schools in two cities were randomly assigned to the intervention or to a minimal classroom intervention that provided students each day with an opportunity for recognition of classroom accomplishments (Prinz, Blechman, & Dumas, 1994). Children were selected via teacher ratings from each class and placed in one of two conditions, an aggressive group or a competent-nonaggressive group. A maximum of four aggressive and four competent-nonaggressive children were selected from each classroom to form a PCS training group, for a total of 12 PCS training groups. The PCS condition included 48 aggressive and 52 competent-nonaggressive children. The no-PCS condition included 47 and 49 children, respectively. Results indicate that for the aggressive children, the program produced a significant reduction in teacher-rated aggression, in comparison to the minimal control condition, maintained through the six-month follow-up. Furthermore, the program was not harmful for the competent-nonaggressive children who participated.

Positive Youth Development is a classroomwide intervention that uses a highly structured, 20-session curriculum designed to promote adolescents' personal and social competence with the ultimate goal of reducing substance use. The curriculum is composed of six units: stress management, self-esteem, problem solving, substances and health information, assertiveness, and social networks. The curriculum is delivered in two 50-minute sessions per week over a 15-week period. One inner city and one suburban school participated in the evaluation. Among the interested pool of teachers, classes were stratified within ability groupings and randomly assigned to program and control conditions. Participation consisted of 282 sixth- and seventh-grade students. Program students, in comparison to control students, improved in coping skills, social and emotional adjustment, problem solving, and intentions to drink. There were no differences in the self-reported frequency of substance use; however, program students were significantly less likely to report *excessive* alcohol use (Caplan et al., 1992).

Sociomoral Reasoning Development Program works with adolescents in middle and high school who are rated as behavior disordered and at high risk for delinquency to increase the average level of maturity of sociomoral reasoning with the ultimate goal of preventing antisocial behavior. Small treatment groups meet once a week for a 45-minute class period for 16 to 20 weeks, facilitated by a group leader. During each session, the leader presents moral dilemmas, in which reasoning and perspective taking are emphasized. Role-plays and discussion are used. A few sessions also focus on listening and communications skills. Seventh- through 10th-grade students in four school districts who were identified by teachers as unruly, aggressive, impulsive, and disruptive participated in the evaluation. The 48 students were rank-ordered on the basis of teacher ratings and then, by coin toss within successive pairs, assigned to treatment or wait-list control condition. There were four treatment and four control groups, with 5 to 8 adolescents in each group. At posttest, intervention students significantly improved, compared to control students, in moral reasoning, disciplinary referrals to the office and police or court contacts, tardiness, and grades in English and Humanities. Teacher ratings of misbehavior were not impacted by the program. These improvements were maintained at one year (Arbuthnot, 1992).

Peaceful Conflict Resolution and Violence Prevention Curriculum, taught once a week for 13 weeks for approximately 50 minutes, includes 13 modules covering problem solving, communication, peer pressure, step-by-step conflict resolution, and expressing anger without fighting. The evaluation included sixth-grade students in two treatment and two control schools with similar demographic characteristics (primarily African-American students living at or near public housing. The program showed short-term effects (two weeks after treatment) on self-reported use of violence and intentions to use violence (DuRant, Barkin, & Krowchuk, 2001). Long-term follow-up is needed to determine how long these outcomes might persist.

Several favorable drug programs, primarily targeting middle and junior school students, emphasize normative education (providing information on the real rates of drug use) and social resistance skills (providing youth with skills to refuse drug offers). Two programs, ***School-Based Smoking Prevention Program*** (Josendal, Aaro, & Bergh, 1998) and ***North Karelia*** (Vartiainen, Paavola, McAlister, & Puska, 1998), were effective in reducing smoking behaviors of adolescents. ***Project Alert*** (Ellickson & Bell, 1990) was most effective in reducing marijuana use, but these gains disappeared by grade 10. The ***Michigan Model for Comprehensive School Health Education*** (Shope, Copeland, Marcoux, & Kamp, 1996) reduced alcohol use, smoking, marijuana, and other drug use, but most of these gains demonstrated at the end of the seventh grade were largely lost by the end of high school (Shope, Copeland, Kamp, & Lang, 1998). Randomized designs were used in these programs, with the exception of the North Karelia project in which three pairs of schools were assigned to three conditions, one to a teacher-led intervention, one to an instructor-led intervention, and one to a control condition.

Cognitive and Social Skills Training Program aims to eliminate behavioral deficits and strengthen effective behavior by improving how people think and solve problems. The 16 one-hour group session programs emphasizes consequences of an action, the alternatives available in a situation, the effect of the individual's behavior on others, an increased understanding of others' points of view, and communication skills. Modeling is used to demonstrate skills, followed by rehearsal of the modeled behavior. The program targets students in high schools with high dropout rates and low family incomes. The evaluation included students who were members of a required ninth-grade health class. Two classes (127 students) were randomly selected to participate in one of three groups. One group of students saw live demonstrations, another saw the same model on videotape, and a control group received no special treatment. At posttest, the experimental groups had a significantly higher number of means used in stories, showed a higher ability to adopt a problem-solving attitude and to be introspective, and generated a greater number of viable alternatives than the control group (Sarason & Sarason, 1981). At one-year follow-up, school data available on 75 students showed that the experimental groups had less tardiness and behavioral referrals than the control group, and the live modeling group had fewer absences than the video modeling and control group.

Reconnecting Youth targets students in grades 9 through 12 who are showing signs of poor school achievement, at risk of dropping out of school, and showing signs of multiple problem behaviors (substance abuse, depression, suicidal ideation, etc.). The curriculum is meant to be delivered as a one-semester (90-day), 55-minute course that specifically targets self-esteem enhancement, decision making for personal problem solving, personal control skills, and interpersonal communication. The class utilizes group leaders and small group work methods. In the first major study of this program, 542 high-risk students from four high schools were invited to participate as either a control or an experimental subject. This resulted in a program class of 101 students and a control group of 158 students. The two conditions at baseline looked very different, with the experimental group more "distressed." Results showed a marginally significant decrease in drug use for the experimental group compared to the control group, as well as decreases in drug control problems and consequences. School bonding, self-esteem, and grade point average also improved significantly for the treatment group, compared to controls (Eggert, Thompson, Herting, & Nicholas, 1994).

Other Instructional Programs

These programs primarily provide classroom instruction without the use of behavioral or cognitive-behavioral techniques, typically making use of more traditional methods of instruction such as lecture, workbooks, and some classroom discussion.

Promising Programs   *Athletes Training and Learning to Avoid Steroids (ATLAS)* is a school-based program designed to intervene with and prevent anabolic androgenic steroid use among student athletes. The program uses educational and skill-training sessions to address risks and benefits of steroid use. ATLAS is integrated into team practice sessions and consists of an educational classroom curriculum and weight room skill-training sessions. The educational component covers subjects such as risk factors of steroid use and strength training, as well as skills to refuse steroid and other substances. In addition, nutritional recommendations and false claims of over-the-counter supplements are discussed. The weight room skill-training sessions focus on demonstrating proper techniques for lifting, as well as providing additional contact time to reinforce the classroom curriculum. The program also incorporates an informational session for parents to help them reinforce the knowledge gained by the youth. The evaluation of this program included a large sample ($n = 3,207$) of males participating in high school football programs in Portland, Oregon (Goldberg et al., 2000). Findings demonstrated favorable effects on the reduction of anabolic steroid use. Significant longitudinal results indicate that this program enhanced healthy behaviors, reduced factors that encouraged steroid use, and lowered intent to use steroids and other substances over a one-year follow-up period following the intervention. Although the reported use of alcohol and other drug use (marijuana, amphetamines, and narcotics) was not lower for the experimental group at program completion, it was significantly lower compared to the control group at the one-year follow-up.

Favorable Programs   *Woodrock Youth Development Project* includes several broad school-based components such as peer mentoring, extracurricular activities, home visits, and parenting classes; however, the core of the program is a Human Relations and Life Skills class conducted by two youth advocates. Classroom activities focus on raising awareness about the danger of drug use, promoting healthy attitudes about drug use, fostering self-esteem through enhancing images of racial membership groups, and developing an appreciation of other ethnic and cultural traditions. Classrooms within four schools were randomly assigned to treatment or control conditions. Drug use (last year and last month) was reduced among the younger subsample (ages 6–9), and relations with students of other races were improved. In the older subsample (ages 10–14), last month drug use significantly favored the treatment group, but the program had no effect on self-esteem and attitudes about students from other races, and actually promoted unhealthy attitudes toward drug and alcohol use (LoSciuto et al., 1997). These mixed results suggest that this program may be beneficial for only younger students.

Know Your Body, targeting K–9 (Walter, Vaughan, & Wynder, 1989), is a broader, year-round health promotion program that focuses on nutrition, fitness, and the prevention of cigarette smoking. This program, in evaluations with random assignment, has shown to be effective in reducing cigarette initiation through the ninth grade.

Counseling, Social Work, and Other Therapeutic Interventions

Although eight programs were originally identified as candidates for favorable, all were eliminated because of design issues. Two other programs had unfavorable results. A meta-analysis by Lipsey (1992) shows that counseling interventions are among the least effective for reducing delinquency.

Mentoring, Tutoring, and Work Study

Other individually based programs focusing on one-on-one mentoring or tutoring of youth, usually paired with an adult or older adolescent, may be utilized in order to build interpersonal as well as school or employment skills. These programs generally target students at high risk of school failure or dropout and are designed to provide more intensive and individualized support than interventions aimed at the school or classroom level. Mentoring is based on the premise that a predictable, consistent relationship with a stable, competent adult can help youth to cope with and avoid a high-risk lifestyle. Tutoring programs strive to overcome risk factors such as early school failure and the lack of bonding to school by providing intensive efforts to remediate academic deficiencies. Work-study programs aim to promote strong bonds to conventional society, which, in turn, promote moral behavior. The rationale is that helping youth to transition into adult roles, such as the role of worker, strengthens the desire to act prosocially because the costs for engaging in delinquent acts are greater. It is also believed that work creates less time for involvement in antisocial behaviors. Evaluations of these three program types have yielded mixed results, with some success for Mentoring and Tutoring, but no identified Work-Study programs with sufficient methodological rigor to include in this chapter.

Exemplary Programs   *Quantum Opportunities Program (QOP)* is an incentives-based program targeting youth development in education, service, and personal skills. The program targets youth from families receiving public assistance and continues through the four years of high school (grades 9 through 12). Activities available throughout the four-year program include 250 hours annually of educational activities, such as computer-assisted instruction, peer tutoring, and other opportunities to enrich academic skills. Also, youth participating in the program have the opportunity to complete up to 250 hours annually of cultural enrichment and personal development activities, such as life/family skills training, planning for college and advanced training, and job preparation. In addition, youth can complete up to 250 hours annually of community service activities, including helping with public events and volunteering in various agencies. Youth are offered small scholarship and cash incentives in order to provide short-term motivation. The program uses a case management approach, in which a caring adult serves as a mentor and program coordinator for small groups of 20 to 25 youth.

Evaluation of the program occurred in five sites throughout the country, in which 50 students from each site (randomly selected from lists of eighth-grade students from families receiving public assistance) were randomly assigned to an experimental or a control group. Program participants scored higher in all 11 academic and functional skills measured. In addition, average academic skill levels increased more than three levels for 27% of participants, compared with only 14% of the control group, after the second year of high school. Following the end of participation in QOP, participants were more likely to have graduated from high school, more likely to be enrolled in a postsecondary program, and less likely to be dropouts than were control students. The rate of four-year college attendance for QOP participants was more than three times higher than the control group, and their rate of two-year college attendance was more than twice as high.

In addition to favorable academic outcomes, two years after the program ended, QOP youth were less likely to have children (female participants) and were less likely to report trouble with the police. Program participants had half the number of arrests as youth in the control group. On average, control males had conviction rates six times higher than that of males participating in QOP.

Promising Programs   None.

Favorable Programs   *Across Ages* matches young people with older adults (typically 55 and older) in order to improve youth bonding with positive role models and to improve their relationships within their schools, families, and communities. Mentors participate with youth in activities such as schoolwork, class trips, sporting or cultural events, and community activities. In addition, youth perform community service with visits to frail elderly persons. A 26-session school curriculum is provided with the project that teaches life and resistance skills for youth. Sixth-grade classes within three schools ($n=729$ students) were randomly assigned to one of three groups: a control group, a treatment group that included all components, and a treatment group that included all but the mentoring component. Overall, 562 students completed participation in the evaluation. Youth receiving all three components of the project (mentoring, community service, and the curriculum) demonstrated better attitudes toward school, the future, and the elderly than both the control group and students not receiving the mentoring component of the project. This group also had higher scores on a well-being scale, better reactions to situations involving drug use, and higher involvement in community service than youth in the control group. The students with mentoring also had significantly fewer days absent than those in the other two groups, and those highly involved with mentors had the fewest days absent. There was, however, no difference between the mentored and control groups on frequency of substance use (LoSciuto et al., 1996).

   Coca-Cola Valued Youth Program, unlike many mentoring and tutoring programs, targets behavioral changes in youth serving as tutors, rather than those being tutored. This program matches limited-English-proficient middle school students at risk of dropping out with children at least four years younger. Tutors take specialized classes to improve academic and tutoring skills and spend four hours per week tutoring younger children, with teacher supervision and support. Tutors ($n=101$) were selected from a pool taken from four campuses in two public school districts (based on class scheduling and availability) based on limited English proficiency and reading below grade level on standardized tests. Comparison students were randomly selected from the remaining pool ($n=93$). There were no baseline differences between groups, with the exception that tutors had significantly lower lunch eligibility. Tutors increased their reading skills over two program years and showed greater self-confidence during the first year, when compared with control students. In addition, tutors showed significantly greater increases in "quality of school life" scores in the first year than did their control group counterparts. Additionally, only 1% of tutors had dropped out of school at the end of the second year, compared to 12% of the controls (Cardenas, Montecel, Supik, & Harris, 1992).

Recreation, Community Service, Enrichment, and Leisure Activities

These programs are designed to provide fun and enriching alternatives to adolescents who might otherwise "hang out" with delinquent peers and engage in delinquent acts. These programs have a special interest in intervening with youth during times when they would have no other adult supervision. They include sports, recreational activities, cultural enrichment, community arts, and wilderness challenge. No school-based programs were identified in this category.

DISCUSSION

Individually focused programs that teach students self-control and social and problem-solving skills are very effective. Lipsey (1992; Lipsey & Wilson, 1998) discovered the importance of these programs in a meta-analysis of 400 delinquency treatment studies and a second meta-analysis of 200 programs serving serious juvenile offenders in and out of the juvenile justice system. Meta-analysis is a statistical technique for aggregating the findings of many studies. Programs were categorized into types, much as this chapter has done, and the strongest program types were identified based on average effect sizes. Findings in both studies showed that behavioral and skills-building programs were most effective. This chapter also identifies several effective programs that include parents, as well as the child, as a target of the intervention. Intervening with both the child and the parents helps to generalize and reinforce the skills learned by the child into the home. Multicomponent programs, such as these, are also identified by Lipsey as extremely effective.

Although a couple of instructional programs are listed, the relative lack of programs on this list suggests that programs using didactic methods, such as lecture to disseminate information, are relatively unsuccessful. This is borne out in past research, which shows that some of the earliest drug programs that made use of information dissemination and scare tactics were unsuccessful in reducing substance use (Botvin, 1990). Gottfredson and colleagues (2000) found that self-control or social competency instruction without the use of cognitive-behavior or behavior instructional methods was ineffective in impacting anti-social/aggressive behavior and dropout and truancy. The results were mixed for crime and alcohol and drug use, but the effect sizes were lower than those found for programs that used the more interactive techniques of instruction, such as coaching, behavioral modeling, and behavioral rehearsal.

There are no identified counseling or recreational programs identified in this chapter that achieve the methodological rigor set for selection. Although eight counseling programs were initially identified that had used a randomized or matched control design, other problems in the evaluations prompted their removal. In fact, two other counseling programs originally identified had unfavorable results (i.e., they harmed rather than helped the child). In Lipsey's (1992) meta-analysis of delinquency treatment programs, he also shows that individual counseling interventions are among the least effective for reducing delinquency (effect size of -0.01 in non-juvenile justice studies and 0.08 in juvenile justice studies). Although recreation programs, in general, show a moderate effect size of 0.18 (Wilson & Lipsey, 1999), the most successful of these programs have not typically been implemented within the school system and, thus, none are identified in this chapter.

There are mixed findings with regard to mentoring, tutoring, and work-study programs. A separate review of 10 mentoring programs indicates that, while they may have some impact on improving school attendance and academic achievement, they do not reduce problem behavior (Brewer, Hawkins, Catalano, & Neckerman, 1995; Thompson & Kelly-Vance, 2001). The only mentoring program with a strong evaluation that has achieved reductions in drug use and delinquency is the well-structured community-based mentoring program, Big Brothers Big Sisters (BBBS). Although many BBBS agencies are incorporating school-based mentoring into their community program, it is unknown how successful these efforts may be. The findings thus far suggest that school-based mentoring alone may not be enough to reduce behavioral problems. The mentoring/tutoring programs described in this chapter are more comprehensive. The Quantum Opportunities Program combines mentoring, done by the case manager of the program with all program participants, with tutoring and other educational and cultural enhancements. Across Ages combines mentoring with a life skills curriculum. The Coca-Cola Valued Youth Program enrolls tutors into specialized classes to improve their own academic skills. No school-based work-study programs are identified in this chapter, and research shows mixed results regarding the effectiveness of these programs (Bushway & Reuter, 1997). The most effective work-study programs, such as Job Corps, remove youth from their home environments and work intensely with them, both academically and vocationally, in a residential setting over the course of a year. Because most work-study programs target high-risk youth, especially dropouts, intensive effort is required to build academic and vocational skills. Short-term, less comprehensive efforts that focus on work alone are not believed to be strong enough to overcome the academic deficits that many of these youth cope with and have not been effective in reducing crime. In fact, there is evidence that work prior to age 18 increases substance use rates in the short and long term, through ages 27 and 28 (Mihalic & Elliott, 1997). The Quantum Opportunities Program, which targets youth at risk of dropping out of school, recommends against youth working, preferring instead to focus on the academic skill building that will ultimately provide job market skills.

Finally, the adoption of effective programs is likely to have little impact on delinquency and substance use if attention is not given to implementation. First and foremost, schools must commit to any prevention efforts undertaken. This means a willingness to allocate resources to materials, obtain teacher buy-in, send teachers to training, troubleshoot and resolve problems that arise, and support and reinforce the efforts of teachers and other implementing staff. In the absence of a strong commitment and determination by school administrators to make a program successful, implementation will often be watered down or terminated as time becomes a scarce resource. While obstacles are unavoidable, careful planning that involves all concerned parties can help to alleviate the resistance and fear that often arise when initiating a new program. Ultimately, many of these programs will not only reduce violence and other behavior problems in school but also help to create a positive learning environment through improved school climate and attachment to school.

REFERENCES

Arbuthnot, Jack (1992). Sociomoral reasoning in behavior-disordered adolescents: Cognitive and behavioral change. In J. McCord and R. Tremblay (Eds.), *Preventing antisocial behavior* (pp. 283–310). New York: Guilford Press.

Botvin, Gilbert (1990). Substance abuse prevention: Theory, practice, and effectiveness. In M. Tonry & J. Q. Wilson (Eds.), *Drugs and crime.* Chicago: University of Chicago Press.

Botvin, Gilbert, Mihalic, Sharon, & Grotpeter, Jennifer (1998). *Life Skills Training.* In D. S. Elliott (Series Ed.), *Blueprints for Violence Prevention* (Vol. 5). Boulder, CO: Center for the Study and Prevention of Violence, Institute of Behavioral Science, University of Colorado.

Brewer, Devon, Hawkins, J. David, Catalano, Richard, & Neckerman, Holly (1995). Preventing serious, violent, and chronic juvenile offending. In J. Howell, B. Krisberg, J. D. Hawkins, & J. Wilson (Eds.), *A sourcebook: Serious, violent, & chronic juvenile offenders.* Thousand Oaks: Sage.

Bry, B. H. (1982). Reducing the incidence of adolescent problems through preventive intervention: One- and five-year follow-up. *American Journal of Community Psychology, 10,* 265–276.

Bry, B. H., & George, F. E. (1980). The preventive effects of early intervention on the attendance and grades of urban adolescents. *Professional Psychology, 11,* 252–260.

Bushway, Shawn, & Reuter, Peter (1997). Labor markets and crime risk factors. In L. Sherman, D. Gottfredson, D. MacKenzie, J. Eck, P. Reuter, & S. Bushway (Eds.), *Preventing crime: What works, what doesn't, what's promising?* College Park, Ma.: University of Maryland.

Caplan, M., Weissberg, R. P., Grober, J. S., Sivo, P. J., Grady, K., & Jacoby, C. (1992). Social competence promotion with inner-city and suburban young adolescents: Effects on social adjustment and alcohol use. *Journal of Consulting and Clinical Psychology, 60,* 56–63.

Cardenas, Jose, Montecel, Maria, Supik, Josie, & Harris, Richard (1992). The Coca-Cola Valued Youth Program: Dropout prevention strategies for at-risk students. *Texas Researcher, 3,* 111–130.

Conduct Problems Prevention Group (Karen Bierman, John Coie, Kenneth Dodge, Mark Greenberg, John Lochman, Robert McMahon, & Ellan Pinderhughes) (1999a). Initial impact of the Fast Track Prevention Trial for conduct problems: II. The classroom effects. *Journal of Consulting and Clinical Psychology, 67,* no. 5, 648–657.

Conduct Problems Prevention Group (Karen Bierman, John Coie, Kenneth Dodge, Mark Greenberg, John Lochman, Robert McMahon, & Ellan Pinderhughes) (1999b). Initial impact of the Fast Track Prevention Trial for conduct problems: I. The high-risk sample. *Journal of Consulting and Clinical Psychology, 67,* no. 5, 631–647.

Davis, Leslie, & Tolan, Patrick (1993). Alternative and preventive interventions. In P. H. Tolan & B. J. Cohler (Eds.), *Handbook of clinical research and practice with adolescents.* New York: John Wiley & Sons.

DuRant, Robert, Barkin, Shari, & Krowchuk, Daniel (2001). Evaluation of a Peaceful Conflict Resolution and Violence Prevention Curriculum for Sixth-Grade Students. *Society for Adolescent Medicine, 28,* 386–393.

Dusenbury, Linda, & Falco, Mathea (1995). Eleven components of effective drug abuse prevention curricula. *Journal of School Health, 65,* 420–425.

Eddy, J. M., Reid, J. B., & Fetrow, R. A. (2000). An elementary-school based prevention program targeting modifiable antecedents of youth delinquency and violence: Linking the Interests of Families and Teachers (LIFT). *Journal of Emotional & Behavioral Disorders, 8,* 165–176.

Eggert, Leona, Thompson, Elaine, Herting, Jerald, & Nicholas, Liela (1994). Prevention research program: Reconnecting at-risk youth. *Issues in Mental Health Nursing, 15,* 107–135.

Elias, M. J., Gara, M. A., Schuyler, T. F., Braden-Muller, L. R., & Sayette, M. A. (1991). The promotion of social competence: Longitudinal study of a preventive school-based program. *American Journal of Orthopsychiatry, 61,* 409–417.

Elias, M. J., Gara, M., Ubriaco, M., Rothbaum, P. A., Blabby, J. F., & Schuyler, T. (1986). Impact of a preventive social problem solving intervention on children's coping with middle school stressors. *American Journal of Community Psychology, 14,* 259–275.

Ellickson, Phyllis, & Bell, Robert (1990). Drug prevention in junior high: A multi-site longitudinal test. *Science, 247,* 1299–1305.

Flay, Brian (2001). Effects of the Positive Action Program on achievement and discipline: Two matched-control comparisons. *Prevention Science, 2,* 71–89.

Fraser, Mark W. (1996). Cognitive problem solving and aggressive behavior among children. *Families in Society: The Journal of Contemporary Human Services, 77,* 19–32.

Goldberg, Linn, MacKinnon, David, Elliot, Diane, Moe, Esther, Clarke, Greg, & Cheong, Jeewon (2000). The Adolescents Training and Learning to Avoid Steroids Program: Preventing drug use and promoting health behaviors. *Archives of Pediatric Adolescent Medicine, 154,* 332–338.

Gottfredson, Denise, Wilson, David B., & Najaka, Stacy S. (in press). School-based crime prevention. In D. P. Farrington, L. W. Sherman, & B. Welsh (Eds.), *Evidence-based crime prevention.* United Kingdom: Harwood Academic Publishers.

Gottfredson, Gary, Gottfredson, Denise, & Czeh, Ellen (2000). Summary: National study of delinquency prevention in schools. Ellicott City, MD: Gottfredson Associates, Inc.

Greenberg, Mark, Kusche, Carol, & Mihalic, Sharon (1998). *Promoting Alternative Thinking Strategies.* In D. S. Elliott (Series Ed.), *Blueprints for Violence Prevention* (Vol. 2). Boulder, CO: Center for the Study and Prevention of Violence, Institute of Behavioral Science, University of Colorado.

Henggeler, Scott (1989). Delinquency in adolescence. In A. E. Kazdin (Ed.), *Developmental clinical psychology and psychiatry* (pp. 24–35). Newbury Park, CA: Sage.

Hennessey, Beth A., & Seigle, Pamela (unpublished). Promoting social competency in school-aged children: The effects of the reach out to schools social competency program. Wellesley, MA: Wellesley College.

Josendal, O., Aaro, L., & Bergh, I. H. (1998). Effects of a school-based smoking prevention program among subgroups of adolescents. *Health Education Research, 13,* 215–224.

Kazdin, Alan E. (2000). Treatments for aggressive and antisocial children. *Child and Adolescent Psychiatric Clinics of North America, 9,* 841–857.

Kazdin, Alan E. (1987). Treatment of antisocial behavior in children: Current status and future directions. *Psychological Bulletin, 102,* 187–203.

Kellam, Sheppard G., Rebok, George W., Ialongo, Nicholas, & Mayer, Lawrence S. (1994). The course and malleability of aggressive behavior from early first grade into middle school: Results of a developmental epidemiologically based preventive trial. *Journal of Child Psychology and Psychiatry, 35,* 259–282.

Kosterman, Rick, Hawkins, J. David, Spoth, Richard, Haggerty, Kevin, & Zhu, Kangmin (1997). Effects of a preventive parent-training intervention on observed family interactions: Proximal outcomes from Preparing for the Drug Free Years. *Journal of Community Psychology, 25,* 337–352.

Lipsey, Mark (1992). The effect of treatment on juvenile delinquents: Results from meta-analysis. In F. Losel, D. Bender, & T. Bliesener (Eds.), *Psychology and Law.* New York: Walter de Gruyter.

Lipsey, Mark, & Wilson, David (1998). Effective intervention for serious juvenile offenders. In R. Loeber & D. Farrington (Eds.), *Serious & violent juvenile offenders: Risk factors and successful interventions.* Thousand Oaks: Sage.

Lochman, J. E. (1992). Cognitive-behavioral intervention with aggressive boys: Three-year follow-up and preventive effects. *Journal of Consulting and Clinical Psychology, 60,* 426–432.

LoSciuto, Leonard, Freeman, Mark, Harrington, Evan, Altman, Brian, & Lanphear, Alden (1997). An outcome of the Woodrock Youth Development Project. *Journal of Early Adolescence, 17,* 51–66.

LoSciuto, L., Rajala, A. K., Townsend, T. N., & Taylor, A. S. (1996). An outcome evaluation of Across Ages: An intergenerational mentoring approach to drug prevention. *Journal of Adolescent Research, 11,* 116–129.

Mihalic, Sharon, & Elliott, Delbert (1997). Short- and long-term consequences of adolescent work. *Youth and Society, 28,* 464–498.

Pepler, D. J., King, G., Craig, W., Byrd, B., & Bream, L. (1995). The development and evaluation of a multisystem social skills group training program for aggressive children. *Child and Youth Care Forum, 24,* 297–313.

Pepler, D. J., King, G., & Gyrd, W. (1991). A social-cognitive based social skills training program for aggressive children. In D. J. Pepler and K. Rubin (Eds.), *The development and treatment of childhood aggression* (pp. 361–379). Hillsdale, NJ: Lawrence Erlbaum.

Prinz, R. J., Blechman, E. A., & Dumas, J. E. (1994). An evaluation of peer coping-skills training for childhood aggression. *Journal of Clinical Child Psychology, 23,* 193–203.

Reid, J. M., Eddy, J. M., Fetrow, R. A., & Stoolmiller, M. (1999). Description and immediate impacts of a prevention intervention for conduct problems. *American Journal of Community Psychology, 27,* 483–517.

Ross, Robert R., & Ross, Bambi D. (1989). Delinquency prevention through cognitive training. *Educational Horizons,* Summer, 124–130.

Sarason, Irwin G., & Sarason, Barbara R. (1981). Teaching cognitive and social skills to high school students. *Journal of Consulting and Clinical Psychology, 49,* 908–918.

Shope, Jean, Copeland, Laurel, Kamp, Mary, & Lang, Sylvia, (1998). Twelfth grade follow-up of the effectiveness of a middle school-based substance abuse prevention program. *Journal of Drug Education, 28,* 185–197.

Shope, Jean, Copeland, Laurel, Marcoux, Beth, & Kamp, Mary (1996). Effectiveness of a school-based substance abuse prevention program. *Journal of Drug Education, 26,* 323–337.

Shure, Myrna B., & Healey, Kathryn N. (1993). Interpersonal problem solving and prevention in urban school children. Paper presented at the American Psychological Association Annual Convention, Toronto.

Shure, Myrna B., & Spivack, George (1982). Interpersonal problem solving in young children: A cognitive approach to prevention. *American Journal of Community Psychology, 10,* 341–355.

Shure, Myrna B., & Spivack, George (1980). Interpersonal problem solving as a mediator of behavioral adjustment in preschool and kindergarten children. *Journal of Applied Developmental Psychology, 1,* 29–44.

Spivack, G., Platt, J. J., & Shure, M. B. (1976). *The problem-solving approach to adjustment.* San Francisco: Jossey-Bass.

Spoth, Richard, Redmond, Cleve, & Lepper, Heidi (1999). Alcohol initiation outcomes of universal family-focused preventive interventions: One- and two-year follow-ups of a controlled study. *Journal of Studies on Alcohol, 13,* 103–111.

Spoth, Richard, Redmond, Cleve, & Shin, Chungyeol (1999). Randomized trial of brief family interventions for general populations: Reductions in adolescent substance use four years following baseline. Manuscript under review.

Spoth, Richard, Redmond, Cleve, & Shin, Chungyeol (1998). Direct and indirect latent-variable parenting outcomes of two universal family-focused preventive interventions: Extending a public health-oriented research base. *Journal of Consulting and Clinical Psychology, 66,* 385–399.

Thompson, Lynn A., & Kelly-Vance, Lisa (2001). The impact of mentoring on academic achievement of at-risk youth. *Children and Youth Services Review, 23,* 227–242.

Tolan, Patrick, & Guerra, Nancy (1994). What works in reducing adolescent violence: An empirical review of the field. Boulder, CO: University of Colorado, Institute of Behavioral Science.

Tremblay, Richard E., Masse, Louise, Pagani, Linda, & Vitaro, Frank (1996). From childhood physical aggression to adolescent maladjustment: The Montreal Prevention Experiment. In R. D. Peters & R. J. McMahon (Eds.), *Preventing childhood disorders, substance abuse, and delinquency.* Thousand Oaks: Sage.

Tremblay, Richard E., McCord, Joan, Bioleau, Helene, Charlebois, Pierre, Gagnon, Claude, LeBlanc, Marc, & Larivee, Serge (1991). Can disruptive boys be helped to become competent? *Psychiatry, 54,* 149–161.

Tremblay, Richard E., Vitaro, Frank, Bertrand, Lucie, LeBlanc, Marc, Beauchesne, Helene, Bioleau, Helene, & David, Lucille (1992). Parent and child training to prevent early onset of delinquency: The Montreal Longitudinal Experimental Study. In J. McCord & R. Tremblay (Eds.), *Preventing antisocial behavior: Interventions from birth through adolescence.* New York: Guilford Press.

Vartiainen, Erkki, Paavola, Meri, McAlister, Alfred, & Puska, Pekka (1998). Fifteen-year follow-up of smoking prevention effects in the North Karelia Youth Project. *American Journal of Public Health, 88,* 81–85.

Walter, Heather, Vaughan, Roger, & Wynder, Ernst (1989). Primary prevention of cancer among children: Changes in cigarette smoking and diet after six years of intervention. *Journal of the National Cancer Institute, 81,* 995–999.

Webster-Stratton, Carolyn, & Hammond, M. (1997). Treating children with early-onset conduct problems: A comparison of child and parent training interventions. *Journal of Consulting and Clinical Psychology, 65,* 93–109.

Webster-Stratton, Carolyn, Mihalic, Sharon, Fagan, Abigail, Arnold, David, Taylor, Ted, & Tingley, Charles (2001). *The Incredible Years: Parent, Teacher and Child Training Series.* In D. S. Elliott (Series Ed.), *Blueprints for Violence Prevention* (Vol. 11). Boulder, CO: Center for the Study and Prevention of Violence, Institute of Behavioral Science, University of Colorado.

Wilson, Sandra, & Lipsey, Mark (1999). Wilderness challenge programs for delinquent youth: A meta-analysis of outcome evaluations. *Evaluation and Program Planning, 23,* 1–12.

13

Policing and School Violence: Perceptions or Reality—Either Way There Will Always Be the Need for Safety

Cindy N. Berner and M. L. Dantzker

This final chapter is designed to pull together all of the proceeding chapters into a coherent whole. Additionally, this chapter offers some survey data from 244 high school students regarding their perceptions of "fear for their lives while at school." In this survey, 70% of the respondents indicated that they felt "safe while in school." The authors conclude that there may be significant differences between perceptions of school crime and the reality of school crime, while noting the need for additional research on this question.

During the first three months of 2001, there was no shortage of actual or potential school-related violent incidents. Some examples were:

California: A 15-year-old high school student killed 2 and wounded 13 other students after firing a .22 caliber revolver from a boy's bathroom.

Colorado: A 14-year-old high school student was arrested after police found two pipe bombs in his home.

Delaware: An 11-year-old student was arrested after leaving a bomb-threat note on a school bus.

Pennsylvania: A 14-year-old girl shot a female classmate in the shoulder following an ongoing dispute between the two girls.

Other similar incidents occurred and more are yet to follow.

Throughout this text, there have been a myriad of discussions for supporting the need for improving safety in schools as well as creating doubt as to the need for improvement. For example, in Chapter 1, Snyder and Sickmund offered data on juvenile crime for 1999. The authors suggested that the data demonstrate a marginal improvement of conditions regarding juveniles as both offenders and victims. Manganaro and Longoria followed Snyder and Sickmund's views with their discussion on school crime in Chapter 2.

Analyzing data from two major reports on school crime, conclusions from Manganaro and Longoria regarding school crime may best be summarized as follows:

1. The data clearly show that middle schools are a problem for both teachers and students.
2. There has been an overall decline in rates across different types of school crime.
3. Policy and decision makers need to consider the reliability of the available data.
4. Convergence of victimization rates among all schools suggests both the effectiveness of strategies in urban and suburban schools and the need for response among school and community leaders in rural areas.
5. Effective data collection and sound program analysis of school crime should be used to pinpoint particular problem areas in all schools, thereby lowering programmatic costs.

In essence, the findings of these authors may suggest that although some specific areas may need to be addressed regarding the school crime and violence issues, overall, the problem is not as grand as advertised.

It is readily agreed among experts that statistics play an important role in establishing policies and procedures. The first two chapters support the need and the use of these statistics. To reinforce this position, both Chapters 3 and 4 focused on the process of reporting school crime in our two biggest states, California and Texas.

Aultman-Bettridge, in Chapter 3, discussed the need for comprehensive and reliable information on the prevalence of crime in our country's schools. She suggests that school incident reporting can do the following:

1. Serve to assist officials in sharing all available information about youth who may be demonstrating a need for prevention or intervention efforts
2. Track trends and patterns in crime in order to assess the exact nature and extent of crime
3. Serve a vital function—safe school planning

She then went on to discuss how California has a mandated standardized reporting system and how it works, providing results from five years of collected data. Ultimately, she concluded that collected data can serve many purposes, including policy making, individual school needs, resource allocation, and progress.

In Chapter 4, Mack and Longoria took a similar approach to that of Chapter 3 and discussed their examination of school crime in Texas. Their study concluded that:

1. School crime in Texas is not as bad as perceived.

2. No statistically significant relationships were found between poverty, adult educational levels, percentage of urban residents, and percentage of Hispanics with school crime.

3. Still, there is a big desire for continued programs, training, and so on to address school crime.

At this point, we want to offer some additional data to muddy the waters. The previously discussed crime statistics chapters tend to lean toward suggesting that perhaps crime in schools is not nearly as bad as perceived. There is, however, the quandary—the matter of perception. "The perception of risk is often greater than the reality, as schools have been largely successful in keeping students and staff safe from harm" (Small & Tetrick, 2001, p. 3). Perhaps for some, one criminal incident is too much, while for another, even a murder may not be too extraordinary. Yet, the media, particularly in more recent years in light of the various school shootings, may be influential in heightening perception, thus raising the question, How do students perceive their safety in school? We offer just one possible response to this.

A QUESTION OF PERCEPTION?

Since the Columbine tragedy on April 20, 1999, violence in U.S. schools has been pushed to the forefront of our minds. The media have taken this concern and turned it into a horrifying tale. Current perceptions of violence in schools have Americans believing they should be terrified to send their children to school for fear they will be murdered there. Society has been bombarded with statistics that seem to be outrageous. But how true are these statistics? Is school violence really something that parents should stay up late worrying about? Or have a few instances skewed our perceptions and clogged our minds with opinion rather than fact, and of course fear? The media have expended many hours and much airtime and money to spread this phobia to every American. Is this really a new uprising problem, or has it always plagued schools? Most importantly, however, do students really fear for their lives while in school? Our study examined students' perceptions of school violence, focusing on how students felt about their safety while in school, regardless of what societal perceptions may have become. This was accomplished through a students' perception of school violence study conducted at a local high school.

Within society there are many socialization agents that influence our perceptions, such as friends, family, and the media, whether visual or print (Dantzker & Waters, 1999). When looking at criminal justice issues and how society perceives them, previous research has shown that the media play an influential role in how these instances are viewed (Bailey & Hale, 1998; Kappeler, Blumberg, & Potter, 1996; Surrette, 1992). As a result, public perceptions of school violence peaked after the Columbine tragedy in 1999, when the media blanketed networks with coverage. A report published after the Columbine incident by the Justice Policy Institute (1999) stated that "rather than providing context, the media's linking of school shooting as a 'trend' has tended to exacerbate people's fears about the safety of their children and youth in schools" (p. 1).

Historically, school violence can be traced back to colonial times. Then, violence was associated with teachers who inflicted pain, and it has since graduated into the occasional school shootings and muggings by students that we see today (Crews & Countes, 1997). In 1978, a three-year Safe School Study showed that 8% of all school administrators reported serious problems in their schools. Furthermore, these administrators believed that the violence that occurred in the 1960s and early 1970s had leveled off during the previous five years (Rubel, 1978). Even with these reported incidents, within the last 15 years there has been a substantial increase in the public's perception of violence in schools. For instance, in 1982, 3% of Americans surveyed viewed violence in schools to be a serious problem, as opposed to in 1994, when more than 50% viewed it as a problem (Gumpel & Meadan, 2000). Is the increase in society fear based on an increase in violence or on an increase in the media's reporting?

According to the U.S. Department of Education, National School Safety Center, in 1992 and 1993, 76 students were slain in school, and prior to the Littleton shootings on April 20, 1999, 9 students had been killed at schools nationally during the 1998–1999 school year (U.S. Department of Education, National Safety Center, 1999). Furthermore, in a survey of 1,234 U.S. public schools in 1997, more than half reported experiencing at least one crime incident during the 1996–1997 school year (U.S. Department of Education, National Center for Education Statistics, 1998). Additionally, in 1996, a study conducted by the Centers for Disease Control found that less than 1% of all homicides among school-aged children occurred in or around school grounds (Centers for Disease Control and Prevention, 1999).

These and other studies conducted throughout the years indicate that there has not been a dramatic increase in school violence since the 1970s (Anderson, 1998). Therefore, it can be hypothesized that because school violence itself has not increased, perceptions of violence in school should not be as dramatic as the media have portrayed it.

Previous research has shown that perceptions are not as dramatic as the media dictate. In 1994, the California School Climate and Safety Survey organization administered a survey to approximately 7,000 students representing 32 public schools that examined students' perceptions of school violence. Here it was found that more than 51% of respondents felt safe while at school (Morrison, Furlong, & Morrison, 1994). Furthermore, in 1996 it was reported in *Education Week* that students actually felt that schools were less violent than they had been the two years prior, despite national reports that school violence had increased (Portner, 1996). Additionally, the 2000 Annual Report on School Safety stated, "since 1995 there has been a welcome decline in students' fear of attack or harm at school" (p. 5).

To further address the idea of students' perceptions of school violence, and to examine if students were actually as fearful in school as society had perceived, a study was conducted at a local high school during a summer session in 1999. All students in attendance in English classes during the selected time frame were surveyed.

Methodology

The purpose of our study was to examine if students actually were fearful for their lives while at school. To accomplish this task, a 10-question survey was designed using items taken from other surveys previously published in the National Institute of Justice and

U.S. Department of Education documents. The questionnaire was distributed to all students enrolled in English classes during a summer session of an Edinburg, Texas, high school. These students were chosen as a result of a decision as to which would be the least disruptive, and yet, most representative of the students enrolled at the time. Regarding the survey, all 10 questions were designed in a closed-ended manner to make quantification easier for analysis. Three hundred surveys were distributed to students in grades 9 through 12, with 244 usable surveys returned.

Findings

Among the 244 student respondents, the gender distribution only slightly favored males (51.2% to 47.1%, respectively). Ethnically, whites comprised 16.8% (n=41) and Hispanics 75.8% (n=185). Regarding the ages of the students, 10.6% (n=26) were between the ages of 12 and 14; 25.8% (n=63) were 15; 29.5% (n=72) were 16; 22.9% (n=55) were 17; and 9.4% (n=23) were between the ages of 18 and 20. By classification type, 20.5% (n=50) were freshmen; 32.0% (n=78) sophomores; 29.5% (n=72) juniors; and 16.4% (n=40) were seniors (see Table 13.1).

Because this study originated as purely descriptive in nature and its goal was to examine students' perceptions as a whole about school violence, only frequencies are reported. When respondents were asked if in the last year violence in their school had increased, decreased, or stayed about the same, 47.1% (n=115) felt that the violence had stayed about the same (see Table 13.2). When acts of violence did occur in school, 54.9% (n=134) of respondents felt they happened in the school building (see Table 13.3). Students were also asked, "If violence does happen within the school, where does it most often occur?" Respondents were given 11 choices with the opportunity to check as many as applicable. The top two areas chosen were hallways (75.4%, n=184) and the cafeteria (75.0%, n=183) (see Table 13.4). In addition, students were asked whether they thought gang violence in school was a very serious problem, a somewhat serious problem, a not very serious problem, or not a serious problem at all. Fifty-four percent (n=131) of respondents believed that gang violence was somewhat of a very serious problem (see Table 13.5). With regard to weapons in school, 52.9% (n=112) of students surveyed believed that weapons in school was not a very serious problem at all (see Table 13.5). When asked whether or not they felt safe while in school, 70.1% (n=171) of students felt somewhat or very safe in school (see Table 13.6). Additionally, when asked how safe students felt at school as compared to their neighborhood, 53.7% (n=131) of respondents felt safe in both places (see Table 13.7). Being physically attacked in school also seems to be a fear in society's mind. When asked how worried they were about being physically attacked in or around school, 64.8% (n=158) of students surveyed indicated that they are not very worried or not worried at all (see Table 13.8). Students were also asked if they thought students brought weapons to school, what were some of the reasons? Fourteen choices were provided allowing the respondent to choose all that were applicable. The top two reasons were to threaten someone (66.4%, n=162) and because it was gang related (65.8%, n=158) (see Table 13.9). Finally, when students were asked if they had ever carried an illegal weapon in or around their school, 86.1% (n=210) of students stated no, they had never taken an illegal weapon to school.

TABLE 13.1   Students' Perceptions of School Violence Demographics–Survey Respondents

Characteristic	Percent[a]/($n=244$)
Gender	
Male	51.2 (125)
Female	47.1 (115)
Ethnicity	
White	16.8 (41)
Hispanic	75.8 (185)
African-American	1.2 (3)
Indian	.8 (2)
Asian	2.5 (6)
Other	1.2 (3)
Missing	1.6 (4)
Age of Students	
12–14	10.6 (26)
15	25.8 (63)
16	29.5 (72)
17	22.5 (55)
18–20	9.4 (23)
Missing	2.0 (5)
Classification	
Freshman	20.5 (50)
Sophomore	32.0 (78)
Junior	29.5 (72)
Senior	16.4 (40)
Missing	1.6 (4)

[a]Percents may not sum to 100 due to rounding.

TABLE 13.2   Students' Perception of School Violence In the past year, has the level of violence at your school . . .

Responses	Percent[a]/($n=244$)
Increased	29.1 (71)
Decreased	20.5 (50)
Same	47.1 (115)
Missing	3.3 (8)

[a]Percents may not sum to 100 due to rounding.

TABLE 13.3   Students' Perception of School Violence
Where do most acts of violence in or around your school occur?

Responses	Percent[a]/($n=244$)
In the school building	54.9 (134)
On the school grounds	28.3 (69)
In the school neighborhoods	11.9 (29)
Missing	4.9 (12)

[a]Percents may not sum to 100 due to rounding.

TABLE 13.4   Students' Perceptions of School Violence
When acts of violence happen in the school building,
where do most of them occur?

Responses	Percent[a]/($n=244$)
Hallways or staircase	75.4 (184)
Lunchroom or cafeteria	75.0 (183)
Classrooms	26.6 (65)
Locker rooms	36.1 (88)
Gym	20.5 (50)
Boys bathroom	32.8 (80)
Girls bathroom	24.2 (59)
Library	4.5 (11)
Violence never happens inside	3.7 (9)
Somewhere else	28.3 (69)
Don't know	8.2 (20)

[a]Percents may not sum to 100 due to rounding.

TABLE 13.5   Students' Perceptions of School Violence
Thinking about your school, do you think that each of the
following concerns is a very serious problem, somewhat
serious, not very serious, or not a serious problem at all?

Category	Percent[a]/($n=244$)			
	Very Serious Problem	Somewhat Serious	Not Very Serious	Not a Serious Problem at all
Gang Violence	21.3 (52)	23.4 (79)	29.5 (72)	14.8 (36)
Weapons in School	27.0 (66)	18.9 (46)	34.0 (83)	18.9 (46)

[a]Percents may not sum to 100 due to rounding.

TABLE 13.6   Students' Perceptions of School Violence
How safe do you feel when you are in school?

Responses	Percent[a]/(n=244)
Very safe	19.7 (48)
Somewhat safe	50.4 (123)
Not very safe	15.6 (38)
About as safe	3.7 (9)
Missing	10.6 (26)

[a]Percents may not sum to 100 due to rounding.

TABLE 13.7   Students' Perception of School Violence
Compared to your neighborhood, do you feel . . .

Responses	Percent[a]/(n=244)
More safe in your school building	11.1 (27)
Less safe	31.1 (76)
About as safe	53.7 (131)
Missing	4.1 (10)

[a]Percents may not sum to 100 due to rounding.

TABLE 13.8   Students' Perception of School Violence
How worried are you about being physically
attacked in or around your school?

Responses	Percent[a]/(n=244)
Very worried	10.2 (25)
Somewhat worried	21.3 (52)
Not very worried	36.5 (89)
Not at all worried	28.3 (69)
Missing	3.7 (9)

[a]Percents may not sum to 100 due to rounding.

Conclusions to Our Study

When Americans send their children to school, they want to believe that they will be safe, and until 1999 most Americans believed that was the case. After the tragedy at Columbine, society's perception of violence in schools skyrocketed. A few school shootings blanketed the television and pushed society into believing that schools were dangerous for their children. The purpose of our study was to examine the perception of violence in schools among students.

TABLE 13.9   Students' Perception of School Violence
Why do you think students carry weapons with them to school?

Responses	Percent[a]/($n=244$)
To impress peers/be accepted by peers	60.7 (148)
For protection/self-defense/fear going to and from school	57.4 (140)
For protection/self-defense/fear in school	53.7 (131)
For self-esteem/to feel powerful or important	54.5 (133)
Used for hunting/regular daily equip./culturally accepted	18.0 (44)
Because they want to hurt someone	52.9 (129)
Forgot to leave it at home	23.4 (57)
To intimidate/threatened/frightened	66.4 (162)
Because friends carry weapons	34.0 (83)
Anger/frustration/fear	50.8 (124)
Gang-related	64.8 (158)
Part of work equipment/used as a tool	12.3 (30)
Other	16.8 (41)
Don't know	16.0 (39)

[a]Percents may not sum to 100 due to rounding.

Due to the limitation presented by school administrators of being able to survey only those students enrolled in English classes during the summer, this study was not representative of Texas students generally. In addition, because of time constraints, a pretest was not conducted, raising concerns of validity and reliability. Based on the findings reported, however, there did appear to be support for the initial hypothesis that despite increased reporting of violence in schools, students do feel safe while in school. As the results indicated, 70.1% of the students surveyed felt somewhat to very safe while in school. Additionally, 64.8% of respondents were not very worried or not worried at all about being physically attacked while in school. We believe this study was an excellent example of how society's perceptions are often off base with reality. Obviously, due to the limitations of the study and its exploratory, descriptive nature, additional research is necessary. Furthermore, these findings do not erase the reality that violent acts can and do occur in our schools, and therefore, it is important for society to ensure that our children are as safe as possible when attending school.

SAFETY IN SCHOOLS

More than anything else, the school shootings of recent years have taught us that school safety is not about any one method of control: metal detectors, surveillance systems, or swift punishment. Nor is it about any single risk factor such as dysfunctional homes and inadequate schools. We have learned that we cannot identify with certainty those students who, for reasons clear only to themselves, will assault their teachers and peers. We now understand that safe schools require broad-based efforts on the part of the entire community, including educators, students, parents, law enforcement agencies, businesses, and faith-based organizations (Pollack & Sunderman, 2001:13).

While statistics and perceptions may suggest that schools are safer than believed, any violent act, particularly one by which lives are lost, should be unacceptable. As noted above, safe schools require involvement from various elements of society as well as a plan.

Preparing for safe schools begins with a plan. Stephens, in Chapter 5, offered a "how-to" for developing and implementing a basic plan for a safe school. He began by defining a safe school as "an environment free of intimidation, violence, and fear" and continued with an explanation for the need for a plan. This discussion was then followed with the information on how to go about creating the plan, essential components, legal aspects, community involvement, necessary steps, challenges and obstacles, site assessment, and collecting data. Stephens offered that the plan's content must entail such elements as the physical, social, and cultural environments; personal characteristics of students and staff members; local political atmosphere; and community will. Finally, as with any plan, there is a need to monitor and evaluate the plan. In essence, Stephens advocated that a safe school plan is simply a good idea.

Chapter 5 laid the foundation for establishing and implementing a safe school plan. Stephens followed up this chapter with recommendations for practices for a safe school. In Chapter 6, he described practices dealing with campus access and control, leadership, school climate, student behavior, supervision and management, student involvement, and building community partnerships. This chapter concludes with examples of documentation to assist in planning.

Because one of the first responders to a school violence incident is the police or other law enforcement personnel, how they respond is crucial. The law enforcement response to the shooting at Columbine led to numerous questions and concerns as to how police should respond to such a situation. In Chapter 7, SyWassink outlined the roles of law enforcement not only in reacting to school crime but also in the proactive stages for planning a response. SyWassink identified who should be involved in developing a school violence plan, carrying out the plan, and the responsibility of responders. He concluded that responding to school crime is not just a law enforcement concern but the community's too. In short, he strongly encouraged that a crisis plan be in place.

Chapter 8 and 9 provide perspectives from those adults who are at the "front lines" of school violence, teachers and administrators. In Chapter 8, Ardis offered her personal perspectives as to why there is so much more school violence today than in years past. One of her major concerns was that the lack of parental involvement may be a big factor. Chapter 9 is an excellent source of viewpoints of superintendents. As a compilation of articles, Chapter 9 offers information on students' rights to due process, school safety, student profiling, school architecture and design, school police officers, and alternative education for troubled youth. Both chapters provide pertinent information applicable to design and implementation of a safe school plan.

The continuing advancement of technology opens a new arena for school safety. Green in Chapter 10 discussed the appropriate and effective use of security technologies in schools. In particular, she concentrated on security concepts and operational issues, video surveillance, weapons-detection devices, entry controls, and duress alarms. She concluded that safety and security technology can be only one tool in a comprehensive program that each school must develop to create a safe learning environment.

More and more programs are being tested and implemented in schools in the name of prevention and safety. In Chapters 11 and 12, Mihalic and Aultman-Bettridge identified several factors useful in explaining the interest in and surge in school-based prevention activities. A few such factors included rising rates of violence, new types of violence, public perceptions, and perceptions of lack of security. Addressing these factors is based in prevention programs, several of which they identified and discussed how and why they work, such as School Resource Officers and conflict-resolution education (also see Crawford & Bodine, 2001).

CLOSING THOUGHTS

Statistics and perceptions aside, violence does and will continue to occur in our schools, and not just the "simple" fistfight between two youths. Whether it is a shooting or a bomb threat, the police will be called upon to respond. This response should be based on an in-depth plan created and implemented by all relevant parties. The plan should actually consist of two major components: the school response and the police response. Both parts should be a cooperative effort. It is especially important for today's schools that are incorporating police officers on their campuses, whether as an assigned duty by a local agency or as full-time employees of a school district police agency, which appears to be a growing trend among today's schools.

In February 2001, the U.S. Department of Justice's Office of Community Oriented Policing Services (COPS) awarded $70 million in grants under the COPS in Schools program. These grants were to lead to the hiring of 640 new School Resource Officers among 348 law enforcement agencies throughout cities and towns in 47 states. "School resource officers act as mentors and role models and perform various school functions, including teaching crime prevention and substance abuse classes, monitoring troubled students, and building respect between law enforcement and students" (Office of Community Oriented Policing Services, 2001:30). COPS in schools first began in 1998 and has awarded $420 million to fund and train more than 3,800 School Resource Officers.

Simply having safety measures available or in place does not guarantee complete freedom from a school violence incident, but it undoubtedly will decrease the chances of a violent episode taking place. Just as importantly as the mechanisms of safety is having a plan to respond if and when such an incident occurs. Nowhere may this be any truer than for police agencies.

REFERENCES

Anderson, D. C. (1998). *Curriculum, culture, and community: The challenge of school violence.* Chicago, IL: University of Chicago Press, 317–363.

Bailey, F., & Hale, D. (1998). *Popular culture, crime, and justice.* Belmont, CA: West/Wadsworth.

Centers for Disease Control and Prevention (1999). *Facts about violence among youth and violence in school.* [On line]. Available: www.edc.gov/ncipc/factsheets/schoolvi.htm.

Crawford, D. K., & Bodine, R. J. (2001). Conflict resolution education: Preparing youth for the future. *Juvenile Justice, 8,* no. 1, 21–29.

Crews, G. A., & Countes, M. R. (1997). *The evolution of school disturbances in America: Colonial times to modern day.* Westport, CT: Praeger.

Dantzker, M. L., & Waters, J. E. (1999). *Examining students' perceptions of Policing: A pre- and post-comparison between students in criminal justice and non-criminal justice courses.* In M. L. Dantzker (Ed.), *Readings for research methods in criminology and criminal justice* (pp. 27–35). Butterworth-Heinemann.

Gumpel, T. P., & Meadan, H. (2000). Children's perceptions of school-based violence. *British Journal of Educational Psychology, 70,* 391–404.

Justice Policy Institute (1999). *Deadly statistics. School violence.* [On line]. Available: www.tbwt.com/interaction/shoot/html/2a.htm.

Kappeler, V. E., Blumberg, M., & Potter, G. W. (1996). *The mythology of crime and criminal justice.* Prospect Heights, IL: Waveland Press.

Morrison, R. L., Furlong, M. J., & Morrison, G. M. (1994). Knocking the wheels off the school violence bandwagon. *Thrust for Educational Leadership, 24,* 6–9.

Office of Community Oriented Policing Services (2001). *Juvenile Justice, 8,* no. 1, 30.

Pollack, I., & Sundermann, C. (2001). Creating safe schools: A comprehensive approach. *Juvenile Justice, 8,* no. 1, 13–20.

Portner, J. (1996). Some students report feeling safer at school. *Education Week, 15,* 7.

Rubel, R. J. (1978). Analysis and critique of HEW's Safe School Study Report to Congress. *Crime and Delinquency, 24,* no.3, 257–265.

Small, M., & Tetrick, K.D. (2001). School violence: An overview. *Juvenile Justice, 8,* no. 1, 3–12.

Surette, R. (1992). *Media, crime, and criminal justice: Images and realities.* Belmont, CA: Wadsworth.

U.S. Department of Education, National Center for Education Statistics (1998). *Violence and discipline problems in U.S. Schools: 1996–1997.* Washington, DC: U.S. Government Printing Office.

U.S. Department of Education, National Safety Center (1999). Washington, DC: U.S. Government Printing Office.